HOMER'S TEXT
AND LANGUAGE

 **TRADITIONS**

Homer's Text and Language

GREGORY NAGY

UNIVERSITY OF ILLINOIS PRESS

URBANA AND CHICAGO

© 2004 by the Board of Trustees
of the University of Illinois
All rights reserved
Manufactured in the United States of America

∞ This book is printed on acid-free paper.

C 5 4 3 2 1

Library of Congress Cataloging-in-Publication Data
Nagy, Gregory.
Homer's text and language / Gregory Nagy.
p.   cm. — (Traditions)
Includes bibliographical references and index.
ISBN 0-252-02983-6 (acid-free paper)
1. Homer—Criticism, Textual. 2. Epic poetry,
Greek—Criticism, Textual. 3. Greek language—
Etymology. 4. Homer—Language. I. Title.
II. Traditions (Urbana, Ill.)
PA4037.N348   2004
883'.01—dc22   2004011786

CONTENTS

ACKNOWLEDGMENTS

I offer my warmest thanks to Ryan Hackney, Casey Dué, and Christopher Dadian, to whom I am grateful for all their help in editing the final version of my text. I am also very grateful to Joycelyn Peyton, who created the index. I dedicate this book to my students, who inspire my research.

A through Ω	*Iliad* I through XXIV
α through ω	*Odyssey* i through xxiv
BA/BA²	*Best of the Achaeans* = N 1979/1999 [with new Introduction]
Esametro	Fantuzzi and Pretagostini 1996
GM	*Greek Mythology and Poetics* = N 1990b
GMZ	Grafton, Most, and Zetzel 1985
HQ	*Homeric Questions* = N 1996b
HR	*Homeric Responses* = N 2003a
IC	Janko 1998a
MHV	Parry 1971
N plus year	Nagy plus year
OEI	Blackburn et al. 1989
PH	*Pindar's Homer* = N 1990a
PP	*Poetry as Performance* = N 1996a
PR	*Plato's Rhapsody and Homer's Music* = N 2002a
VMK	*Viermännerkommentar* 'four-man commentary'

The Homer of *Homer's Text and Language* is a metonym for the text and the language of the *Iliad* and the *Odyssey*.[1] The empirical basis for all that we know about Homer is this text, this language. What I offer here is a book about this Homer. It is a set of essays rewritten and reintegrated with one central aim in mind: to show how the text and language of Homer derive from a system, an oral poetic system. That is my deduction.

My overall method, however, which has been shaped by over three decades of research on Homer, is more inductive than deductive. Inductive thinking about the facts of Homeric text and language has become for me a story in itself, and this book is my attempt to tell such a story.

In Homeric studies, there is an ongoing debate centering on different ways to establish the text of Homer, different ways to appreciate the poetry created in the language of Homer. This book takes a stand in the midst of that debate. The stakes are high, not only because Homer remains such an indispensable figure in the canons of world literature but also because so much about Homeric poetry is still unknown or uncertain.

In an age of information technology, the debate has only intensified, and the stakes have been raised ever higher. Two of the essays rewritten in this book appeared originally in an electronic journal, *The Bryn Mawr Classical Review*.[2] The second of these two essays, which was a review of a recent edition of the Homeric *Iliad*,[3] provoked a reply that was published in the same electronic journal.[4] The electronic trail leads further. The writer of that reply went on to incorporate a rewritten version into a printed book,[5] but then, in

1. By "metonym" I mean an expression of meaning by way of connecting something to something else, to be contrasted with "metaphor," which I define for the moment as an expression of meaning by way of substituting something for something else.

2. These essays are N 1998b and N 2000a, rewritten here as Ch.5 and Ch.3 respectively: http://ccat.sas.upenn.edu/bmcr/1998/1998-07-14.html and http://ccat.sas.upenn.edu/bmcr/2000/2000-09-12.html.

3. N 2000a, reviewing West 1998b.

4. West 2001a, replying to N 2000a: http://ccat.sas.upenn.edu/bmcr/2001/2001-09-06.html.

5. West 2001a, incorporated into the printed book of West 2001b, on which I have more to say in Ch.4.

response to my review of that book, which I published in a printed journal,[6] that same writer chose the same electronic journal for a new reply, combining it with his reply to another review of the same book, which had also been published in the same electronic journal.[7] From the start, the technological aspects of this debate caught the attention of popular media: for example, the *Frankfurter Allgemeine Zeitung* took note of the publicity sparked by the electronic publication of my original review.[8]

Electronic publishing has not only intensified the ongoing debate over Homer.[9] It has also accelerated the rush to engage in the debate.[10] All that rush needs to be counterbalanced by a slow and careful rereading of arguments central to the debate. *Homer's Text and Language* addresses such a need by returning to the debate in the form of a printed book, to be complemented by an electronic version of the same book. The printed version offers an opportunity to engage in the kind of slow and careful rereading I have in mind. I should add here my opinion that electronic publishing in the Classics need not be used merely to promote the intensification of debate for the sake of debate: I advocate alternative uses, focusing on enhanced ways of reading and reflecting on ancient texts.[11]

An opportunity to reflect is also an opportunity to reposition the ongoing debate. In practicing the profession of literary historian and critic, I must be both straightforward and open to dialogue. In maintaining a critical outlook, I will need to be direct in some of my criticisms. In developing my central argument, that Homeric poetry derives from a system, an oral poetic system, I find it necessary to highlight my disagreements with some contemporary Classicists. On some points, they too disagree with me—or with each other; on many other points, there is general agreement. If I became preoccupied, however, with tracking all the agreements and disagreements, the aim of my book would be lost. *Homer's Text and Language* tells its own story in the form of a unified positive argumentation.

6. N 2003b, reviewing West 2001b. N 2003b is rewritten here as Ch.4.

7. West 2004, replying to Rengakos 2002 and N 2003b. Both Rengakos and Nagy reviewed West 2001b. N 2003b is rewritten here as Ch.4.

8. Schloemann 2001, assessing the review of West 1998b by N 2000a.

9. For an electronic publication of the Introductions and the Bibliographies for Volumes 1 and 2 of N 2001h, *Greek Literature* (both of these volumes concern mainly Homer), see N 2001g: http://chs.harvard.edu/chs_pubs/ninevol/index.htm.

10. For example, the printed publication by Kullmann 2001 of his review of Latacz 2000a/b/c and 2001 on Homer was soon countered by the electronic publication of counter-arguments by Latacz 2002: http://ccat.sas.upenn.edu/bmcr/2002/2002-02-15.html.

11.A case in point is the concept of "multitext," to which I will turn at a later point.

In the course of my argumentation, I hope to address a wide variety of questions of interest to students of literature in general, not only to Classicists in particular. What do our text of Homer and its variants really stand for? What were the norms of composition, performance, and editing that shaped the poetry as we now have it? How does tradition operate on the interactive levels of synchrony and diachrony?[12]

For my argument to be effective, I need to engage with specialized studies grounded in the realities of Homeric text and language—and with the technical terminology that goes with those studies. The terminology of text criticism is introduced gradually as the reading of Part I proceeds. Then, halfway into the book, Part II begins to introduce a further set of terms having to do with linguistic reconstructions, or "etymologies." To read through the whole book in sequence, then, is to acquire at least two different kinds of complex technical language currently being used in Homeric research. What sustains the reading, however, is not the gradual acquisition of these complex technical languages but the central argument itself, which remains simple in its essence: that the text and language of Homeric poetry derive from oral traditional poetry.

The central argument is driven by three special interests: the systematic nature of oral poetry; the interplay of tradition and innovation in this kind of poetry; and the realities of actual performance. The first interest goes to the heart of my ongoing research on the history of Homeric reception. By combining the insights of Milman Parry and Albert Lord with the general methods of structural linguistics, I aim to show that the system underlying the making of Homeric verse enables us to appreciate the Homeric editorial practices of the ancient world. My second interest, concerning the interplay of innovation and tradition, runs closely parallel to the first: once we recognize the ways in which creative performers analogize and extend analogies within a tradition, we can break free from rigidly confining ideas of a single "Homeric genius" as the ultimate source of a once-and-for-all fixation of the Homeric text. Thirdly, my interest in the dynamics of performance motivates my re-examinations of the "origins" of the hexameter, as well as my analysis of the precious information contained in the Homeric scholia, that is, in the marginal notes we find preserved in ancient papyri and, more pervasively, in medieval manuscripts. In these scholia, traces of generations of past performances can be detected still.

12. On the terms "synchronic" and "diachronic," see Saussure 1916.117: "De même *synchronie* et *diachronie* désigneront respectivement un état de langage et une phase d'évolution."

Chapter One plunges the reader into the intricacies of the Homeric scholia—and what they can tell us about the ancient transmission of Homer. A key to understanding this transmission is the research of one particular ancient expert in the text and language of Homer, Aristarchus of Samothrace, director of the Library of Alexandria in the middle of the second century CE. The first five chapters accentuate the work of this man. Already in the first chapter, I start building an argument about the variant readings attributed by later sources to Aristarchus: most of these readings, as I strive to show, derive from his practice of comparing and collating Homeric scrolls available to him. Aristarchus relied as much on such outside information as he did, famously, on explaining Homer "out of Homer" (*Homēron ex Homērou saphēnizein* 'clarify Homer out of Homer')—that is, on applying his intuitions about the underlying system that animates the poetry.[13] If my argument holds, I will be justified in saying that the work of Aristarchus has preserved for us traces of authentic variations in the performance of ancient Homeric poetry.

Chapter Two offers a clarification of the term "multiform" and its applications in the study of traditional oral poetics. It makes a connection between Lord's notion of multiformity and the variations we find in the Homeric text as we know it. Some of these variations are insignificant, while others are of great significance. One sure sign of significant variation in Homeric poetry is the occasional highlighting of a given variant by the poetry itself: for example, a variant can be rhetorically "focalized" in contrast with other variants.

Chapter Three is more technical in content, examining in detail Martin West's edition of the Homeric *Iliad*. The results of this examination are essential for the overall argument initiated in Chapters One and Two: that the variations in wording as we find them in Homeric *texts* stem ultimately from variations in formulaic composition stemming from many centuries of ongoing Homeric *performances*.

Chapter Four continues an ongoing debate with West by articulating some essential differences between his view of the Homeric text and mine. I argue that this text reflects a poetic system, and that editors of Homer need to work out a system of their own in their ongoing efforts to understand that system. For West, on the other hand, the Homeric text reflects no system, and he feels no obligation to articulate his own approach to this

13. The wording comes from Porphyry *Homeric Questions* [*Iliad*] 297.16 ed. Schrader 1890; see also scholia D at *Iliad* E 385. On the Aristarchean provenance of the wording, see Porter 1992.70-74 (who effectively addresses the skepticism of Pfeiffer 1968.225-227).

text—except to affirm and reaffirm, over and over again, his reliance on his own personal judgment of what is right and wrong.[14] Against the backdrop of this debate, Chapter Four spells out what is ultimately at stake: are the Homeric poems to be read once and for all as a uniform text determined by one editor who knows best—or are they to be read and re-read in light of the multiform oral traditions that had shaped their history and prehistory? I contend that the emergent uniformity of the Homeric *Iliad* and *Odyssey* cannot be appreciated if we fail to understand the submerged multiformity of oral traditions that gave life to these poems. I resist the idea that Homeric poetry will somehow be safer in the hands of editors who seek to flatten out that multiformity. What saved this poetry in the distant past was the system of its oral traditions, in all its multiformity. To keep it safe, future editors need to maintain an active engagement with the history and prehistory of that system. It matters less, then, for me to worry about overextended claims, assumptions, and negative rhetoric about problems inherent in the study of Homeric poetry.[15] It matters more to find common ground.[16] And, ultimately, it matters even more to find answers to some basic questions. What did the Aristarchean critic Didymus know—or not know—about the editorial work of Aristarchus? How did Aristarchus himself use the earlier work of Aristophanes of Byzantium? What role did the "city" texts of Homer play in the evaluations of ancient editors?

Chapter Five confronts, in detail, thirty-three examples of readings claimed to be "authentic" in the Homeric text—as opposed to alleged "conjectures" made by Aristarchus and others. Here I put to the test a point I am making throughout Part I of this book about Homeric poetry as a system: if this poetry is in fact a system, and if the variants reported by Aristarchus can be shown to be part of such a system, then these Aristarchean variants cannot be dismissed as mere "conjectures"—as opposed to non-Aristarchean variants that are alleged to be "authentic." If my demonstration is successful, then the Aristarchean as well as the non-Aristarchean variants can be considered authentic—that is, authentically generated by the system of oral traditional poetry. All such variants can be considered to be part of the overall system. And the evidence to be used to demonstrate such common authenticity can be found in the text of Homer as we have it. An Aristarchean variant as attested in a given Homeric verse can be validated by way of matching

14. West 2001b.

15. The overextension seems particularly noticeable in West 2004, where he replies to Rengakos 2002—as also to N 2003b.

16. To cite just one example: as we will see, West and I agree more than disagree on the reading of *Iliad* O 64-71.

it with identical non-Aristarchean variants attested in other Homeric verses. On the basis of the vast number of variants that survived in Homeric textual history, we have enough evidence to conclude that the attestations of variation in the text are traces of variation in the traditional system underlying that text. Aristarchean variants are no exception: they are native to this traditional system, and they cannot be dismissed as alien guesswork.

Chapter Six inaugurates Part II of the book, shifting from questions about text to questions about language. As in Part I, the questions center on the derivation of Homeric poetry from oral traditions. As we shift from text to language, the idea that Homeric poetry is a traditional system can be seen in a new light. We can start thinking about the individuality of specific performances, not only about the evolution of a monumental composition toward a final fixed textual form. We can also start thinking about how individual performers may have contributed to such an evolution. Any synchronic view of individuality in performance, however, needs to be counterbalanced with a diachronic view, which brings us back to the realities of oral traditional poetry as a system that keeps on changing over time. That system, further, needs to be viewed linguistically as an interaction of individual *parole* and collective *langue*.[17] The first case in point is the etymology of the name of Achilles, which is the main concern of Chapter Six. In studying the deeply pervasive interaction between the meaning of this etymology and the meaning of the overall plot of the Homeric *Iliad*, we can see the precision and cohesion of Homeric poetry as a system. A recognition of such precision and cohesion exemplifies the links between Parts I and II, and it gives the book its unity.

Chapter Seven matches Chapter Six in focusing on the etymology of a name. This time it is the name of the god Apollo. The meaning of this name reveals Apollo as god of the sacred speech act and, by extension, of all speech acts. This quintessential Greek god embodies the sacred function of speech itself. As god of language, Apollo has absolute control of language. He is the god of linguistics. Within the framework of Homeric poetry as a system, the linguistic power of the god comes to life. Apollo, through his Muses, becomes the force that animates the medium of Homeric poetry.

Chapter Eight focuses on the formal medium of Apollo, as also of Achilles and Homeric characters in general—even of Homer himself as a speaker of heroic verse. That medium of heroic verse is the dactylic hexameter, the etymology of which is relevant to the driving idea of Homeric poetry as a system. In using the word "etymology," what I am really saying is that the problem of the "origins" of the hexameter is fundamentally a linguistic prob-

17. *HQ* 15, following the terminology of Saussure 1916.

lem. In linguistics, studying the etymology of any given word needs to be a holistic undertaking: it requires attention to all levels of speech, from phonology to morphology to syntax to semantics. A holistic approach is needed also for studying the "etymology" of the hexameter. This chapter offers a review and reconfiguration of my cumulative work on the forms and preforms of the hexameter, summarizing the results of my research since the publication of my original book on meter and comparative metrics in 1974.[18] In this chapter, as in other chapters, I append corrections of factual as well as typographical errors in my previous publications.

Ellipsis—as concept and as practice—is reserved for the final essay of this book, Chapter Nine. Ellipsis is also relevant to all eight of the previous essays—and in fact it is relevant to all my research as it has evolved over the last thirty years. Ellipsis has to do with something quite fundamental about ancient Greek civilization: every instantiation of this civilization, be it an utterance, a poem, or an image, is highlighted as well as shaded over by ellipsis—by what is elided in the time or space of performance. Ellipsis highlights the cosmos of meanings that generations of audiences experienced by way of participating in cultural acts, such as hearing Homer. Ellipsis, then, is a powerful *metaphor* for that whole cosmos, just as it works as a *metonym* within its own context (highlighting by hiding). While the examples I give in Chapter Nine are meant to focus on specific Homeric stylistic conventions, they also embody a much broader aesthetic, and ultimately, a confirmation that the Homeric text was shaped by a deep structure of meanings, constantly available for reactivation at all linguistic levels: phonology, morphology, syntax, semantics. The ultimate ellipsis is the one that produces the illusion of an "original" poet, who is in reality the shimmering, constantly re-energized (we might say holographic) image of every performer of the poetry itself.[19]

Readers who are already familiar with my work will, I hope, see most clearly in this final essay the rapidly shifting kaleidoscope of Homeric themes to which I have attended in my older publications. Each of those themes has been given a new twist, however, in the new environment of this book. To readers who are new to my work, the ninth essay is meant to give an overview of the depth and vitality of the ancient Greek poetic treasure that is Homer.

As for the nine essays taken all together, each of them elaborates on that same depth and vitality, viewing Homer as an endless stream of variegated

18. N 1974.

19. For the nuances of this last sentence, I am indebted to one of the two anonymous referees of my book, whose suggested wordings have powerfully affected my own.

moments in the actual reception of Homer. My essays, then, are rethinkings and refinements, as well as supplements to the debates they started. As such, they are meant to be the opposite of a scholarly reprint, for their purpose is not to memorialize older positions but to try to keep pace with the eternal newness of Homeric studies.

HOMER'S TEXT
AND LANGUAGE

PART I

Text

The Quest for a Definitive Text of Homer: Evidence from the Homeric Scholia and Beyond

As of this writing, Homeric scholarship has not yet succeeded in achieving a definitive text of either the *Iliad* or the *Odyssey*. Ideally, such a text would encompass the full historical reality of the Homeric textual tradition as it evolved through time, from the pre-Classical era well into the medieval. The problem is that Homeric scholarship has not yet reached a consensus on the criteria for establishing a Homeric text that is "definitive." The ongoing disagreements reflect a wide variety of answers to the many serious questions that remain about Homer and Homeric poetry. Crucial to most of these questions is the evidence provided by the Homeric scholia.

The relevance of the scholia (plural of *scholion*), that is, of annotations that accompany the text of Homer in a wide variety of manuscripts, was first made manifest to the world of modern Homeric scholarship in 1788, when Jean Baptiste Gaspard d'Ansse de Villoison published the tenth-century Venetus A codex manuscript of the *Iliad* of Homer (codex Marcianus 454).[1] In his *Prolegomena*, Villoison assesses the impact of the Venetus A scholia on Homeric scholarship:

> By way of these scholia, never before published, the greatest light is shed on Homer's poetry. Obscure passages are illuminated; <u>the rites, customs,</u>

---

* The original version of this essay is N 1997d.
1. Villoison 1788.

mythology, and geography of the ancients are explained; the original and genuine reading is established; the variant readings of various codices and editions as well as the emendations of the Critics are weighed. For it is evident that the Homeric contextus, which was recited by the rhapsodes from memory and which used to be sung orally by everyone, was already for a long time corrupt, since it would have been impossible for the different rhapsodes of the different regions of Greece not to be forced by necessity to subtract, add, and change many things. That Homer committed his poems to writing is denied by Josephus at the beginning of Book I of his *Against Apion*, and this opinion seems to be shared by an unpublished Scholiast to Dionysius Thrax, who narrates that the poems of Homer, which were preserved only in men's minds and memory and were not written, had become extinct by the time of Peisistratos, and that he accordingly offered a reward to those who would bring him Homeric verses, and that, as a result, many people, greedy for money, sold Peisistratos their verses as if they were Homeric. The Critics left these spurious verses in the Edition, but they did so in a special way, marking them with the obelus.[2]

This assessment in Villoison's 1788 *Prolegomena* anticipated in some significant details the ultimately far more influential views of Friedrich August Wolf in his *Prolegomena ad Homerum*, published in 1795[3] (English-language edition 1985).[4] In other details, however, Wolf's assessment diverged radically from that of Villoison. This divergence is crucial for weighing the importance of the Homeric scholia and, by extension, even for establishing the text of Homer. The point of disagreement centers on what the scholia tell us about the ancient *kritikoi* or Critics, as Villoison refers to them in the passage just quoted.

These critics are the scholars responsible for the textual transmission of Homer in the Library of Alexandria, founded in the early third century BCE,

2. Villoison 1788.xxxiv; the translation and the underlinings are mine. I leave untranslated his use of the Latin noun *contextus*, which conveys the metaphorical sense of 'fabric, structure'; compare the Latin verb *contexere* 'weave, restart weaving where one had left off weaving'. *Here and everywhere, I use single rather than double quotes for translating the meanings of words and phrases.* On the *rhapsōidoi* or 'rhapsodes', professional performers of Homeric and other archaic poetry, see below. The obelus is a horizontal mark, placed next to a verse in the left-hand margin of a text, to indicate the editor's doubts about the authenticity of the verse. I will have more to say about this sign as the discussion proceeds.

3. Wolf 1795.

4. Grafton, Most, and Zetzel 1985; hereafter abbreviated as GMZ. Besides translating Wolf's original Latin text into English, GMZ have written an introduction and notes focusing on Wolf's influence on Homeric scholarship. GMZ 7–8 give their own translation of the passage from Villoison p. xxxiv quoted above. They do not stress Wolf's fundamental

the era of Zenodotus of Ephesus, who is credited with the first Alexandrian "edition" of Homer. There were subsequent "editions" by Aristophanes of Byzantium, who became director of the Library around the beginning of the second century BCE, and by a later director, Aristarchus of Samothrace, the culmination of whose work is dated around the middle of the second century BCE. It is the "edition" of Homer by Aristarchus, as frequently cited by the scholia of the Venetus A manuscript, that constitutes the primary authority behind these Homeric scholia.

Here we come to the central point of divergence between Villoison and Wolf: whereas Villoison viewed the Venetus A scholia as an authoritative witness to an authoritative edition of Homer by Aristarchus, Wolf swerved from this position by questioning the authoritativeness of the Homeric scholia and, more fundamentally, the authority of Aristarchus as an editor of Homeric poetry. This swerve away from Villoison's position is reflected in the fullest single collection of data currently available on the Homeric scholia, Hartmut Erbse's edition of the *Iliad* scholia.[5]

Erbse's edition aims to encompass two main components of the scholiastic tradition on Homer: (1) "Ap.H.," the archetype of the Venetus A scholia and a main source for the twelfth-century Homer commentator Eustathius (as also for the *Etymologicum Genuinum*),[6] and (2) c, the archetype of the b and the T scholia.[7] Erbse's edition excludes, however, the so-called D scholia.[8] Erbse also excludes the material from the *Homeric Questions* of Porphyry (third century CE).[9]

---

debt to this specific formulation by Villoison. On that subject, see Pierron 1869 I xxiii and II 509n1.

5. Erbse 1969–1988. More below on the other scholia. On the problems of dating the origins of compilations of scholia in general, see Wilson 1967.244–256; also the reactions in the addenda of Erbse 1969–1988 II 547, with specific reference to the Homeric scholia.

6. Erbse 1969–1988 I xlvii. See pp. xlv–xlvi on the wording in Eustathius I 76 8: ἐν τοῖς Ἀπίωνος καὶ Ἡροδώρου εἰς τὸν Ὅμηρον ὑπομνήμασι 'in the Homer commentaries of Apion and Herodorus [probably corrupted from "Heliodorus"]', whence the abbreviation "Ap.H." On Heliodorus, see Dyck 1993a.2n6. Editions of Eustathius: van der Valk 1971–1988, Stallbaum 1825.

7. Erbse I p. li traces the b scholia (the family of the B manuscript, as also of C, E³, and others) and the T scholia back to a larger family c, which may also have been a source for Eustathius.

8. For more on the D scholia (formerly known, wrongly, as the Didymus scholia), see below; also Haslam 1997.61 and n17. These scholia are mixed in with the A and B scholia, as printed in the edition by Dindorf, volumes I–VI (1875–1888); volumes V–VI, edited by Maass (1887–1888), contain the T scholia. The D scholia have been edited by van Thiel 2000b and published electronically in the form of a "Proecdosis," on which see van Thiel 2000a.

9. See Schrader 1880–1882 and 1890. See also Sodano 1970.

Erbse divides what he calls the "major scholia" of Homer, as represented by A, b, and T, into two categories: (1) the data culminating in A, stemming from the so-called *Viermännerkommentar*, that is, the "four-man commentary," or "VMK" for short, and (2) the data culminating in c, archetype of b and T, the so-called "exegetical" scholia.[10] As for the D scholia, they are assigned by default to a more amorphous category, the "minor scholia," about which I will have more to say later. Also, there are Homeric "scholia" in papyri from the Hellenistic and Roman periods, some of which are cognate with but qualitatively different from the D scholia.[11] I will have more to say later on the papyrus scholia as well.

Erbse's categories of Homeric scholia apply also to the textual tradition of the *Odyssey*, not just the *Iliad*, but here we find much less textual evidence. The two earliest minuscule manuscripts of the *Odyssey*, G (tenth century) and F (eleventh century), are without scholia.[12] There is nothing remotely comparable to the A scholia of the *Iliad* in the textual history of the *Odyssey*. Nor is there an edition of the *Odyssey* scholia that matches the scale of Erbse's work on the *Iliad* scholia.[13]

Focusing on the A scholia of the *Iliad*, Erbse traces their data back to the VMK.[14] The *subscriptio* that we find at the end of each of the 24 books (except for a lacuna at the end of Book 17 and an omission at the end of Book 24) of the Venetus A *Iliad* gives the basic information about the VMK: παράκειται τὰ Ἀριστονίκου σημεῖα καὶ τὰ Διδύμου Περὶ τῆς Ἀρισταρχείου διορθώσεως, τινὰ δὲ καὶ ἐκ τῆς Ἰλιακῆς προσῳδίας Ἡρωδιανοῦ καὶ ἐκ τοῦ Νικάνορος Περὶ στιγμῆς 'placed in the margins are the signs of Aristonicus and the work of Didymus entitled "On the Aristarchean edition [*diorthōsis*]," and some material also from the "Iliadic prosody" of Herodian and from the work of

---

10. Erbse 1969–1988 I xi–xii. The c scholia may also contain fragments of the VMK (p. lii). Although these scholia often reflect views that contradict those advocated by the school of Aristarchus at the Library in Alexandria, they are not necessarily to be traced back to the rival school of Crates at the Library in Pergamon: see Erbse I xii. See also Haslam 1994.44, arguing that the c scholia derive from commentaries and that the term "exegetical" is a misnomer.

11. Erbse 1969–1988 I xiii. See also Erbse 1960.170–1.

12. Haslam 1997.94.

13. An early edition: Dindorf 1855. See also Ludwich 1888–1890.

14. Erbse 1969–1988 I xii, xlvii.

15. Erbse 1969–1988 I xv; see also p. xlvii, where he argues that the source of the VMK data in A is an archetypal codex that had merged the four distinct commentaries. (Erbse adduces scholia A at *Iliad* K 398, ἐν μέντοι τῇ τετραλογίᾳ Νεμεσίωνος οὕτως εὗρον περὶ τῶν στίχων τούτων 'this was my finding about these lines, in the tetralogy of Nemesion', and he conjectures that Nemesion lived in the 5th or 6th century CE.) There is reason

Nicanor entitled "On punctuation'".[15] Thus the VMK combines the Homeric scholarship of Didymus (on variant textual readings),[16] Aristonicus (on critical signs),[17] Nicanor (on punctuation),[18] and Herodian (on accent).[19] The VMK authors are to be dated as follows: Didymus flourished in the second half of the first century BCE and beginning of the first CE; Aristonicus was a contemporary of Didymus; Nicanor lived in the era of Hadrian; Herodian flourished about 200 years after Didymus, in the era of Marcus Aurelius. The data provided by the VMK are based ultimately on the Homer edition and commentary of Aristarchus, as we learn from the testimony of the first of the "four men" I list here, Didymus, as mediated by the scholia.

On the basis of data derived primarily from the Homeric scholia, Rudolf Pfeiffer reconstructs the history of Aristarchus' edition of Homer as follows: first, Aristarchus made a *hupomnēma* or 'commentary' on the *ekdosis* or 'edition' of Homer produced by his immediate predecessor as head of the Library of Alexandria, Aristophanes of Byzantium; then, Aristarchus produced his own 'edition' and made a revised 'commentary' to accompany it; later, members of his school produced a revised 'edition'.[20]

Here we return to the divergence of opinions, going all the way back to Villoison and Wolf, about the value and even the nature of the work accomplished by the 'editors' of Homer, especially Aristarchus, in transmitting the Homeric textual tradition. Depending on how we interpret the information attributed by the Homeric scholia to Aristarchus and other such scholars, there is room for a wide variety of different ideas about what exactly the definitive text of Homer may have been, and even whether there had existed such a thing as a "definitive" text.

In order to grasp the essence of this divergence, we may focus on the wording of Villoison's original formulation, as highlighted in the passage quoted at the beginning. According to Villoison, the Homeric scholia provide essential background on the following three aspects of the Homeric

---

to dispute this argument, on the basis of comparative evidence discussed by Haslam 1978.71.

16. Schmidt 1854; Ludwich 1884.175–631.

17. Friedländer 1853; Carnuth 1869.

18. Friedländer 1850. Cf. Blank 1983.

19. Lentz 1867–1870. Cf. Dyck 1993b.

20. Pfeiffer 1968.217. On the second *ekdosis* 'edition' of Aristarchus, supposedly produced by his students, see Apthorp 1980.132. On his *hupomnēma* 'commentary', see Lührs 1992.10, who describes it as a combination of an *apparatus criticus* and a *commentarius criticus*. In Ch.4 (p. 85) I discuss a more developed scenario for reconstructing the Homer editions of Aristarchus, with special reference to the work of Montanari 1998. I will also discuss the existence of two *ekdoseis* 'editions' attributed to Aristarchus in the post-Aristarchean era.

tradition: (1) the historical context, (2) the text itself, and (3) the oral traditions underlying but also "undermining" that text.

Starting with the first aspect, we see that Villoison valued the Homeric scholia for their providing a background on "the rites, customs, mythology, and geography of the ancients." For Villoison, the Homeric scholia put the Homeric text back into its historical context(s):

> Villoison's hopes for the usefulness of the scholia—and the wide interest his huge, highly technical edition of them provoked—owed much to views of Homer that sprang up largely outside the professional tradition in philology, and in particular to a new sense of the poet's *historicity* that grew out of the criticisms of him voiced during the Quarrel of the Ancients and Moderns.[21]

Turning to the second aspect, the Homeric text, we have already noted that the "Critics" to whom Villoison's formulation primarily refers are the three Homer scholars of the Library or Museum at Alexandria who were credited with producing "editions" of Homer: Zenodotus of Ephesus, Aristophanes of Byzantium, and, especially, Aristarchus of Samothrace. The publication of Venetus A and its scholia, with well over 1,000 references to Aristarchus, produced a quantum leap of information about the premier Alexandrian editor of Homer. There was a sense of euphoria about prospects of recovering the Homer edition of Aristarchus, along with the commentary produced by his school. Villoison could hope to establish "the original and genuine reading," on the basis of examining "the variant readings of various codices and editions as well as the emendations of the critics." The A scholia of Homer seemed to bring Aristarchus back to life.

As we can see from his quoted formulation, however, Villoison's optimism about restoring, through the scholia, the "original and genuine" text of Homer was tempered by his intuition about an oral tradition that transmitted but also "corrupted" this "text." Here we come to the third of the three aspects of Homeric tradition highlighted by Villoison. His point about an oral Homeric transmission by way of *rhapsōidoi* (ῥαψῳδοί) 'rhapsodes' was seized on by Wolf, whose own elaborations on this third aspect of the Homeric tradition led ultimately to a destabilization of scholarly perspectives on the second and even the first aspects, concerning the Homeric text and its contexts as elucidated by the scholia. To this day, the destabilization continues, and most experts fail to agree on a unified explanation for the instabilities inherent in the ancient Homeric textual tradition.

21. GMZ 8. The italics are mine. The contributions of the A scholia to an understanding of the historical context are more than matched by the bT scholia: for an illuminating survey, see Schmidt 1976. On the mythological world of the D scholia, see Lünstedt 1961.

Wolf's reformulation of Villoison's assessment centers on the testimony of Josephus *Against Apion* 1.12–13, as invoked by Villoison in the passage quoted above. Josephus (first century CE), in his polemics with the Homer expert Apion (also first century), seems to be arguing from the premise that no *original text* of Homer survived. Wolf infers that the Homer scholars of Alexandria must have accepted this premise. Otherwise, Wolf reasons, Josephus could not get away with arguing, against an authoritative Homer expert like Apion (he was a student of the Aristarchean Didymus), that Homer did not write. Here is Wolf's interpretation of the Josephus passage:

> ... the ancients themselves ascribed the *origin* of variant readings to the rhapsodes, and located in their frequent performances the principal source of Homeric *corruption and interpolation*. And this judgment, which began with the Alexandrian critics [footnote 76], is clearly supported by consideration of the nature of the case (Ch.25).[22]

At footnote 76, Wolf cross-refers to an earlier part of his treatise (Ch.18), where he argues not only that Homer did not use writing in composing his poetry but also that the Homer scholars of Alexandria must have known this:

> This [= the passage cited from Josephus] is the only clear, authoritative testimony about the question. But it is weightier because it was written against the most learned Homeric commentator [= Apion], and no ancient defender of a different or contrary opinion survives. Therefore, however the overall credibility of Josephus may be assessed, that passage [of Josephus] will have all the force that clear words have. Recently he was reinforced by a certain scholiast [footnote 39], a coadjutor unworthy of any mention had he not gathered his tale, one soon corrupted by the stories of later grammarians, from the same Alexandrian remains. For it is clear that they did not draw it from Josephus (Ch.18).[23]

In his footnote 39, Wolf specifies that this additional testimony comes from the scholia to Dionysius Thrax published by Villoison himself in his *Anecdota Graeca* 2.182 [*Grammatici Graeci* 3.179]: the Greek text of the scholiast is translated thus: "For the works of Homer were lost, as they say. For in those days they were not transmitted by writing, but only by training so that they might be preserved by memory, etc."[24]

The implications of Wolf's inference are far-reaching: if he is right, then the Homer text inherited by the scholars of Alexandria has been "corrupted"

22. GMZ 111. The italics are mine.
23. GMZ 94–95.
24. GMZ 95n39.

by oral transmission, and whatever "corrections" they make are likely to be conjectures. By extension, the evidence of the scholia, which reflect the work of the Alexandrian scholars, is devalued.

The Greek text of Josephus *Against Apion* 1.12–13, as we have seen it invoked by both Villoison and Wolf, is as follows:

> ὅλως δὲ παρὰ τοῖς Ἕλλησιν οὐδὲν ὁμολογούμενον εὑρίσκεται γράμμα τῆς Ὁμήρου ποιήσεως πρεσβύτερον, οὗτος δὲ καὶ τῶν Τρωϊκῶν ὕστερος φαίνεται γενόμενος, καί φασιν οὐδὲ τοῦτον ἐν γράμμασι τὴν αὑτοῦ ποίησιν καταλιπεῖν, ἀλλὰ <u>διαμνημονευομένην</u> ἐκ τῶν ᾀσμάτων ὕστερον <u>συντεθῆναι</u> καὶ διὰ τοῦτο πολλὰς ἐν αὐτῇ σχεῖν τὰς <u>διαφωνίας</u>·

> In general, no commonly recognized writing is found among the Greeks older than the poetry of Homer. But he too seems to have been later than the Trojan War, and they say that not even he left his poetry in writing, but it was <u>preserved by memory</u> [= verb *diamnēmoneuein*] and <u>assembled</u> [= verb *suntithenai*] later from the songs. And it is because of this that there are so many <u>inconsistencies</u> [*diaphōniai*] in it.[25]

As we see from the wording of Josephus, he claims that the poems of Homer were preserved by memory *and assembled later from the songs*. The idea of an 'assembling' of a text 'from the songs' suggests that the premise of Josephus' argumentation is the existence of stories that told of a recension of the Homeric poems commissioned by the Athenian tyrant Peisistratos.[26] We may treat these stories as a historical reality in their own right, even if we do not choose to believe the contents of the stories. In other words, the historical reality is not necessarily what the stories say about a Peisistratean Recension, as Wolf argues, but merely the stories themselves—or, better, the narrative tradition. It can be argued, *pace* Wolf, that the stories of the Peisistratean Recension result from a political myth, fostered by the dynasty of Peisistratos himself, that pictured the tyrant as a culture hero who rescued and restored the poems of Homer, which had formerly become neglected, fragmented, and even lost.[27] It can also be argued that such stories are characteristic of a type of charter myth, attested not only in other archaic Greek traditions but also in those of a wide variety of different cultures, that serves

25. GMZ 94.

26. On the stories about a "recension" commissioned by Peisistratos or at least by a member of the dynasty of the Peisistratidai, see *HQ* 65–106. See also *HQ* 103–105 for arguments in support of dating the story of the Peisistratean Recension at least as far back as the fourth century BCE, the era of Dieuchidas of Megara (*FGH* 485 F 6, by way of Diogenes Laertius 1.57).

27. *HQ* 70–75.

to explain the genesis of a centralized oral tradition in the metaphorical terms of written traditions, so that the gradual evolution of an oral tradition into a centralized institution is imagined by the myth as an instantaneous re-creation of a lost book—or of an obsolete archetype of an ultimate Book.[28]

There is reason, then, for resisting what both Villoison and Wolf infer from the stories of the Peisistratean Recension. These stories center on the notion of a lost text, and they make no explicit reference to the reality of oral transmission by Homeric performers called *rhapsōidoi* (ῥαψῳδοί) 'rhapsodes'. Although there is indeed evidence to support both Villoison and Wolf in their arguing for the concept of a rhapsodic phase in the history of Homeric transmission,[29] the point is that the Alexandrian scholars argued for an altogether different concept: for them, especially for Aristarchus, the idea of an original written text of Homer was not so much a metaphor but a supposed reality.[30] For Aristarchus, it appears that Homer was an Athenian who lived around 1000 BCE, in the time of the so-called Ionian Migration (scholia A at *Iliad* N 197);[31] moreover, the scholiastic tradition stemming ultimately from Aristarchus implies that Homer *wrote* his poems (scholia A at *Iliad* P 719) and that Hesiod actually had a chance to *read* them (scholia A at *Iliad* M 22a).[32] Although earlier traditions did indeed accept the

28. *HQ* 70–75. Cf. Tzetzes *Anecdota Graeca* 1.6 ed. Cramer.

29. There is valuable information in the scholia at Pindar *Nemean* 2.1e (ed. Drachmann) about the rhapsode Kynaithos of Chios. I note especially the usage of *apangellein* in the sense of 'perform publicly', with reference to the performance of rhapsodes in the circle of Kynaithos (οἱ περὶ Κύναιθον ... τὴν Ὁμήρου ποίησιν ... ἐμνημόνευον καὶ ἀπήγγελλον 'Kynaithos and his school ... made a practice of ... the remembering of the *poiēsis* of Homer, and they performed it publicly'), to be compared with the usage of the same word *apangellein* in Herodotus 7.142.1 in a similarly performative context. I also draw attention to the association of *mnēmoneuein* 'practice the remembering of ... with *apangellein* 'perform publicly'. On the relationship of master and disciple in the traditions of the rhapsodes (cf. οἱ περὶ Κύναιθον), see Ritoók 1970.23–24.

30. *PP* 150–151.

31. As a supplement to scholia A at *Iliad* N 197 see Proclus περὶ Ὁμήρου 59–62 ed. Severyns 1938: τοῖς δὲ χρόνοις αὐτὸν οἱ μὲν περὶ τὸν Ἀρίσταρχόν φασι γενέσθαι κατὰ τὴν τῆς Ἰωνίας ἀποικίαν, ἥτις ὑστερεῖ τῆς Ἡρακλειδῶν καθόδου ἔτεσιν ἑξήκοντα, τὸ δὲ περὶ τοὺς Ἡρακλείδας λείπεται τῶν Τρωϊκῶν ἔτεσιν ὀγδοήκοντα. οἱ δὲ περὶ Κράτητα ἀνάγουσιν αὐτὸν εἰς τοὺς Τρωϊκοὺς χρόνους 'As for the dating, Aristarchus and his school situate Homer at the time of the Ionian Migration, supposedly sixty years after the Return of the Herakleidai, which in turn was supposedly eighty years after the era of the Trojan War; by contrast, Crates and his school date him back to the era of the Trojan War'. On the rivalry of Aristarchus and Crates as editors of Homer, see below. Further discussion in *PP* 151; Pfeiffer 1968.228; Janko 1992.32n53, 71; Keaney and Lamberton 1996.67n2.

32. See Porter 1992.83.

idea of a rhapsodic transmission of Homer and Hesiod,[33] even picturing the poets themselves as rhapsodes,[34] the later exegetical traditions of scholars like Aristarchus seem to have rejected this model, positing instead a literate Homer and Hesiod.[35]

Thus Wolf seems unjustified in thinking that the Homer scholars of Alexandria posited a phase of oral transmission to account for the variations that they found in the history of the Homeric text. The problem is, Wolf does not make a distinction between earlier and later views of Homer in ancient criticism: the premise of Josephus reflects an earlier Homeric model, while that of Apion promotes a later one, of Aristarchean provenance (to repeat: Apion was a student of the Aristarchean Didymus).[36] Wolf's thinking on this point turns out to be a cornerstone for his overall theory that patterns of relative instability in the earlier phases of the Homeric textual tradition can be explained by positing even earlier phases of Homeric oral tradition. "Like Villoison, he [Wolf] saw the early oral transmission of the Homeric poems as the chief source of early variants and the chief stimulus for the development of textual criticism.... Unlike Villoison, however, Wolf insisted that the ancient critics had not had old enough materials to give their critical work a firm foundation."[37] In other words, Wolf questions, in varying degrees, the reliability of the scholia and of their primary authorities—Zenodotus, Aristophanes, and even Aristarchus—as sources that can lead to the recovery of the "original" Homer text.

Villoison, by contrast, claims that these scholia establish the "original and genuine reading," thereby affirming his conviction that the Alexandrian Homer scholars, especially Aristarchus, did indeed come close to recovering an "original" Homer text. Thus Villoison's Homer text is Aristarchean, in

33. E.g. "Plato" *Hipparchus* 228b–c, Plato *Ion* 531a, 532a.

34. E.g. Plato *Republic* 10.600d.

35. Wolf 1795 Ch.25, in arguing that the textual instability of Homeric poetry was due to the rhapsodes—and that the Alexandrian critics made the same inference—cites an account about the rhapsode Kynaithos of Chios in the scholia at Pindar *Nemean* 2.1c, e (cf. Eustathius I 10 30ff, etc.). Evidently Wolf thought that this account about Kynaithos derives from Aristarchus. I have argued in support of this derivation in N 2000f.99n6, and I will repeat the essentials of my argument later on at p. 29n15 below. According to this account about the rhapsode Kynaithos, as we will see, he "interpolated" his own verses into the poetry of Homer. The idea that Kynaithos was a rhapsode implies an oral tradition, but the idea that he was "interpolating" implies a written tradition, as far as Aristarchus was concerned. For Aristarchus, the task was to "correct" the *textual* instability of Homer.

36. See Jensen 1980.155, who argues explicitly that Josephus accepted an earlier model, which she outlines on p. 150. For Apion, see Neitzel 1977.

37. GMZ 17.

contrast to Wolf's, which is meta-Aristarchean. Essentially, Villoison's claim about the Venetus A text and the Venetus A scholia of the *Iliad* seems to match the goal of Aristarchus himself, who sought to recover an "original" text.[38]

To be sure, we may disagree fundamentally with the premise of Aristarchus, who searched for variants in Homeric textual transmission in order to find in each case *the* authentic variant. Instead, I argue for an evolutionary model, accounting for a plethora of different authentic variants at different stages (or even at any one stage) in the evolution of Homeric poetry *as an oral tradition*; variations in the textual tradition would reflect different stages in the transcribing of this oral tradition.[39]

Such a model is fundamentally at odds with the theories of Villoison, who puts his trust in Aristarchus, validating that Alexandrian scholar's case-by-case search for *the* authentic reading in the text of Homer. Such a model is also at odds with the theories of Wolf, who distrusts Aristarchus' ability to recover authentic readings in general. Whereas Aristarchus—and Villoison—may have gone too far in positing *the* authentic reading in any given case throughout the Homeric text, there is no reason to doubt that any Homeric variant attributed to Aristarchus can be considered *an* authentic reading.[40] For Wolf to cast general doubt on variant readings attributed to Aristarchus may well be going too far in the opposite direction.

In this regard, there is room for disagreement with the editors of the "English Wolf," who set up the following dichotomy between Villoison and Wolf: "where Villoison heaped up without structure or order texts and data from all periods of Greek literature," they claim, "Wolf moved systematically through the scholia, assembling what he took to be characteristic corrections attributed to the ancient readers and critics."[41] This is to put the best light on Wolf's general practice of discrediting not only Zenodotus but also Aristophanes and even Aristarchus.[42] According to this assessment, Wolf's pessimistic formulation supposedly helps put Homer into a historical context. Pursuing this train of thought, the editors of the "English Wolf" quote

38. *PP* 107–152, Ch.5: "Multiform epic and Aristarchus' quest for the real Homer." On the relative disinterest of Aristarchus in the performative traditions of Homeric rhapsodes, see *PP* 130 and 151. For what seems to be a vestigial reference in the Homeric scholia to such performative traditions, see scholia T at *Iliad* Π 131 (where it is prescribed that verses narrating the arming of Patroklos are to be performed at an allegro pace) and the comments of Richardson 1980.287.

39. *PP* 132–149. I will have more to say on this evolutionary model in Ch.2 below.

40. More on this point in Ch.5.

41. GMZ 18.

42. GMZ 8.

the verdict of Pfeiffer on Wolf as the man "who opened the eyes of his contemporaries and of posterity to the unique *historical* position of the Homeric
poetry" [the emphasis is by Pfeiffer].[43]

Ironically, Villoison's optimistic formulation, articulating the goal of
recovering the genuine Homer through Aristarchus, can lead to a clearer
perspective about the earlier history of Homeric transmission, while Wolf's
pessimism about verifying the testimony of the three major Alexandrian
Homer scholars, including Aristarchus, leads to a default mentality that
finds certainty only in the later history of this transmission. To follow this
mentality is to rely mostly on what Wolf considers the only verifiable historical reality, that is, the Homer text that evolved *after* the era of Aristarchus.
Pierre Alexis Pierron, one of Villoison's defenders, says sarcastically that the
Iliad of Wolf is the *Iliad* known to the likes of Porphyry, who composed his
Homeric Questions in the third century CE.[44]

There are other possible approaches to the Homer scholia, and one
of them is even more optimistic than that of Villoison: we may consider
any variant—whether it is found in the textual traditions or is attributed
by the scholia to Zenodotus, Aristophanes, Aristarchus, or other Homer
scholars—to be a *potentially* authentic written reflex of the oral poetic system of Homeric diction.[45] Let us focus for the moment on the three major
Alexandrian Homer scholars. For Wolf, whenever Aristarchus is "right"
about a reading and Zenodotus is "wrong," or the other way around, the
inference is that *neither* can be trusted. From the standpoint of oral poetics,
however, I will argue that we cannot establish which given reading is "right"
and which is "wrong" as we study the variants that survive in the Homeric
textual tradition: all we can determine is what seems to be authentic or not,
and we may even leave room for more than one authentic reading in any
given situation—if we take into account the evolution of Homeric poetry in
performance.

In investigating the historical layers separating the Homeric scholarship
of Zenodotus, Aristophanes, and Aristarchus, Wolf manages to discredit all
three to the extent that none of them can lay claim to be the consistent trans-
mitter of *the* authentic reading. Here is where a return to Villoison helps
broaden the perspective. His text of the *Iliad*, relying on the Venetus A scho-

43. Pfeiffer 1968.214, quoted in GMZ 29.
44. Pierron 1869 I p. cxl.
45. *PP* 132–149, defending the validity of editorial testimony attributed to Zenodotus
and Aristophanes as well as to Aristarchus. For the editorial methods of Zenodotus, see
the indispensable work of Nickau 1977. For an overall work on Aristophanes of Byzantium,
see Slater 1986.

lia, helps reconstruct the earlier history of Homeric transmission, even if he overprivileges the testimony of Aristarchus against that of Zenodotus and Aristophanes, let alone the earlier Athenian transmission.[46]

In this light it is instructive to study, as a historical model, the editorial work of Pierre Alexis Pierron on the Iliadic text.[47] Pierron builds on the work of Karl Lehrs, the moving force of the "Königsberg School," who consistently defended the value of Aristarchus' Homeric scholarship as transmitted primarily through the A scholia.[48] Pierron's edition represents an approximation, however fragmented, of Aristarchus' own editorial work on the *Iliad* text.[49] Such an Aristarchean edition of Homer, achieved primarily by way of the A scholia, is valuable not so much for its avowed goal of pinpointing the singular text that Aristarchus had hoped to recover but for its illustrating the variety of multiple readings that were apparently still available to this ancient scholar in his ongoing quest to find in each case the one true reading. What the Homeric scholia reveal, however imperfectly, is that Aristarchus' attempt to reconstruct the single truth of an original Homeric text had led him to scan a multiplicity of existing Homeric texts.[50] Attracted to the idea of that singularity, Villoison placed his trust in Aristarchus. Facing the reality of multiple Homeric textual transmission, Wolf despaired of ever recovering the original Homer text.

The differences between Villoison and Wolf in weighing the importance of the Homeric scholia have left to this day a legacy of uncertainty about the criteria needed for editing Homer. The Homer edition used until recently by most English-speaking Classicists as the definitive or near-definitive text, the Oxford Classical Text of T. W. Allen (with D. B. Monro), has been called into question.[51] For example, Helmut van Thiel, the editor of a rival edition of Homer (both the *Iliad* and the *Odyssey*),[52] condemns Allen's earlier edi-

46. That Zenodotus, in the process of editing Homer, did indeed produce his own *text* is argued by Rengakos 1993.12–14. He also argues that Aristarchus had direct access to the Homer edition of Zenodotus, even if Didymus and Aristonicus may not have (p. 14). So too Apollonius of Rhodes and Callimachus, both contemporaries of Zenodotus, had access to such a text (ibid.). See also Montanari 2002.

47. Pierron 1869.

48. Lehrs 1882.

49. See especially Pierron 1869 II.564n2, referring to the criticism of Wolf by Lehrs (1833) in his second edition of his work on Aristarchus.

50. More on this point in Ch.4.

51. Janko 1990.332 and 334 on the Monro and Allen edition of 1920. See also Janko p. 332n19 on the editorial strategy of the *editio maior* of Allen 1931. Even the intellectual integrity of Allen as editor has been called into question: see Wilson 1990. For a more balanced assessment of Allen's methods, see Haslam 1997.89–90.

52. van Thiel 1991 and 1996.

tion as fundamentally defective in its methodology,[53] and he reinforces his condemnation by deliberately making his manuscript sigla different from those of Allen.[54]

It is open to question, however, whether van Thiel's own Homeric editions are any more definitive than Allen's: as Michael Haslam points out, with specific reference to van Thiel's *Odyssey* (1991), such an edition "is founded on the premise of the exclusive authority of the vulgate."[55] By his shorthand reference to the "vulgate" text of Homer, Haslam means the medieval transmission, as distinct from readings attested in the scholia, in papyri, or in the indirect tradition (Homer-quotations and the like).[56] The editorial method espoused by van Thiel is to treat as mere conjectures the variants attributed by the scholia to the Alexandrian editors.[57] In response to current descriptions of such a method as "conservative," Haslam adds, parenthetically: "... not that there is actually anything conservative about preferring medieval manuscripts to ancient ones."[58] It is also essential to keep in mind, as Haslam succinctly puts it, that many medieval variant manuscript readings are "infiltrators from the scholia."[59] Also, there were many Homeric readings that the medieval tradition simply did not preserve.[60]

Even the inconsistencies of modern usage in applying the word "vulgate" to various different phases of a reconstructed Homeric text illustrate the ongoing uncertainties in establishing a definitive text of Homer. For Arthur Ludwich, the "vulgate" Homeric text is pre-Alexandrian, derived from an Athenian prototype, which is the ultimate source for the medieval manuscript tradition.[61] Similarly for Marchinus van der Valk, a pre-Aristarchean "vulgate" had "preserved the authentic text," and this text "was also transmitted by the vulgate of the medieval manuscripts."[62] For both Ludwich and van der Valk, this "vulgate" is distinct from the Homer "editions" of the Alexandrians, especially that of Aristarchus. For van der Valk, however, the readings of the "vulgate" are generally more authentic than the variant readings attributed by the Homer scholia to scholars like Aristarchus, which he generally takes to be "conjectures"; for Ludwich, by contrast, such vari-

---

53. See especially van Thiel 1991 iii; cf. Haslam 1997.95.
54. Haslam 1997.95.
55. Haslam 1997.100.
56. Haslam 1997.63.
57. See especially van Thiel 1991 ix–xiii.
58. Haslam 1997.100n133.
59. Haslam 1997.95.
60. Haslam 1997.96.
61. Ludwich 1898; cf. Allen 1924.327.
62. See van der Valk 1963/1964 I 609.

ants are not "conjectures" but authentic readings preserved by the scholia from the Alexandrian editions of Aristarchus and others.[63] For Ludwich, the Alexandrian "edition" of Aristarchus represents a quantum leap beyond the pre-Alexandrian "vulgate"; for van der Valk, by contrast, the pre- and post-Alexandrian "vulgate" text is relatively superior to the Alexandrian "edition" of Aristarchus, which may not even be deserving of the term "edition."[64]

The term "Wolfian vulgate" has been applied to post-Wolf editions of Homer that tend to discount the judgments of Alexandrian critics, especially with reference to criteria of excluding lines in the Homeric corpus.[65] Such an edition is the Monro-Allen 1920 Oxford Classical Text of the *Iliad*. In other respects, though, this edition follows the criteria of Aristarchus, occasionally adopting the variant readings attributed by the Homer scholia to Aristarchus or to his Alexandrian predecessors.[66] By contrast, the more recent Homer editions of van Thiel go beyond Monro-Allen and most other previous editions in moving toward the "Wolfian vulgate" as the definitive text. Ironically, the impetus toward privileging the "Wolfian vulgate" and challenging most of the Alexandrian editorial criteria transmitted by the scholia has been championed by the editor of the major *Iliad* scholia, Hartmut Erbse.[67] Rudolf Pfeiffer, in his summary of the efforts of Lehrs and others to rehabilitate the authoritativeness of Aristarchus as editor of Homer, singles out Erbse's minimizing the authority of the Alexandrian editors.[68] Pfeiffer begins by saying: "it looks to me as if by a sort of unconscious counter-revolution Wolf has now been put back on the throne from which Lehrs had driven him."[69]

It may well be an overstatement to say that Wolf has been reinstated as the driving force behind Homeric studies. Still, the "Wolfian vulgate" version of the Homeric text is once again ascendant in some quarters, culminating in the Homer editions of van Thiel. A key to this ascendancy is the work of Erbse, culminating in his edition of the *Iliad* scholia. As we have seen, the centerpiece of Erbse's edition, as also of Villoison's, is the testimony of the A scholia. Much as Villoison had supplemented the testimony of the A scholia with those of the B scholia, so also Erbse with that of the c branch comprised of the b and T scholia.

63. Cf. *PP* 185.
64. *PP* 185.
65. Apthorp 1980.xiii, enhancing the arguments of Bolling 1925.
66. Janko 1990.332–334.
67. Cf. Erbse 1959.275–303.
68. Pfeiffer 1968.214–215.
69. Pfeiffer 1968.215.

And yet, Erbse's edition cannot provide a complete picture of the Homer scholia. The corpus encompassed by this edition, massive as it is, preserves but a fraction of the information that had once been available and is still sporadically visible in the Homer commentaries of papyri from the Hellenistic and Roman eras. Moreover, Erbse's edition omits the D scholia, as we have already noted. This is a major loss, since these scholia supplement considerably the picture of ancient Homeric scholarship.[70]

To be sure, there are counter-trends to the trend of accepting the default of a "Wolfian vulgate." There are those who systematically argue for validating the editorial standards of the Alexandrians (Zenodotus and Aristophanes as well as Aristarchus), especially with reference to their choices of variant readings.[71] As of this writing, they are in a minority. Still, some aspects of their views are gaining ground: a case in point is the growing acceptance of arguments for the validity of Aristarchus' criteria in establishing an "authentic" *numerus versuum*, a fixed number of verses deemed genuine in the text of the Homeric poems.[72]

New editorial work on the D scholia will considerably enhance our knowledge of ancient Homeric scholarship, though the results of this work too will fall far short of the whole picture.[73] Moreover, the textual history of these scholia is even more complicated than that of the A scholia. In order to grasp the essence of the D scholia, we must start with the broader concept of "minor scholia," a category that includes the D group. The "minor scholia" can be divided into four categories:[74]

1 scholia written in papyrus texts of Homer (some of these scholia derive from school-texts, others from learned disquisitions) and interlinear scholia written in medieval manuscripts; the interlinear scholia found in the Homer texts of A and T, which stem from the D scholia, were published in the editions of Dindorf and Maass[75]
2 Homeric glossaries found in papyri and in medieval manuscripts; the basic format is to start with a *lēmma*, that is, with an individual word or phrase taken from the Homer text, and then to explain that *lēmma*
3 Homeric lexica, found in papyri and in medieval manuscripts
4 running paraphrases in prose, found in papyri and in medieval manuscripts

70. For a "Proecdosis" of the D scholia, see now van Thiel 2000a and 2000b.
71. See especially Rengakos 1993.
72. See especially Apthorp 1980.
73. On the D scholia, see again van Thiel 2000a.
74. This classification follows the valuable analysis of Henrichs 1971/1974. See especially Henrichs 1971.100–101.
75. Dindorf, volumes I–VI (1875–1888); volumes V–VI, edited by Maass (1887–1888). Cf. Henrichs 1971.101n11.

The *lēmmata* of the papyrus "scholia" can sometimes be traced back to the writings of Alexandrian scholars, though much of the information found in these texts comes from less scholarly sources.[76] We may note in general that the papyrus "scholia," like the medieval ones, often omit the name of the scholar whose authority had been invoked, and that the actual sources range from sophisticated scholarly epitomes and disquisitions (some of which must have had direct access to the work of Alexandrian scholars) to relatively unsophisticated schoolmasterly or schoolboyish paraphrases.[77]

What is remarkable about the medieval D scholia corresponding to the papyrus "scholia" is their tendency to preserve the relatively more learned versions of the ancient sources.[78] Also, the D scholia sometimes "have lemmas not represented in the direct transmission of the poems."[79]

The bulk of the "minor scholia" transmitted by the "archetype" of the medieval manuscript versions of the D scholia—as well as the codex of the lexicon of Apollonius Sophista and the codex of the lexicon of Hesychius—must have been very similar to what is already a fairly consolidated corpus of information as reflected in the Homer papyrus scholia of the Roman period (most of the Homer papyri stem from this period).[80] This much said, it is important to keep in mind that the D scholia preserve only a part of the traditions reflected in the Homer papyrus scholia.[81]

Finally, the D scholia tradition preserves another important component of scholarly heritage stemming from the period of Alexandrian Homer scholarship, drawing on the scholarly genre of the mythological *historia*; the chief source is a "complex" known as the Mythographus Homericus.[82]

We may perhaps detect a general sense of hesitation on the part of most Homer scholars today about the prospect of tracing the information found in medieval manuscript scholia back to corresponding information in papyrus scholia. Such reluctance can be explained in part as a lingering reaction to the excesses of earlier scholars who thought that they had recovered from

76. Henrichs 1971.102.

77. See especially Haslam 1997.94 on the medieval manuscript Genavensis 44, containing exegetical scholia at *Iliad* Φ that are "miraculously matched" by a second-century papyrus commentary on the same book.

78. Henrichs 1971.105.

79. Haslam 1997.96.

80. Henrichs 1971.106–107. Cf. Haslam 1997.60–61.

81. Henrichs 1971.109. There are two branches of sources for the Iliadic D scholia: a-1, edited by de Marco from select manuscripts (1932, 1941), and a-2, edited by Lascaris (1517). There is an edition by Asulanus (1528) of the Odyssean D scholia. See now also van Thiel 2000a and 2000b.

82. Montanari 1979.14; also p. 24n35 on the contributions of van der Valk in defining the Mythographus Homericus. Cf. Haslam 1997.61n17. Also Haslam 1990 and 1996. For an example of a *historia* preserved by way of the D scholia, see Haslam 1991.37.

the scholia the apparatus of Aristarchus himself. Constructions of stemmata linking the readings found in the scholia of papyri with the readings in the scholia of medieval manuscripts are nowadays deemed to be impossible even in the case of the "beloved" Venetus A manuscript, since "collation spreads readings unsystematically: there are no separate lines of transmission."[83] The point is well taken, though there may be a danger in going too far in the other direction by not crediting the readings found in the scholia of the Venetus A manuscript with an authority comparable to that of readings in other scholia, especially the D scholia. In the case of the D scholia, it has been said with some justification that their "authority" is often "bolstered by papyri."[84]

There is perhaps a further danger: an undervaluing of the Venetus A scholia leads to an undervaluing of the Homer editions of Aristarchus, Aristophanes, and Zenodotus, which in turn leads to an overvaluing of the "Wolfian vulgate." In order to find a balance, we may consider the testimony of the Homer scholia themselves on the concept of the "vulgate."

Applications of the term "vulgate" to various aspects of the Homeric textual tradition can be traced back ultimately to the usage of Aristarchus—or at least of Didymus, the epitomator of Aristarchus—as reflected especially in the Homer scholia. According to the scholia, the *khariesterai* (χαριέστεραι) or 'more elegant' texts of Homer were (1) the manuscripts that were "edited" by previous scholars and (2) the so-called *politikai* (πολιτικαί) or 'city editions' stemming from Massalia / Marseille (= ἡ Μασσαλιωτική [*Massaliōtikē*]), Chios (= ἡ Χία [*Khia*]), Argos (= ἡ Ἀργολική [*Argolikē*]), Sinope (= ἡ Σινωπική [*Sinōpikē*]), Cyprus (= ἡ Κυπρία [*Kupria*]), and Crete (= ἡ Κρητική [*Krētikē*]), while the texts of Homer that were *dēmōdeis* (δημώδεις) 'popular' or *koinai* (κοιναί) 'common' did not belong to the previous two privileged categories.[85] In the context of such negative comparisons, the usage of plural *koinai* (κοιναί) and singular *koinē* (κοινή) 'common' has been equated with Latin *vulgata* or 'vulgate.'[86]

But the biblical Latin analogy can mislead: in Jerome's *Epistle to Sunnia and Fretela*, the word *koinē*, which he glosses in Latin as the *vulgata* or 'vulgate', is applied to two 'common' Greek versions of the Hebrew Bible, one of which is the *editio* or 'edition' of one Lucian while the other is the *edi-*

---

83. Haslam 1997.95.

84. Haslam 1997.96.

85. More on these categories in Ch.4. See also Haslam 1997.71. For a defense of the authenticity of variant readings found in the *politikai* 'city editions', see PP 147–148, following Citti 1966; cf. Haslam 1997.69–71.

86. Allen 1924.317.

tio of Origen of Alexandria (late second to mid-third century CE)—that is, the Septuagint as edited in the *Hexapla* of Origen.[87] As in the usage of the Homer scholia, there is an element of negative comparison here as well: conceding that the Greek term *koinē* is applicable to both of the Greek-language biblical 'editions' in question, Jerome goes on to contrast the 'old corrupt edition' of Lucian with the 'uncorrupted and immaculate' version that serves as the source for Jerome's Latin vulgate translation:

> κοινή autem ista, hoc est communis, editio ipsa est quae et septuaginta, sed hoc interest inter utramque quod κοινή pro locis et temporibus et pro voluntate scriptorum vetus corrupta editio est, ea autem quae habetur in ἑξαπλοῖς et quam nos vertimus ipsa est quae in eruditorum libris incorrupta et immaculata septuaginta interpretum translatio reservatur.

> This *koinē*, that is, this common edition, is the same thing as the edition of the Seventy, but there is this difference between the two: that the *koinē*—in line with different times and different places and different whims of people who wrote it down—is an old and corrupt edition, whereas by contrast the one that is found in the *Hexapla* and which we have translated is the same thing as the actual translation [into Greek from Hebrew] of the Seventy interpreters, which has been conserved without corruption and without blemish in the books of the erudite.

> Jerome *Epistles* 106.2

In other words, the 'edition' of the Septuagint that Jerome uses as his own textual source is *koinē* to the extent that it is a 'common'—in the sense of 'general' or even 'universal'—text, but it transcends the designation of *koinē* to the extent that it is a 'corrected' text, freed from 'corruptions' associated with a text that is 'common'—in the sense of 'vulgar'. The word *koinē* has the aura of an authoritative but relatively 'uncorrected' text.

Similarly in the case of Aristarchus, it can be argued that his category of *koinai* or 'common' texts of Homer, mentioned throughout the Homeric scholia, may be traced back to an authoritative but relatively 'uncorrected' textual source, and the most likely reconstruction is an Athenian "City Edition," as current in the fourth century.[88]

A piece of evidence that may be cited in favor of this reconstruction is the fourth-century Athenian usage of the adjective *koinos* as 'common' in the

87. Jerome *Epistles* 106.2, as discussed by Allen 1924.317, 319. See in general Neuschäfer 1987. Cf. also Lührs 1992.8 on Origen's editorial policy of avoiding personal emendations or conjectures in editing the text of the Septuagint.

88. *PP* 187–200, following (in part) Jensen 1980.109. This possibility is entertained but ultimately rejected by Haslam 1997.71.

ideological sense of 'general, standardized, universalized';[89] such a description would fit the *Iliad* and *Odyssey* as "owned" by the Athenian State, on
the occasion of seasonally-recurring performances at the Festival of the
Panathenaia.[90]

Another piece of evidence comes from the patterns of fluctuation that we
see between plural *koinai* and singular *koinē* in the medieval Homer scholia:
there are cases where the plural *koinai* in these medieval texts is matched
by the distinctive singular *koinē* in the testimony of annotations written in
papyrus texts of Homer.[91] Here too, as in Jerome's assessment of the word
koinē, we may detect the aura of an authoritative but relatively 'uncorrected'
text.[92]

Thus the argument that the *koinē* Homer text stems from an Athenian
"City Edition" cannot be countered by suggesting that Aristarchus would
have actually preferred an Athenian "City Edition," if indeed he had access
to such a thing, over other editions.[93] The Homer scholia make it clear that
Aristarchus' criterion for distinguishing a superior from an inferior *ekdosis*
or 'edition' is the variable scholarly quality of the editing process, that is, of
diorthōsis or 'correction'—in the sense of *restoring 'genuine' or 'original' readings to a 'corrupted' text.* Accordingly, I propose to use 'corrective editing' as
a working translation of *diorthōsis*.[94]

To the extent that the *koinē* Homer is 'common' in the uneroded and privileged sense of a 'general, standardized, universalized' text stemming from

89. Cf. Lycurgus *Against Leokrates* 102 and Demosthenes 18.170; also Isaeus 7.16, on the
care taken in legitimizing texts recorded by the state of Athens: only after full verification
'are they to be written down into the *koinon grammateion*' (εἰς τὸ κοινὸν γραμματεῖον
ἐγγράφειν). This usage confirms that the expression ἐν κοινῷ goes with *both* γραψαμένους
and φυλάττειν in "Plutarch" *Lives of the Ten Orators* 841f, as discussed in *PP* 175n77: in this
context, what is recorded and preserved by the Athenian state in standardized form is the
corpus of tragedies attributed to Aeschylus, Sophocles, and Euripides. See also Bollack
1994.

90. *PP* 189. More in Ch.2 about the Panathenaia.

91. Haslam 1997.71 and n35.

92. Haslam 1997.71 notes that the relatively fuller and more accurate reporting of singular
koinē vs. plural *koinai* in the papyri indicates "the severely reduced nature of the scholia."
I should point out, however, that singular *koinē* is also attested in the medieval Homer
scholia, as for example at *Iliad* E 461b and M 404a1. Such usages of the singular, relatively
more common in the papyri and less common in the medieval scholia, can I think be
traced back to an era that predates Aristarchus himself. By the time of Aristarchus,
for whom there was evidently no need to posit a single *surviving* authoritative text of
Homer, there would be no need to specify a singular *koinē* except perhaps in terms of a
reconstruction.

93. I am paraphrasing here (and disagreeing with) the suggestion of Haslam 1997.71.

94. See further at Ch.4, p. 85.

an earlier past, we can expect Aristarchus to value it; to the extent that this same *koinē* is 'common' in the eroded and non-privileged sense of 'vulgar', we can expect him to prefer the more 'corrected' editions from the more recent past, including those of Aristophanes and Zenodotus. This pattern of preference could only be expected to intensify in the post-Aristarchean era, by which time the privileged sense of *koinē* would have eroded further.

According to an explanation that differs from the one offered here, the mentions of plural *koinai* in the Homer scholia refer simply to "the early Ptolemaic papyri that we may see as specimens of the 'common' text(s)."[95] This is to assume, however, that plural *koinai* and the more distinctive singular *koinē* mean 'common' only in the eroded sense of 'vulgar'. It is also to assume that *koinē* is merely a foil, an inferior copy. Rather, it may be an authoritative point of departure for the process of scholarly *diorthōsis* 'corrective editing' that ostensibly leads to the edition of a superior text.[96]

The authenticity of *koinē* readings, where the designation *koinē* is actually made explicit by the scholia, can be confirmed on the basis of two independent criteria: (1) comparative linguistics and (2) oral poetics.[97] But this is not to discredit the authenticity of non-*koinē* readings that the scholia attribute to the *diorthōsis* or 'corrective editing' of scholars like Aristarchus. In many instances, the variant readings attributed to Aristarchus or Aristophanes or Zenodotus can likewise be confirmed on the basis of those same two independent criteria of comparative linguistics and oral poetics.[98] Thus it is unjustified to assume, as have many Homeric scholars, that the variant readings resulting from the *diorthōsis* 'corrective editing' of Alexandrian critics are as a rule scholarly conjectures. As I will show at a later point in the book, many of these variants stemming from the learned editions prove to be just as authentic, from the standpoint of oral poetics, as the variants stemming from the "City Editions" or from the *koinē* texts in general.

Ironically, an assumption that Wolf had made about oral traditions led him to accept one of the two working assumptions of Alexandrian critics like Aristarchus. These critics assumed both that the Homeric text was 'corrupted' and that they could 'correct' these corruptions by combining the internal evidence of Homeric diction with the external evidence of variant manuscript traditions. Though Wolf did not accept the assumption of the Alexandrian critics that they had the means to 'correct' the 'corruptions', he took as a given their assumption that there were indeed 'corruptions'

95. Haslam 1997.71, following S. West 1967.26.
96. For more on *diorthōsis* as a process of 'corrective editing', see Ch.4, p. 85.
97. Janko 1992.26.
98. *PP* 148–149; cf. Muellner 1976.58–62. Also Bird 1994.

in the first place. For a scholar like Aristarchus, such 'corruptions' were a matter of textual traditions that had gone wrong. For Wolf, they became something else, a matter of oral traditions that had made the textual traditions go wrong.

The study of living oral traditions, as we shall see in the chapters that follow, refutes this assumption: the process of composition-in-performance, typical of oral traditions, does not 'corrupt' an 'original' composition. Even the concept of 'original' misleads in the context of this argumentation, in that any performance in an oral tradition can re-create a given composition into a new 'original'—though of course the degree of re-creation may vary considerably, depending not only on the nature of the given tradition but also on a wide variety of historically-determined contingencies.

In the chapters that follow, I have more to say about oral traditional poetry and about the process of recomposition-in-performance. I will argue that different authentic variants can be generated by the same oral tradition at different historical points of its evolution. I will also argue that the principle of variation affects not only the content but even the length of a given recomposition-in-performance.

The Homer scholia are a most valuable source for reconstructing the evolution of Homeric textual traditions from oral traditions. As we shall see, however, such reconstruction cannot recover any single definitive text. Different Homeric texts may have been definitive at different historical moments, but no single Homeric text can be deemed definitive beyond its own historical context.[99]

99. Haslam 1997.95 argues that the text of A merits no greater respect than the text-family of BCE³ or the text of T or the underlying text of D.

CHAPTER 2

The Homeric Text and
Problems of Multiformity

The multiformity of Homeric poetry is a sign of its prehistory as oral traditional poetry. This insight stems from the work of Milman Parry[1] and Albert Lord.[2] Multiformity, according to Lord, is a basic feature of oral traditional poetry.[3]

In his writings, lectures, and conversations, Lord preferred to use the terms *multiformity* and *multiform* instead of *variation* and *variant* in order to emphasize the fluidity of oral poetry, to be contrasted with the fixity of written texts. Lord was worried that those who are unfamiliar with the workings of any given oral tradition might easily be misled to think of its variants exclusively in terms of a pre-existing fixed text:

[I]f one believes in a fixed text, then the idea of variants—even the word— indicates a deviation from a fixed entity. In one's thinking of the composition of oral traditional poetry, the word *multiform* is more accurate than 'variant', because it does not give preference or precedence to any one word or set of words to express an idea; instead it acknowledges that the idea may exist in several forms.[4]

* The original version of this essay is N 2001a.
1. Collected papers in Parry 1971, = *MHV*.
2. Lord 1960, 1991, 1995.
3. Lord 1960.100.
4. Lord 1995.23. In this posthumously published work, Lord also refers to his extensive

This concept of multiformity, as Lord acknowledges, challenges the student of literature with a basic problem:

> Our real difficulty arises from the fact that, unlike the oral poet, we are not accustomed to thinking in terms of fluidity. We find it difficult to grasp something that is *multiform*. It seems to us necessary to construct an ideal text or to seek an *original*, and we remain dissatisfied with an ever-changing phenomenon. I believe that once we know the facts of oral composition we must cease trying to find an *original* of any traditional song. From one point of view each performance is an *original*.[5]

As we see from Lord's formulation, the concept of "original" is relative in terms of oral traditions. In what follows I argue that multiformity in oral traditions likewise needs to be defined in relative rather than absolute terms.

Let us begin by applying both synchronic and diachronic perspectives to the concept of oral composition.[6] This concept can be understood as a process of recomposition in the context of each new performance. From a synchronic point of view, oral composition at any given time and place may be relatively more or less multiform, along a graded continuum extending from relatively more fluid to relatively more rigid systems of recomposition-in-performance; from a diachronic point of view as well, the process of oral composition may be more or less multiform at different phases of its history.[7] Proposing an evolutionary model for the making of Homeric poetry, I have argued that the *Iliad* and *Odyssey* were relatively more multiform in earlier

---

discussions of multiformity in his earlier work (especially Lord 1991). For more on multiformity, see also *PP*, especially Ch.5, "Multiform epic and Aristarchus' quest for the real Homer." In *PP* 9, I explicitly accept Lord's understanding of *multiform* while continuing to use the term *variant* as an equivalent. The usefulness of speaking in terms of variation—without implications of an *Urform*—is vividly illustrated by the metaphorical world of *poikilia* 'variation': see *PP* Ch.1: "The Homeric nightingale and the poetics of variation in the art of a troubadour." Lord himself (1995.23) uses *variant* and *multiform* as synonyms: "The very existence of these thousands of variants or multiforms is dramatic proof of the fluidity of the Latvian oral *daina* tradition."

5. Lord 1960.100. The italics are mine. Quoted in *PP* 9. In the original printed version of *PP*, I committed three errors in reproducing this single paragraph, which is one of Lord's most valuable formulations. For the record, here are my errors: p. 9 line 4, "It seems to us necessary" not "It seems ideal to us"; p. 9 line 8, "From one point of view" not "From an oral point of view"; p. 9 line 9, "is an" not "is." These errors, corrected in later versions of *PP*, illustrate (at my expense) the dangers of extreme familiarity with the original of a fixed text. There is an irony in my having made perhaps the worst typographical errors of my career in reproducing a passage that was most familiar to me.

6. On the terms "synchronic" and "diachronic," see again Saussure 1916.117.

7. For more on synchronic and diachronic perspectives in analyzing oral traditions, see *PR* 3–4 and *HR* 1.

phases and relatively less so in later phases of developments that resulted ultimately in the Homeric texts as we now have them.[8]

The progressive reduction of multiformity in Homeric poetry resulted primarily from the passage of this poetry through an Athenian phase of development—a "Panathenaic bottleneck."[9] In view of continuing debate over the very concept of multiformity as applied to the Homeric poems, it is timely to reassess the evolutionary model in general and the theory of a Panathenaic bottleneck in particular.

In response to the challenge posed by Lord's concept of multiformity, the evolutionary model presents an alternative to the numerous attempts at reconstructing an 'original' text of Homer. In terms of this model, I envisage five periods of progressively less fluidity, more rigidity:

1 a relatively most fluid period, with no written texts, extending from the early second millennium into the middle of the eighth century in the first millennium BCE.

2 a more formative or "Panhellenic" period, still with no written texts, from the middle of the eighth century to the middle of the sixth BCE.

3 a definitive period, centralized in Athens, with potential texts in the sense of *transcripts*, at any or several points from the middle of the sixth century to the later part of the fourth BCE; this period starts with the reform of Homeric performance traditions in Athens during the régime of the Peisistratidai.

4 a standardizing period, with texts in the sense of transcripts or even *scripts*, from the later part of the fourth century to the middle of the second BCE; this period starts with the reform of Homeric performance traditions in Athens during the régime of Demetrius of Phalerum, which lasted from 317 to 307 BCE

5 a relatively most rigid period, with texts as *scripture*, from the middle of the second century onward; this period starts with the completion of Aristarchus' editorial work on the Homeric texts, not long after 150 BCE or so, which is a date that also marks the general disappearance of the so-called "eccentric" papyri.

By the time of period 3, Homeric poetry reaches a phase that can be described in terms of "textualization"—without our having to posit an orig-

8. *PP* 151–52, 109, and *HQ* 103–4. This is not to say that fluidity and rigidity are necessarily characteristic of earlier and later phases of any system. My "evolutionary model" differs from various other models, such as the "dictation theory" of Janko 1982.228–231, who proposes 750–725 BCE and 743–713 BCE as definitive dates for the text-fixation of the *Iliad* and *Odyssey* respectively. It also differs from the modified dictation theory of West 1995.203–219, who argues for a terminus post quem of either 688 or perhaps 678 BCE.

9. The term was introduced in N 1999b.271–272 (see now *HR* 69–70); also N 1999f.68. For more on the general concept behind the term, see also *PH* 23, *HQ* 43, and *PP* 77.

inal "text." A key to this concept of textualization is the factor of *diffusion*, complementing the two more basic factors of oral poetics, *composition* and *performance*.[10] This third factor of oral poetics, *diffusion*, can in some cases involve a process of centralization—even if in other cases it is a process of decentralization, of atomized dispersal.[11] In period 3 of the evolutionary model, the hypothetical point of "textualization," I posit a clearly defined center for the diffusion, or "broadcasting," of Homeric poetry. The centralized diffusion would have involved centripetal as well as centrifugal forces —"a centralized context for both the coming together of diverse audiences and the spreading outward of more unified traditions."[12] This center of diffusion was the seasonally recurring festival of the Panathenaia at Athens.

In the era that I am calling "period 3," the Homeric *Iliad* and *Odyssey* were performed by professional rhapsodes at the Athenian state festival of the Panathenaia, just as tragedies were performed by professional actors (and by nonprofessional choruses) at the Athenian state festival of the City Dionysia.[13] Though there are many uncertainties, there have survived some valuable pieces of information about the seasonally recurring Panathenaic performances of Homeric poetry.[14] Also, there is one certainty that turns

10. To quote from my earlier work (*HQ* 40): "I continue to describe as *text-fixation* or *textualization* the process whereby each composition-in-performance becomes progressively less changeable in the course of diffusion—with the proviso that we understand *text* here in a metaphorical sense."

11. For models of centralized and decentralized diffusion, see *OEI*, especially S. H. Blackburn, "Patterns of Development for Indian Oral Epics," *OEI* 15–32.

12. *HQ* 43.

13. See *PP* 81 for more on the "functioning institutional complementarity, in Athens, between the performance of drama by actors and chorus at the City Dionysia on the one hand and, on the other, the performance of Homeric epos—and of Homeric hymns that serve as preludes to the epos—by rhapsodes at the Panathenaia." The most important references to the Athenian institution of rhapsodic performances of Homeric poetry at the Panathenaia are "Plato" *Hipparkhos* 228b–c, Lycurgus *Against Leokrates* 102, and Dieuchidas of Megara (fourth century BCE) *FGH* 485 F 6 via Diogenes Laertius 1.57. For a correlation of the information provided by these passages, see *PP* 70–91. As for the references to the *epē* of Homer, as found in all three passages, I offer the working translation 'verses'. More precisely, the *epē* are the poetic 'lines' of Homer (on *epos* as a distinct poetic unit or 'line', see Koller 1972). For Aristotle, the *epē* of Homer become 'epic' by default, whence the term *epopoiia* 'making of epic', as in the beginning of the *Poetics*, 1447a: see N 1999e.27. The implicit preoccupation with 'lines' as the poetic units or building blocks of *epē* has to do with an ongoing question that engaged the ancient transmitters of the Homeric tradition: which 'lines' are genuine compositions of Homer and which 'lines' have been 'interpolated' (one word for which is *emballein*, as in Diogenes Laertius 1.57)? For more on this specific concern, see the next note.

14. Especially important is the information to be derived from the ancient commentaries on Pindar *Nemean* 2.1 as preserved in the scholia (ed. Drachmann). This information, I

out to be vital for understanding the overall history of the Homeric tradition: the *Iliad* and the *Odyssey* eventually became the only epic poetry to be performed by rhapsodes at the Panathenaia, that most important of all Athenian festivals.[15]

For period 3, it is useful to picture the Athenian or "Panathenaic" phase of Homeric poetry as a "bottleneck" that affects the flow of ongoing oral traditions. In terms of this metaphor of a "Panathenaic bottleneck," we may envisage a movement from decentralized multiplicity toward centralized unity. The living South Slavic oral traditions described by Lord are decentralized,

argue, was mediated by the school of Aristarchus (middle of second century BCE), whose thinking affects an important reference to Hippostratus, = *FGH* 568 F 5, in the scholia to *Nemean* 2.1c. Hippostratus (ca. third century BCE) is being cited here as the source for information concerning Kynaithos of Chios as the first rhapsodic performer of the *epē* of "Homer" in the polis of Syracuse, within the timeframe of the sixty-ninth Olympiad (= 504–1 BCE). It seems to me misleading to claim that all the information we read in the scholia about the rhapsodic performance of Kynaithos "derives" not from Aristarchus but from Hippostratus, as if we needed to make an exclusive choice between the two sources. Janko 1998a makes this claim with specific reference to what I said in HS 110 (see p. 12n35 above), where I discussed the scholia to Pindar *Nemean* 2.1c. The fact that one detail in the scholiastic information about Kynaithos (that is, the dating of his rhapsodic performance at Syracuse) "derives" from Hippostratus cannot be used to rule out the school of Aristarchus as an intermediary source for that information—or even as a direct source for other information about Hippostratus. Besides the reference to Hippostratus in the scholia for Pindar *Nemean* 2, we see four explicit references to Aristarchus in the scholia for the same poem: 9a, 17c (twice), and 19. We may note too the reference to Hippostratus *FGH* 568 F 2 in the scholia at Pindar *Pythian* 6.5a. This reference happens to occur immediately next to an explicit reference to Aristarchus, again at 5a. In all, we find over seventy references to Aristarchus in Drachmann's edition of the Pindaric scholia (and five to Hippostratus). These references, as casual as they are frequent, lead me to conclude that Aristarchus' overall critical presence was taken for granted in the Pindaric exegetical tradition that culminated in the scholia. Returning, then, to the scholia for Pindar *Nemean* 2.1c: I maintain that the learned discussion in this section reflects primarily the agenda of Aristarchus, not of Hippostratus (whose work concentrated, after all, on sorting out the genealogies of Sicilian dynasties). Thus I follow the view of Wolf 1795 Ch.25, who discerns the agenda of "the Alexandrians" in the claim, reported by the scholia for Pindar *Nemean* 2.1c, that Kynaithos and his followers 'interpolated [emballein] many of the *epē* that they had composed to be placed inside the composition [poetry] of Homer' (οὕς φασι πολλὰ τῶν ἐπῶν ποιήσαντας ἐμβαλεῖν εἰς τὴν Ὁμήρου ποίησιν).

15. The wording of Lycurgus *Against Leokrates* 102 makes it clear that only the *epē* of "Homer" were performed at the Panathenaia. Also, in the scholia to Pindar *Nemean* 2.1d, it is mentioned *en passant* that the rhapsodes of Homeric poetry have as their repertoire the *two* poems (ἑκατέρας τῆς ποιήσεως εἰσενεχθείσης); the source of information in this context is named: Dionysius of Argos (ca. fourth or third century BCE) = *FGH* 308 F 2. In my view, this reference to Dionysius was mediated by the school of Aristarchus; compare the reference to Hippostratus (ca. third century BCE) = *FGH* 568 F 5 in the scholia to Pindar *Nemean* 2.1c, as discussed in the note above.

abounding in a multiplicity of thematic and formal variants. A similar type of multiplicity can also be posited for period 1 in the evolutionary model for ancient Greek oral poetry and, to a lesser degree, for period 2. In period 3, however, such multiplicity becomes "gradually squeezed into a centralized unity that allows for only minimal variation."[16] In terms of the evolutionary model, only the *Iliad* and the *Odyssey* pass through the "Panathenaic Bottleneck," starting in the sixth century BCE; other archaic Greek epic traditions, most notably the "Cyclic" poetry of the *Cypria*, the *Aithiopis*, the *Little Iliad*, and the *Iliou Persis*, are exempt.

The wording "minimal variation" is intended to reflect an inherent relativity in the concept of multiformity: by the time we reach period 3, in terms of the model described, the multiformity of the Homeric poems is already relatively minimal. In period 4 and period 5, the relative multiformity is even further reduced.

Whereas this model views the multiformity of the Homeric poems in relative terms, others imagine a binary opposition between multiformity and "uniformity," arguing that the *Iliad* and the *Odyssey* are uniform to start with—and positing an "original" written text in order to explain such uniformity. In the words of one commentator:

> All our sources [of the *Iliad*] basically agree over matters of dialect, plot, episodes and so forth; other oral epics recorded in writing have a far wider range of textual variation, e.g. the *Nibelungenlied, Chanson de Roland, Mahabharata,* or *Digenes Akrites.* All of our MSS [of the *Iliad*] *somehow go back to a single origin* [italics mine], and have passed through a single channel; it is improbable that more than one "original" of the *Iliad* ever existed, even if different rhapsodic performances and editorial interventions have led to the addition or (rarely) omission of verses here and there. This basic fixity needs to be explained.[17]

In terms of this formulation, the notion of the "fixity" of the *Iliad* is to be explained by the hypothesis of an "original" text dictated by an eighth-century Homer.[18] The evolutionary model, recalling Lord's view that "we must cease trying to find an original of any traditional song," obviates the need to posit such an "original." It sees the "fixity" of the Homeric poems as relative, resulting from a progressive decrease in multiformity, not from an "original" uniformity.[19]

16. N 1999b.271, *HR* 69–70.
17. Janko 1992.29.
18. Janko 1992.37–8.
19. N 1999b.269–72. See now also *HR* Ch.3.

The idea of Homeric "fixity" has led to assumptions of a rigid distinction between multiformity and uniformity, so that Lord's concept of multiformity as applied to the Homeric *Iliad* is rejected—while it is accepted for the Epic Cycle, as exemplified by the *Cypria*.[20] It is worthwhile to address the assumptions inherent in such an absolutizing notion of multiformity, given the disparity between this view and the concept of multiformity as formulated by Lord. For the moment, however, let us concentrate on a contrasting concept, "uniformity."

To argue that the *Iliad* is "uniform" in contrast to the *Cypria*, which is multiform, requires a special explanation for the exempting of Homeric poetry:

> It follows, then, that while [...] the fixation of oral poems in writing does not necessarily affect their multiform character or produce a variant that is more authoritative than the others, [t]his conclusion fits the Cyclic epics rather than the poems of Homer [= the *Iliad* and the *Odyssey*]. Obviously, some additional factor, and not simply their fixation in writing, was responsible for the remarkable uniformity of the Homeric poems.[21]

The fundamental issue here is the concept of multiformity itself. What is described as "the remarkable uniformity" of the *Iliad* and the *Odyssey* could instead be viewed as a matter of relatively less multiformity in terms of these poems' evolution, as opposed to relatively more multiformity in the *Cypria* and in the rest of the Cycle. Multiformity and "uniformity" as polar opposites cannot simply be mapped onto oral and written poetry respectively.

What is the "additional factor" at work in making the Homeric poems distinct from the Cycle? In terms of the evolutionary model, the factor of the Panathenaia and the "Panathenaic bottleneck," beginning at period 3, is critical. Some time in the second half of the sixth century BCE, around the starting point of this period, the evolution of the Homeric poems diverges radically from the evolution of the Cycle. By "Homeric poems" I mean the *Iliad* and the *Odyssey* only—to the exclusion of the Cycle.[22]

Two important clarifications are needed.

20. Finkelberg 2000; Janko's formulation of "fixity" in terms of an "original" uniformity is quoted at p. 4.

21. Finkelberg 2000.9.

22. N 1999b.271, *HR* 70. For further bibliography on the Panathenaia as the defining context of the *Iliad* and the *Odyssey*, see p. 65 of Lowenstam 1997. Although Finkelberg (2000.9) evidently agrees with me about the Panathenaia as a factor that distinguishes the Homeric poems from the Cycle, she chooses not to engage with my evolutionary model (more specifically, with the formulation of "period 3" and the "Panathenaic bottleneck").

First, in terms of the evolutionary model, only the *Iliad* and the *Odyssey* pass through the "Panathenaic bottleneck." Only the *Iliad* and the *Odyssey* pass through periods 3, 4, and 5. By contrast, the poetry of the Cycle—including the *Cypria*—is exempt from periods 3, 4, and 5. Consequently, the evolutionary model allows for far more fluidity—or let us say multiformity—in the case of the *Cypria* and far less in the case of the *Iliad*.

Secondly, if indeed the *Iliad* and the *Odyssey* were shaped by the Panathenaia, unlike the *Cypria* and other poems of the Cycle, we must still be wary of assuming that the Homeric poems of the second half of the sixth century BCE were already the written "originals" of our *Iliad* and *Odyssey*.

With these reflections in mind, we may move from problems of "uniformity" to the related problems of multiformity. When Lord spoke of multiformity, he was thinking of oral traditions. Others are thinking of written traditions when they speak of "different versions of the *Cypria* through the period of one thousand years, from Herodotus in the fifth century BCE to Proclus in the fifth century [CE]" and when they contrast what they describe as the multiformity or fluidity of the *Cypria* with the "uniformity" or rigidity of the Homeric poems.[23] I see conceptual and methodological difficulties with such descriptions of the *Cypria* as "a written multiform text."

It is striking that scholars should argue for a textual multiformity that lasts a thousand years. Such an emphasis on *longue durée* suggests that, in the case of the *Cypria*, the argument needs a stark contrast with the textual history of the *Iliad*, which takes up roughly the same time span. According to this argument, the Cycle in general and the *Cypria* in particular stayed multiform for a thousand years in contrast to the *Iliad*, which was supposedly "uniform" from the very start: "But there has always been only one version of the *Iliad*."[24] Yet, as argued above, the multiformity of the *Cypria* is not some kind of absolute: all we can say is that the *Cypria* was relatively more multiform than the *Iliad*.[25] Second, there is no evidence for the claim that the *Iliad* was a "uniform" text dating from the second half of the sixth century BCE.

Moreover, there is evidence against such claims about the *Iliad*. The testimony of vase paintings shows clear traces of thematic multiformity in the

23. Finkelberg 2000.11.

24. Finkelberg 2000.11. In this context, she compares the Homeric tradition to the Hebrew Bible, citing with approval West 1998a.95. In terms of my "evolutionary" model, a scriptural analogy is apt not so much for the sixth century BCE, as Finkelberg and West think, but more for the second and thereafter: see Ch.7 of *PP*, "Homer as 'Scripture.'"

25. See Burgess 1996, especially p. 90n51. Moreover, much of the multiformity claimed for the *Cypria* can be explained in other ways: it is possible that there were several or at least two compositions entitled *Cypria* (cf. Finkelberg 2000.8n26).

Iliad tradition up to the early fifth century BCE; to quote Steven Lowenstam: "with regard to Iliadic and Odyssean myth, the versions of the epic tradition preserved in our inherited written texts do not have authoritative status for the vase-painters of the sixth and early fifth centuries."[26]

We may consider the clear traces of multiformity in the textual history of the *Iliad*—and of the *Odyssey*—down to the middle of the second century BCE. As I have argued extensively in other works, many of the textual variants that we do find surviving in the Homeric poems are in fact the reflexes of formulaic and even thematic multiforms that characterize oral poetry.[27] Such textual traces of multiformity in the Homeric poems cannot be expected to match—in degree—any corresponding textual traces of multiformity in the Cycle, not to mention the multiformity of living oral traditions as recorded by today's ethnographers. Still, many of the variants we see in the attested phases of the Homeric textual tradition are survivals of multiforms stemming from unattested phases of the Homeric oral tradition. As we work our way forward in time, to be sure, we find that the degree of textual multiformity becomes minimal. Still, even in the latest phases of the ancient textual history, it is a question of degrees: we find ever less multiformity, not absolute "uniformity."

Perhaps it would be useful for us to reverse, as it were, our temporal direction. If we work our way backward in time, not forward, as we trace the textual history of the Homeric poems, the implausibility of a "uniform" Panathenaic text of the *Iliad* and the *Odyssey*, continuing unchanged from the second half of the sixth century BCE all the way to the second half of the second, can be intuited more easily. What we see is a marked increase in degrees of multiformity as we move back from the fifth to the fourth to the third periods—from "scripture" to "script" to "transcript."

For a brief survey, let us start with the "vulgate" version of the Homeric poems, the version that Aristarchus accepted as the base text (*texte de base*) for his edition of the *Iliad* and *Odyssey* in the middle of the second century BCE. Even this "vulgate" was not a "uniform" text—as far as Aristarchus himself was concerned. In his Homeric commentaries or *hupomnēmata*, he frequently adduced textual variants that he considered more likely to be

---

26. Lowenstam 1997.66. Finkelberg 2000.9n27 cites Lowenstam's article, though this citation actually undermines the general claim that she is making at p. 9 where she says: "no fluctuations in the names of the characters or in the order of the episodes like those observed [in the *Cypria*] have ever been attested for the *Iliad* subjects." Lowenstam documents such fluctuations (see especially his p. 66n145 concerning variations on the Briseis theme and other such multiformities). On Homer and the vase-painting tradition, see also Shapiro 1993 and Snodgrass 1998.

27. See Ch.4 and Ch.5 below.

Homeric than the corresponding textual forms that he actually retained in his base text, in the "vulgate."[28] Similarly, though he athetized some verses—that is, marked them with an obelus to indicate that he considered them non-Homeric—he nevertheless retained such verses in his base text because the manuscript evidence at his disposal did not permit him to do otherwise. Aristarchus was persuaded that such verses, although he athetized them, really did belong in the base text that we call the "vulgate."[29]

Aristarchus treated the "vulgate" Homer text in much the same way that a neo-Aristarchean editor like Origen treated the Septuagint in his *Hexapla* edition of the Hebrew Bible: the Septuagint was Origen's base text.[30] By analogy, we may say that the Homeric "vulgate," as the base text of Aristarchus, had achieved the status of "scripture."[31]

It was essentially the "vulgate" version of the Homeric poems, and not the textual variants adduced by Aristarchus, that survived into the medieval manuscript tradition.[32] For this reason, it has been inferred that the "vulgate" version of the Homeric poems represents a textual continuum derived directly from what is supposed to be a sixth-century Panathenaic archetype.[33]

It must be pointed out, however, that Aristarchus himself—as frequently paraphrased in such sources as the Venetus A scholia of the *Iliad*—did not speak of a "vulgate" in terms of any single textual tradition. Instead, he studied the evidence of *koinai*, 'common' manuscripts reflecting a textual consensus that presumably went back to some kind of 'standard' version.[34] For Aristarchus there was no single unified *koinē* manuscript that could possibly approximate the status of a definitive archetype.[35]

From the standpoint of classical Athenian civic terminology, *koinē* in the double sense of 'standard' and 'common to all' could indeed have been used as a suitable term for a Panathenaic tradition of Homeric poetry.[36]

28. *PP* Ch.5.

29. In Ch.4 below, I introduce the terms of "horizontal" and "vertical" variants: in the first case, the ancient editor had to choose between different wordings that make up a single line of Homeric poetry, while in the second case he had to choose between fewer or more lines that make up a given sequence of lines (cf. also *PP* 139–40).

30. *PP* 194–5.

31. For the hermeneutic model of Homer as "scripture," see *PP* Ch.7.

32. See Haslam 1997, especially pp. 63–78.

33. Finkelberg 2000.2n2 (also p. 10) evidently uses the term "vulgate" with this understanding.

34. See Ch.1 p. 23; cf. *PP* 117, 133–134.

35. More on *koinē* in what follows.

36. On the *koinē* as a virtual 'standard' text derived from Panathenaic competitions in performing the Homeric poems, see *PP* 152–6, 185–90, 193–5, 198, 205.

Nevertheless, such a tradition would be more a matter of performance than of text. At best, we may think of such a Homeric tradition in terms of a Panathenaic "script."[37]

Any Panathenaic "script," however, could be subject to some degree of change each time the *Iliad* and the *Odyssey* were reperformed on the occasion of each quadrennial recurrence of the Great Panathenaia.[38] For an analogy, we may compare the design woven into the Peplos of the goddess Athena on the occasion of each successive quadrennial recurrence of the Great Panathenaia: this design, controlled by elected officials called the *athlothetai*, was institutionally subject to change.[39]

Just as Aristarchus had no single unified *koinē* manuscript but a multiplicity of *koinai* for establishing his base text, so also for us it turns out to be an impossibility to recover a single unified "vulgate," stemming from some notionally "uniform" Panathenaic text of Homer written as early as the second half of the sixth century BCE.[40] Such a text is nothing more than a virtual reality. More realistically, we may posit multiform "transcripts" stemming from a multiplicity of seasonally recurring performances of Homeric poetry at each successive Panathenaic festival. By "transcript" here I mean a text that merely records a given performance and that has no direct bearing on the traditions of performance, as in the case of a "script."[41]

It remains to ask how we may distinguish more precisely between "transcripts" and "scripts" of Homeric performances at the Panathenaia. In terms of my evolutionary model, moving forward rather than backward in time, I can draw the line only imprecisely, somewhere around the third and the fourth periods, characterized by relatively more and less fluidity or multiformity. For a more precise distinction between "transcript" and "script," however, we may look to the principle of *numerus versuum*, a strict system of regulating the number of Homeric verses. As the pioneering work of Michael Apthorp has demonstrated, this principle was observed by Aristarchus in establishing the base text of his Homeric edition around the middle of the second century BCE.[42] The principle of regulating the number of Homeric verses seems to be at work already in the fourth century, possibly as early as the time of Plato.[43]

As Apthorp has also demonstrated, Homeric verses that were athetized

37. For the hermeneutic model of Homer as "script," see *PP* Ch.6.
38. *PR* 7–8.
39. *PR* 91.
40. *PP* 117, 152–6, 185–6.
41. For the hermeneutic model of Homer as "transcript," see *PP* Ch.5.
42. Apthorp 1980.
43. *PP* 143.

by Aristarchus nevertheless "counted": they were included in the base text of his edition. In other words, they were considered to be part of the official *numerus versuum*. By contrast, verses that were deleted by Aristarchus from his base text fell outside the count, as it were, and they were not part of the *numerus versuum*.[44] These deleted verses, nowadays known as "plus verses," can be called "interpolations" from the standpoint of the Homeric textual tradition as understood by Aristarchus.[45] They are multiforms, however, from the standpoint of the Homeric oral tradition as we understand it from analyzing the formulaic and thematic repertoire of Homeric poetry as a system. This Homeric "system" is represented not only by those textual variants that happen to fit an immediate context, established by the text of the Homeric poems as we know them. It is represented also by all textual variants that can be shown to be formulaic multiforms.

Some textual variants, that is, stem from relatively earlier phases of an evolving oral tradition, while other textual variants stem from later phases. In terms of my evolutionary model, plus verses of Homeric poetry may belong to a phase so early that they predate the system of *numerus versuum*. If we contemplate the later phases, when this system of verse-counting was being introduced, we can see the emergence of a principle that regulates performances, not texts per se. The passage from unregulated to regulated verse-counts in the performance tradition would correspond to a passage from "transcript" to "script" in the text tradition. In other words, the principle of *numerus versuum* had to be performative before it became purely textual. Moreover, the passage from performative to purely textual verse-counting would correspond to a passage from "script" to "scripture."

The plus verses are a most valuable test case. As a rule, they do not fit, either textually or thematically: we find that there is usually something "off" about them in terms of the overall text as we know it from viewing the Homeric poems through the lens of the "vulgate" version. But there is nothing "off" about these same plus verses in terms of the overall system as we know it from viewing Homeric poetry through the lens of its formulas and themes inherited from a continuing oral poetic tradition.

A striking example is *Iliad* E 808, where Athena says to Diomedes that she helped his father, Tydeus, emerge victorious in a confrontation with the Thebans. As Apthorp has demonstrated on the basis of the external manuscript evidence, line 808 was a plus verse, and had been deleted by Aristarchus from his base text, though the verse had subsequently crept back into the post-Aristarchean versions of the "vulgate," including the text of the

---

44. I say "delete" and not "omit" for reasons that I will clarify in Ch.3.
45. Apthorp 1980.47–56.

Venetus A.[46] Not only is there external evidence, in terms of a documented history of "weak" manuscript attestations, that this verse is anomalous, there is internal evidence as well, in terms of the immediate context of the Iliadic text as we have it: Athena seems to be saying to Diomedes that she is present and ready to help him fight the Trojans, whereas—by implication—she was not present and did not help Tydeus fight the Thebans. In terms of this implication, verse 808 would contradict what Athena is saying.

From the synchronic perspective of "our" *Iliad*, stemming from the "vulgate" version, this verse is thus an "interpolation." From the diachronic perspective, however, *Iliad* E 808 is a precious vestige of a phase of Homeric poetry that predates the institution of the *numerus versuum* at the Panathenaia. From a diachronic perspective, this verse is not at all anomalous: as we see from *Iliad* Δ 390, Athena was indeed present and did indeed help Tydeus fight the Thebans.

Since the speaker of *Iliad* Δ 390 is Agamemnon while the speaker of *Iliad* E 808 is Athena, the argument can be made that the "focalizations" of the two verses represent an intentional contrast or even mismatch.[47] True, Agamemnon's perspective is different from Athena's in the two different contexts of the text—*as we have it*. But the point is, we see here the building blocks of two different traditional ways of constructing the speech of Athena: she can make either a parallel or a contrast between the father and the son. In the "vulgate" version of the *Iliad*, she chooses to make a contrast; in another, earlier, version as reflected by *Iliad* E 808, she could choose to make a parallel, just as Agamemnon makes a parallel at *Iliad* Δ 390. We see here a glimpse of multiformity in repertoire, and the potential for different plot constructions in different times.

Such traces of multiformity lead to different ways of viewing Homeric poetry, as I have argued in my earlier work on Homeric multiforms. If you accept the reality of multiforms, you forfeit the elusive certainty of finding the original composition of Homer but you gain, and I think this is an important gain, another certainty, an unexpected one but one that may turn out to be much more valuable: you recover a significant portion of the Homeric repertoire.[48]

In earlier work, where I first applied the scheme of Homeric periodization that I am reapplying in this chapter, I argued that the study of Homeric multiforms helps the reader develop a sense of different Homers for differ-

46. Apthorp 2000. Again I say "delete" and not "omit," for reasons that I will clarify in Ch.3.

47. Apthorp 2000.9. On Homeric "focalization," see Jong 1985 and 1989.

48. *PP* 151–152.

ent times, such as a relatively "proper Homer" for the late fourth century and thereafter, periods 4 and 5, as opposed to a "primitive Homer" in, say, periods 1 and 2, the era before the reforms of the Peisistratidai. As for period 3, the most appropriate description may be the "common" Homer—or let us say the Homer of the *koinē*.[49]

In general, the variant readings reported by the three most eminent editors of Homer at the Library of Alexandria—Zenodotus, Aristophanes, and Aristarchus—stem from such multiforms.[50] The same goes for the variant readings reported by the most eminent editor of Homer at the Library of Pergamon, Crates.[51] On the basis of these multiforms adduced by the ancient editors, in addition to the multiforms that survive directly in the textual traditions of Homer, I maintain that there can be no "original" version for us to reconstruct.[52] The textual evidence allows us to reconstruct a Panathenaic tradition, relatively less multiform than other epic traditions, but this evidence cannot be reduced to a single "uniform" Panathenaic text.

To claim an original uniformity for the Homeric poems requires minimizing radically the multiformity inherent in the recorded textual variants.[53] In a project still to be published, I produce a detailed inventory of Homeric textual variants that reveal multiforms of relatively major thematic significance. For the moment, I mention three examples that I explored in earlier work:

1 A "hymnic" prooemium of the *Iliad*, attested by Crates, as opposed to the non-hymnic prooemium in the "vulgate."[54]

49. *PP* 152.

50. Whether some of these variant readings are conjectures made by the editors themselves is a question I addressed in N 1998b, the argumentation of which is recast as Ch.5 below.

51. N 1998a.

52. For an acute discussion of multiforms attested in fourth-century "quotations" and in early papyri, see Dué 2001.

53. Such claims are reflected in assessments like the following (Pelliccia 1997.46; quoted by Finkelberg 2000.2n5): "the variant recordings that we know of from papyri and the indirect sources ... are for the most part too boring and insignificant to imply that they derived from a truly creative performance tradition.... [W]e are still left wondering if the banal repetitions and expansions that we find in various papyrus scraps really require us to accept, in order to explain them, a full-blown oral performance tradition." Once again we see an absolutizing notion of multiformity, viewed as typical of "a truly creative performance tradition" and "a full-blown oral performance tradition." In terms of the assessment just quoted, the choice is once again between oral and non-oral, multiform and "uniform"—or at least near-uniform except for variants that are banal, boring, and insignificant.

54. N 1998a.215–23.

2 Contexts of dual-for-plural in the "Embassy Scene" of *Iliad* I, attested by Zenodotus, as opposed to contexts of dual-for-dual-only in the "vulgate"; the edition of Homer by Zenodotus regularly accepted textual variants that required dual-for-plural meanings.[55]

3 A "happy outcome" for the Phaeacians in *Odyssey* v 152 (they are fated to escape from being sealed off forever by a mountain that threatens to envelop their city), attested by Aristophanes of Byzantium, as opposed to the "unhappy outcome" in the "vulgate" (they are fated not to escape).[56]

A fourth example, the detailed analysis of which I save for a future publication, is a pair of variant reading in *Odyssey* α 93 and α 285, attested by Zenodotus (scholia to *Odyssey* γ 313), where Telemachus goes not to Sparta—which is his destination in Scroll δ of "our" *Odyssey*—but instead to the island of Crete. One Classicist refers to the alternative verses in *Odyssey* α 93 and α 285 as "what many would regard as the most disconcertingly suggestive of all ancient Homeric variants."[57] In my future publication, I interpret these variants as multiforms stemming from oral traditions localized in Crete.

As the foregoing examples indicate, multiformity in ancient Greek epic must be understood as a matter of degrees. A more precise specification of these degrees—both formally and historically—seems a most rewarding new line of research.

55. N 1999b.259–260, *HR* 50–55. See the scholia at *Iliad* A 567, Γ 459, Z 112, Θ 503, N 627, O 347, Π 287, Ψ 753; *Odyssey* α 38, θ 251, as analyzed by Broggiato 1998. See also Matthaios 1999.378ff and the comments of Rengakos 2002.

56. N 2001c.

57. S. West 1996; see also West 1998.43–44. Finkelberg (2000.10) treats these variants simply as "significant changes proposed by ancient scholars," discounting them because they did not become "part of the vulgate."

CHAPTER 3

Editing the Homeric Text: West's *Iliad*

Martin West's edition of the Homeric *Iliad* (volume 1 / 1998; volume 2 / 2000) is not, and cannot be, the last word. Still, it serves its purpose in presenting a reconstruction of what one man deems to be the definitive text. The question remains, though: how do you define what exactly is definitive when you set out to reconstruct the text of the Homeric *Iliad*? How you edit Homer depends on your definition of Homer.

West says that Homer did not exist.[1] In denying the existence of Homer, he is not arguing, as I have, that Homer the poet is a mythical construct.[2] For West, only the name of Homer is mythical.[3] The *Praefatio* of West's edition makes it explicit that the poet of the *Iliad* was not a mythical but a real historical figure, even if we do not know his name; this poet was the "primus poeta," and he was "maximus."[4]

Here is West's scenario for the *Iliad* of this master poet. The poem was written down in the course of the poet's own lifetime.[5] Even during his

---

* The original version of this essay is N 2000a, reviewing West 1998b.
1. West 1999b.
2. *HQ* 111–112.
3. Again, West 1999b.
4. West 1998b.v.
5. West 1998b.v.

career, the poet had the opportunity to make his own changes in his master poem: there were major interpolations, says West, that the poet himself introduced into his written text from time to time.[6] After the master's death, the scrolls (*volumina*) of his *Iliad* were abandoned to the whims of *rhapsōidoi* (ῥαψῳδοί) 'rhapsodes', who kept varying the text in their varied performances, much like the actors of a later era who kept varying the text left behind by Euripides ("rhapsodorum ... qui Iliadem nihilo magis sacrosanctam habebant quam histriones Euripidem").[7] The opportunities for introducing more and more interpolations kept widening. Meanwhile, the master's composition eventually made its debut at the festival of the Panathenaia in Athens toward the end of the seventh century, but only in bits and pieces at the start.[8] In the late sixth century, the era of the tyrant Hipparchus of Athens, the text was formally adopted for Panathenaic recitations and divided up into 24 rhapsodies; in other words, this system of division had nothing to do with the "primus poeta" himself.[9] The Athenian phase of transmission was consolidated in the sixth through the fourth centuries, with teachers playing a particularly significant role.[10] Throughout this period of Homeric transmission, the text suffered from Athenian accretions.[11]

Here ends my summary of West's scenario, which serves as the premise for his edition of the *Iliad*. The editor's task, in terms of this premise, is relatively straightforward: West sets out to reconstruct the seventh-century Ionic text of the master poet, which needs to be purged of its Athenian accretions, its rhapsodic variations, its editorial interpolations. I will now proceed to evaluate West's premise, and his edition, against the historical background of previous editions of the Homeric *Iliad* and *Odyssey*.

The very idea of establishing the definitive text of Homer was destabilized over two centuries ago when Friedrich August Wolf published his *Prolegomena* to his editions of the Homeric *Iliad* and *Odyssey* (*Prolegomena* 1795; *Iliad* 1804; *Odyssey* 1807).[12] The ground has been shifting ever since. For Wolf, there was no Homer to recover. He argued that the Homeric text had emerged out of oral traditions, which could not be traced all the way

6. West 1998b.v.
7. West 1998b.v.
8. West 1998b.vi.
9. West 1998b.vi n3; cf. West 1999b.382.
10. West 1998b.vi.
11. West 1998b.vi.
12. Wolf's *Iliad* and *Odyssey* editions are not nearly as well known as the separately published *Prolegomena*: cf. Janko 1998d (= *BMCR* 98.6.17) correcting Janko 1998a (= *BMCR* 98.5.20), where he had denied the existence of these editions in the context of attempting

back to some "original" single author. How far back, then, in terms of Wolf's argumentation, could we trace the oldest of ancient Greek texts, the *Iliad*, if not all the way back to Homer? In other words, if we work backward from the surviving medieval textual tradition of Homer, just how far back can we go in reconstructing that tradition? Here I recall again the sarcastic remark of a rival editor of the *Iliad*, Pierre Alexis Pierron, who says that the *Iliad* edition of Wolf takes us no farther back than around the third century CE, the era of Porphyry's *Homeric Questions*.[13]

For the likes of Pierron, we could indeed go farther back, at least as far back as the era of Aristarchus of Samothrace, head of the Library of Alexandria around the middle of the second century BCE, who produced what Pierron thought was the definitive edition of the Homeric *Iliad*. Pierron's own edition of the *Iliad* (1869) was meant to be the closest thing to an edition of the *Iliad* by Aristarchus.

So what was so special about the Homer edition of Aristarchus? As far as the ancient world was concerned, Aristarchus' produced a *diorthōsis* of Homer, which represented an authoritative attempt to restore the original text of the *Iliad* and *Odyssey*. The modern understanding of *diorthōsis* is "edition," but such a rendering does not do justice to the essence of ancient editorial procedures. As far as Aristarchus himself was concerned, his *diorthōsis* of Homer was an attempt to restore the true text of Homer by way of 'correction', that is, 'corrective editing'.[14] Such a restoration depended on finding the best surviving textual evidence, which he thought would ultimately lead back to whatever it was that Homer himself had written down sometime around 1000 BCE—if we convert the Aristarchean chronological reckoning to our own (Proclus περὶ Ὁμήρου 59–62).[15]

In attempting to reconstruct the *Iliad* of Aristarchus, Pierron was following a tradition established by the *Iliad* edition of Jean Baptiste Gaspard d'Ansse de Villoison (1788), whose earlier attempt at recovering Aristarchus' edition was based primarily on the text and scholia of the tenth-century manuscript of the *Iliad* commonly known as Venetus A (codex Marcianus 454), which Villoison himself had discovered in Venice.[16] The text and textual apparatus of the Venetus A, according to Villoison, could lead us back to the text and

---

to correct what I had to say (N 1997d = Ch.1 in this book) about the influence of Wolf's editions on later Homer editions like the Oxford Classical Text of Monro and Allen 1920.

13. Pierron 1869.cxl.

14. See Ch.1, p. 22.

15. For the quotation from Proclus and for further references, see Ch.1, p. 11n31.

16. See again Ch.1.

textual apparatus of Aristarchus' very own edition of the *Iliad*. For Villoison too, as for followers like Pierron, the recovery of Aristarchus' *Iliad* would have been the closest thing to the recovery of Homer's own *Iliad*.

At this point, a major question emerges: how are we to deal with the historical chasm separating Homer from Aristarchus? Villoison anticipated Wolf by imagining an oral tradition, perpetuated by *rhapsōidoi* (ῥαψῳδοί) 'rhapsodes', which must have "corrupted" an original composition of Homer. For Villoison, as for Wolf later, the wording of Josephus *Against Apion* 1.12–13 could be interpreted to mean that this "original" composition of Homer had been oral, not written.[17] For Villoison, the "original" oral composition of Homer had been eventually rescued from the "corruptions" of rhapsodic transmission, thanks largely to the research of scholars at the Library of Alexandria, especially Aristarchus. The text of the Venetus A codex of the *Iliad* was for Villoison the eventual result of this ongoing rescue operation. Even if we could never recover an original *Iliad*, we could at least reconstruct the next best thing, that is, a prototype of the Venetus A text of the *Iliad*. For Villoison, such a prototype represented the recovery of the *Iliad* through the editorial efforts of Aristarchus in Alexandria and, secondarily, of such Alexandrian predecessors as Aristophanes of Byzantium and Zenodotus of Ephesus. The "original" composition of Homer seemed within reach.

Wolf's *Prolegomena* changed all that. He challenged the authority of the Venetus A text and its scholia by questioning the credibility of Zenodotus, Aristophanes, and even Aristarchus as sources that could lead to the recovery of the "original" Homer text. For Wolf, most of these Alexandrian editors' readings, wherever they differed from the readings that continued into the medieval text traditions, were mere conjectures. The historical chasm separating Homer from Aristarchus had dramatically reasserted itself.[18]

Wolf's pessimistic views on the validity of the Alexandrian editions of Homer led to a prevailing "default mentality" that relied primarily on the

17. The relevant passage from Josephus, *Against Apion* 1.12–13, quoted above, needs to be interpreted in its own right, aside from the interpretations of Villoison and Wolf; as far as Josephus himself is concerned, the point he is making is that the ancient Greeks, unlike the Jews, did not have a continuous written tradition going all the way back to a prototypical authorship (see Wyrick 1999). Josephus leaves it open whether there had been an "original" Homeric text, and his wording points to a variation on the theme of the Peisistratean Recension, which I view as a cultural construct based on the mythical idea of a prototypical text that had disintegrated on account of neglect, only to be reintegrated later by an enlightened ruler (N 1998a.227–228; in this discussion I include references, with bibliography, to the alternative view that the Recension was a historical event).

18. See again Ch.1.

post-Alexandrian textual traditions. Wolf's pessimism was most unsettling for the likes of Pierron, as we have seen from that editor's sarcastic remark: the *Iliad* of Wolf is the *Iliad* of Porphyry.[19]

As we also saw in the first chapter, the editions of Homer by Helmut van Thiel (*Odyssey* 1991, *Iliad* 1996) represent an extreme case of such pessimism. This editor systematically privileges the readings attested in the medieval manuscripts at the expense of variant readings attributed to the Alexandrians, which he generally dismisses as editors' conjectures. A more moderate case is the Homer edition used up to now by most English-speaking Classicists, the Oxford Classical Text of T. W. Allen (with D. B. Monro).[20]

Yet another case of pessimism is West's edition of the *Iliad*. He too is generally pessimistic about the Alexandrian editions of Homer. On the other hand, West is relatively optimistic about his own edition. He seems confident that he has recovered the closest thing to the putatively original *Iliad*. To that extent, he is like Villoison and his followers. Unlike Villoison, however, West has attained his own version of the "original" without relying on Aristarchus as a primary source of support. West's *Iliad* shares with van Thiel's version a general stance of diffidence about the textual variants that go back to Aristarchus—not to mention Alexandrian variants in general.

Granted, West is not as extreme as van Thiel is in this regard. Occasionally, he goes out of his way to defend a variant that goes back to Alexandrian sources, even when that given variant is weakly or not at all attested in the existing manuscript traditions. A notable case in point is *Iliad* I 394, where West opts for the Aristarchean reading γε μάσσεται instead of γαμέσσεται, which is the reading transmitted by the existing manuscripts.[21] As West remarks, with reference to this case and a handful of others: "de bona traditione agitur, non de coniecturis" (also with reference to I 397, M 218, 412).[22] Still, in most cases where a given Aristarchean variant is weakly or not at all attested in the existing manuscripts, West opts for a non-Aristarchean variant, as we will see later.

What makes some Aristarchean readings, but not most of the others, a matter of "bona traditio" and not "coniectura"? West's approach to deciding what is good or bad tradition, what is traditional and what is conjectural, does not seem to me systematic. That is, his decisions about good or

19. See again Ch.1.

20. Monro and Allen 1920. For a defense of Allen's overall editorial work, which has been severely criticized by e.g. Wilson 1990, see again Haslam 1997.89–91.

21. More on this reading in Ch.5 below.

22. West 1998b.vii n9.

bad textual traditions are not based on external evidence. I can find no unambiguous instance where West prefers an Aristarchean variant for the simple reason that it stems from one manuscript tradition or another—or at least on the grounds that it derives from an ancient editorial source that guarantees pre-existing manuscript traditions no longer known to us. In the end, it all comes down to whether West believes that any given variant—Aristarchean or otherwise—happens to recover the right wording. It does not matter for him, ultimately, whether such a variant happens to be a "coniectura," putatively deriving from some Alexandrian editor, maybe even from Aristarchus himself, or rather an authentic reading that the Alexandrians might have found preserved in a "bona traditio" no longer known to us. Ultimately, the *goodness* of the given tradition depends on whether West thinks that the given reading is *right* in the first place. He is not concerned whether a reading comes from an ancient source or from a conjecture, ancient or modern, as long as it is *right*. For him, a conjecture offered by, say, Richard Payne Knight (1820) can in theory be just as right as a reading found by Aristarchus in some ancient source.

A typical emendation by Payne Knight, accepted by West, is τεόν for τὸ σόν (which is the reading transmitted by the manuscripts) at A 185, on the analogy of τεόν at A 138; also at A 207 (in this case, both τεόν and τὸ σόν are attested as manuscript variants). The problem is, the syntax of Homeric τό as article—even though it is less archaic than the syntax of τό as a demonstrative pronoun—pervades the formulaic system of Homeric poetry and thus cannot simply be eliminated everywhere by emendation.[23] In general, Homeric diction is linguistically multi-layered, allowing older and newer phenomena to coexist (for example, the older forms τοί and ταί function only as demonstrative pronouns, while the newer forms οἱ and αἱ function either as articles or, by default, as demonstrative pronouns). Thus the sum total of phonological, morphological, and syntactical functions in the formulaic system of Homeric poetry cannot simultaneously be reduced to their oldest phase. Such is the problem with the efforts of Payne Knight (and West) in emending Homeric phrases into a state of conformity with a pre-existing article-free phase of their existence. This kind of effort reveals a general sense of dissatisfaction with the anomalies of existing systems— a dissatisfaction so strong that it verges on an impulse to recover what is irrecoverable. Such an impulse can lead to an overextended idea about what is genuine—and what cannot be so. Payne Knight is the man who said to Elgin about the Acropolis Marbles: "You have lost your labour, my Lord

---

23. On the "article" in Homeric diction, see Schwyzer/Debrunner 1966.20–22.

Elgin. Your marbles are overrated: they are not Greek: they are Roman of the time of Hadrian."[24]

In taking a generally non-Aristarchean stance, West bypasses the neo-Aristarcheans, as represented by the so-called Königsberg school of Karl Lehrs (1st/2nd/3rd eds. 1833 / 1865 / 1882). The work of Lehrs challenged the *Prolegomena* and Homer editions of Wolf by undertaking a large-scale rehabilitation of the editorial methods of Aristarchus. Earlier followers of Lehrs included Pierron, who acknowledged the indebtedness of his *Iliad* (1869) to the neo-Aristarcheans. Among later followers, Arthur Ludwich stands out: his research culminated in a Teubner edition of the *Iliad* (1902; reissued 1995, three years before the appearance of volume I of West's *Iliad*).[25] In order to understand why West bypasses the neo-Aristarcheans, it is instructive to examine the basics of Ludwich's editorial method.

Ludwich's edition of the *Iliad* explicitly follows the editorial method of Aristarchus himself. Essentially, Aristarchus sought to balance the internal evidence of Homeric poetry, as a system of composition and diction, with the external evidence of the Homeric texts, as a sampling of manuscripts. The Aristarchean method is most clearly documented by Ludwich himself (1884, 1885), who went on to apply that method in his own edition of the *Iliad* (1902). Like Aristarchus, he tried to balance two different kinds of evidence. On the one hand, he made editorial decisions based on his own sense of the internal evidence of Homeric composition and diction. On the other hand, such decisions were regulated by the external evidence of the Homeric manuscripts—to the fullest extent of their availability. Here is where we begin to see a major difference between the editorial methods of Ludwich and West.

For the neo-Aristarcheans, the question of the availability of manuscripts is essential. Obviously, the external evidence available to Aristarchus was different from what was available to Ludwich—and what is now available to West. But the essential question remains, what exactly was in fact available to Aristarchus? The general conclusion reached by the neo-Aristarcheans is that Aristarchus himself had access to a wealth of manuscripts, containing a wealth of variant readings, and much of this evidence is no longer available to us. For the neo-Aristarcheans, the central source of this information must be Aristarchus himself.

Here we come back to the question: why is it that West chooses to bypass the neo-Aristarcheans? An answer that now emerges is this: it is because he

24. Cook 1984.80.
25. On Pierron and Ludwich, see Ludwich 1885.82, 91, 168; for more on the Königsberg School, see Ludwich 1885.199.

has chosen also to bypass the authority of Aristarchus as a reliable guardian of the Homeric textual transmission. West's reasons for this radical departure have to do mainly with his theory about an Aristarchean whose work we have already considered, Didymus. For West, as we will now see, it was not Aristarchus but Didymus who must be recognized as the central source of our surviving information about ancient Homeric manuscripts and editions. The implications of this stance are far-reaching. At stake here is the authority of Aristarchus himself as an editor of Homer.

Before we consider the details of West's theory, we need to review some basic information about the methodology of Aristarchus and about the role of Didymus in reporting on that methodology.

Didymus was an Alexandrian scholar who flourished in the second half of the first century BCE and the beginning of the first century CE. For posterity, the primary mediator of the Aristarchean method has turned out to be this man. Didymus' commentary on the Aristarchean *diorthōsis* 'corrective editing' of the *Iliad*, as excerpted mainly in the scholia to Venetus A, has become the central source for reconstructing the editorial method of his Alexandrian predecessor, Aristarchus. Ludwich's 1884 edition of the surviving fragments of Didymus' commentary serves as an essential foundation for his 1902 Teubner edition of the *Iliad* (as Ludwich observes in his *Praefatio*).[26] This foundation has now been challenged by West, who offers a radically different theory about Didymus—a theory that he applies pervasively in his edition of the *Iliad*.

West's theory, as we will see, depends on how you answer this question: what facts can we learn from Didymus about Aristarchus? In order to introduce the theory, I will now highlight two of these facts.

The first fact is the more obvious of the two: the methodology of Aristarchus, as mediated by Didymus, insists on adherence to the internal evidence of Homeric poetry, as a system of composition and diction. This editorial policy is indicated by the scholia A at *Iliad* Π 467c, where Didymus observes that Aristarchus would not leave anything *aparamuthēton* 'uncontextualized [in the mythos]', in other words, that Aristarchus' goal was to make contextual comparisons with all available internal evidence. Aristarchus' rigorous analysis of Homeric poetry as a system was monumentalized by his reputation as an "analogist," in opposition to an "anomalist" like his contemporary, Crates of Mallos, who was head of the Library of Pergamon (Varro *De lingua latina* 8.23). Crates was an editor of Homer in his own right, and his editorial judgments were frequently

26. Ludwich 1884.vii–viii.

contested by Aristarchus.[27] The antithesis between Aristarchus the analogist and Crates the anomalist is liable to various exaggerations, but the basic contrast is valid to this extent: Aristarchus as editor of Homer was more likely than Crates to reject as incorrect a given variant reading that does not fit the rest of the system as he saw it.[28]

Now I confront a second fact—less obvious but more important—about the methodology of Aristarchus as mediated by Didymus: in producing his edition of Homer, Aristarchus did not overprivilege the internal evidence of Homeric diction at the expense of the external evidence of Homeric manuscript transmission. Here I strongly disagree with West, who claims that Aristarchus did indeed prefer to concentrate on the internal evidence of Homeric diction at the expense of the external evidence of Homeric manuscripts.[29]

It does not follow, just because Aristarchus was an analogist, that he would sacrifice the evidence of the manuscripts to his own sense of analogy. There is ample evidence to show that Aristarchus, although he was indeed an analogist, cautiously avoided mechanistic appeals to analogy at the expense of the manuscript evidence.[30]

Ludwich's *Iliad* edition consistently relies on the testimony of Aristarchus wherever an editorial choice has to be made between variant readings, on the grounds that Aristarchus adopted readings based on the external evidence of manuscripts even when he thought that some other reading was "right." Aristarchus' definitive statements on whatever he judged to be right or wrong, better or worse, were originally to be found not in the actual text of his edition but in his *hupomnēmata* (which, I repeat, can best be described as a combination of a modern apparatus criticus and a modern commentary).[31] We may compare the editorial policy of Origen, who formatted the received text of the Septuagint as the fifth *selis* or 'column' of his six-column *Hexapla* edition of the "Old Testament"; the critical signs in the margins of the fifth column (obelus, lemniscus, hypolemniscus, asterisk) would refer the reader to Origen's *hupomnēmata*, where the editor offered his own judgments about the available variants.[32] Similarly, Aristarchus'

27. Broggiato 1998.41; N 1999b.260, *HR* 50–55.
28. N 1998a.219–223.
29. West 1998b.viii.
30. *PP* 129n99.
31. See Ch.1, with reference to Lührs 1992.10. For a persuasive reconstruction of the history of Aristarchus' Homeric *hupomnēmata*, see Montanari 1998.11–20. See further below at p. 85.
32. *PP* 194–195, following Allen 1924.315–320.

hupomnēmata kept track of variants that were signaled by critical signs in the text proper of his edition.[33]

West does not see things this way, as we discover from a closer examination of his theory about Didymus. He seems to be implying that Aristarchus placed his own choices of variant readings into the text proper of his edition; more important, West says explicitly that it was not Aristarchus but Didymus who collected a mass of manuscripts to be collated for purposes of tracking down any non-Aristarchean variant readings.[34] According to West's theory, it was Didymus, not Aristarchus, who developed such criteria as αἱ πλείους 'the majority', πᾶσαι 'all of them', αἱ Ἀριστάρχου ... ἡ δὲ κοινή 'the editions of Aristarchus ... but the common version [*koinē*]' (as in the scholia at *Iliad* M 404a1), αἱ χαριέστεραι 'the more elegant ones' [*khariesterai*], and so forth; it was he, not Aristarchus, who made use of αἱ πολιτικαί 'the city editions' [*politikai*] from Massalia / Marseille (= ἡ Μασσαλιωτική / *Massaliōtikē*), Chios (= ἡ Χία / *Khia*), Argos (= ἡ Ἀργολική / *Argolikē*), and Sinope (= ἡ Σινωπική / *Sinōpikē*).[35]

West's theory about Didymus leaves out of consideration—and is contradicted by—the testimony of Didymus himself, as mediated by the Homeric scholia, concerning the methodology of Aristarchus. A most explicit statement of Aristarchus' editorial policy comes from the scholia A at I 222, where Didymus says ἄμεινον οὖν εἶχεν ἄν, φησὶν ὁ Ἀρίσταρχος, [εἰ] ἐγέγραπτο "ἂψ ἐπάσαντο" ἢ "αἶψ᾽ ἐπάσαντο,"... ἀλλ᾽ ὅμως ὑπὸ περιττῆς εὐλαβείας οὐδὲν μετέθηκεν, <u>ἐν πολλαῖς οὕτως εὑρὼν φερομένην τὴν γραφήν</u> 'it would have been better, says Aristarchus, if it had been written "ἂψ ἐπάσαντο" or "αἶψ᾽ ἐπάσαντο"; nevertheless, because of his extreme caution, he changed nothing, <u>having found in many of the texts this attested way of writing it</u> [= "ἐξ ἔρον ἕντο" instead of "ἂψ ἐπάσαντο"]'. The last part of this statement, as highlighted, is quoted in the apparatus criticus of Ludwich but not in that of West. The wording is crucial: we see here the most explicit testimony, coming from Didymus himself, concerning Aristarchus' practice of comparing variant readings by examining a wide range of manuscripts. At a later point in this book, in another context, I

---

33. As Montanari 1998.10 argues with reference to the procedures of Aristarchus, the margin of his edited text would not have been suitable for displaying variants; it would have been suitable only for critical signs that refer to the relevant discussion in the *hupomnēmata*. To put it another way: when it comes to the transmission of editorial judgments, marginal notes would not be as useful as marginal signs that refer to an authoritative discussion in the *hupomnēmata*.

34. West 1998b.vi.

35. West 1998b.vi.

will argue about this testimony: "The wording assumes that *some* of the texts did indeed feature ἄψ ἐπάσαντο instead of ἐξ ἔρον ἔντο. I infer that Aristarchus 'changed nothing' (οὐδὲν μετέθηκεν) *even though he could have made a change* on the basis of manuscript attestations of a variant reading. Moreover, he is quoted as considering the variant reading as a contrary-to-fact proposition. Accordingly, it seems unjustified to describe such readings as his own editorial conjectures."[36] I should add that the verb *metatithenai* in the Homer scholia means 'emend'—not 'conjecture'—when applied to the editorial activities of Aristarchus.[37] Also, whenever Aristarchus did make conjectures, he did not put them into his edited text.[38]

There is further evidence against West's Didymus theory, provided by the *ipsissima verba* of Aristarchus. Here I cite a quotation from Aristarchus himself, as preserved in the scholia A at *Iliad* A 423–424. The quotation, designated as the *lexis* 'wording' of Aristarchus, is introduced this way: λέξις Ἀριστάρχου ἐκ τοῦ Α τῆς Ἰλιάδος ὑπομνήματος 'here is the *lexis* of Aristarchus, from his commentary [*hupomnēma*] on volume A of the *Iliad*'. The expression λέξις Ἀριστάρχου 'the *lexis* of Aristarchus' here and elsewhere seems to convey the idea that the *hupomnēmata* 'commentaries' of Aristarchus were not only commentaries written down in papyrus scrolls but also, at least notionally, commentaries delivered as lectures by Aristarchus, as if these lectures were meant to be transcribed by his students.[39] As the

36. N 1998b = Ch.5 below.
37. Ludwich 1885.97.
38. Ludwich 1885.92.
39. Here are other survivals of quotations of Aristarchus by Didymus, introduced by the tag '*lexis* of Aristarchus': scholia at *Iliad* B 125, Ἀριστάρχου λέξεις ἐκ τῶν ὑπομνημάτων … 'the *lexeis* of Aristarchus, from his *hupomnēmata*…'; at *Iliad* B 245, οὕτως αἱ Ἀριστάρχου λέξεις ἐκ τοῦ Β τῆς Ἰλιάδος … 'this is the way the *lexeis* of Aristarchus have it, from volume B of the *Iliad*…'; at *Iliad* Γ 406, προσθήσειν μοι δοκῶ καὶ τὴν Ἀριστάρχου λέξιν οὕτως ἔχουσαν… 'I think the *lexis* of Aristarchus will also add [to the evidence], which has it this way…'. See also at *Iliad* B 111, ἔν τινι τῶν ἠκριβωμένων ὑπομνημάτων γράφει ταῦτα κατὰ λέξιν … 'in one of the *hupomnēmata* that have been corrected for greater accuracy, he [= Aristarchus] writes this, and I quote according to the *lexis*…' (again, a quotation from Aristarchus follows; earlier in this context, we read in the discussion of Didymus: παρ' ὃ δὴ καὶ κατά τινα τῶν ὑπομνημάτων μετειλῆφθαι τὸ μέγα ἀντὶ τοῦ μεγάλως. τὸ δὲ οὐκ ἔχει τἀκριβὲς οὕτως. εἰ γὰρ τὰ συγγράμματα τῶν ὑπομνημάτων προτάτ[τ]οιμεν, ἕνεκα γοῦν τἀκριβοῦς γράφοιμεν κατὰ Ἀρίσταρχον… 'here, according to some of the *hupomnēmata*, the sense of 'great' has been switched to 'in a great way'; but it is not accurate this way; for if we prefer his [= Aristarchus'] monographs [*sungrammata*] to his commentaries [*hupomnēmata*], then we should write, for the sake of accuracy, in following the judgment of Aristarchus,…'). In this last example, the expression γράφει ταῦτα κατὰ λέξιν 'he [= Aristarchus] writes this, and I quote according to the *lexis*' implies that Aristarchus is 'speaking' (hence κατὰ λέξιν = verbatim) the exegetical remarks that are about to be

quotation proceeds, it is difficult to determine exactly where the words of Aristarchus himself leave off, to be picked up by the words of Didymus.[40] This much is certain, however: the person who is being quoted, after expressing his preference for the variant reading κατὰ δαῖτα instead of μετὰ δαῖτα, goes on to say: οὕτως δὲ εὕρομεν καὶ ἐν τῇ Μασσαλιωτικῇ καὶ Σινωπικῇ καὶ Κυπρίᾳ καὶ Ἀντιμαχείῳ καὶ Ἀριστοφανείῳ 'this is the way we found it in the *Massaliōtikē* and the *Sinōpikē* and the *Kupria* and the *Antimakheios* [Ἀντιμάχειος = text of Antimachus of Colophon] and the *Aristophaneios* [Ἀριστοφάνειος = text of Aristophanes of Byzantium]'.[41] As Ludwich argues, the context of οὕτως δὲ εὕρομεν 'this is the way we found it' makes it clear that the subject of this verb is Aristarchus, not Didymus.[42] The first person of εὕρομεν 'we found' comes from the direct quotation of words 'spoken' (notionally and I would say perhaps even literally) by the master teacher. In other words, the rhetoric of the quotation is set in the mode of a master's *ipse dixit*.[43]

The distinction between what was said by Aristarchus and what defaults to Didymus is collapsed in the apparatus criticus of West, who reports (and chooses for his text proper) the variant κατὰ δαῖτα at *Iliad* A 424 on the authority of the following (I list them in the order given by West): Antimachus of Colophon, Aristophanes of Byzantium, Aristarchus, Callistratus, Dionysius Sidonius, Ixion, four papyrus fragments, Apollonius Sophista, manuscripts "V" (= V1 Allen) and "Z" (= Ve1 Allen). In other words, Aristarchus is represented here and elsewhere as a source, not as a collator of sources. West juxtaposes (and rejects) the variant μετὰ δαῖτα, reported on the authority of three papyrus fragments, various ancient Homer-quotations, and the "Ω" family of manuscripts (more on which later: this family approximates Ludwich's concept of "vulgate"). A casual reader of West's apparatus is left with the impression that it was Didymus, not Aristarchus, whose collation of manuscripts set the framework for choosing between the variants, and that it was Didymus who chose κατὰ δαῖτα while all along being fully aware of μετὰ δαῖτα—to which variant West applies his ubiquitous formula: "novit Didymus."

---

quoted, but he is also 'writing' (hence γράφει) these remarks in the sense that they are now being read in the quotation. We may paraphrase in English: 'he writes, and I quote from what he says'. My point is, the expression κατὰ λέξιν insists on the idea of *ipse dixit*.

40. See Ludwich 1884.194–196; cf. also Erbse 1969–1988 I 119–120.

41. The Homer edition of Antimachus of Colophon seems to have been a specially prized possession of the Library of Alexandria, treated as a counterweight to the Homer edition of Euripides, a prized possession of the Library of Pergamon: see Bolling 1925.38–39.

42. Ludwich 1884.194–196.

43. More on this passage in Ch.4.

In his apparatus criticus at *Iliad* Γ 406, West applies the tag "omnes boni libri Didymi" on the basis of the following report of Didymus in the A scholia (*Iliad* Γ 406a): καὶ οὐ μόνον ἐν ταῖς ἐκδόσεσιν, ἀλλὰ καὶ ἐν τοῖς συγγράμμασιν ἁπαξάπαντες οὕτως ἐκτίθενται. προσθήσειν μοι δοκῶ καὶ τὴν Ἀριστάρχου λέξιν οὕτως ἔχουσαν 'and not only in the *ekdoseis* but also in the monographs [*sungrammata*], all feature it this way [= ἀπόεικε in place of ἀπόειπε]; I [= Didymus] think the *lexis* of Aristarchus will also add [to the evidence], which has it this way [= which has ἀπόεικε]' [what follows here is the quotation of the *ipsissima verba* from Aristarchus' exegesis].[44] I submit that the tag "omnes boni libri Aristarchi" would be more apt. From the wording of the scholia here at *Iliad* Γ 406a, I interpret the report of Didymus this way: first he refers to the external evidence as transmitted by Aristarchus, and then he follows up by quoting the master's exegesis of the internal evidence.[45]

West's theory about Didymus also leaves out of consideration another basic aspect of Aristarchean methodology, one that I highlighted already in Chapters One and Two. It is the criterion of *numerus versuum*, as analyzed by Michael Apthorp.[46] West's general bypassing of Alexandrian editorial methodology is most strikingly exemplified by his lack of engagement with this criterion and with the work of Apthorp, who is nowhere cited in volume I of West's *Iliad*. Apthorp builds on Aristarchus' methodology in establishing an "authentic" *numerus versuum*, that is, a fixed number of verses that the Alexandrian editor had deemed genuine in the text of the Homeric poems. This methodology has to do with the external evidence of stronger vs. weaker attestations in the available manuscripts of the Homeric text, not just with the internal evidence of Homeric diction and composition.

The far-reaching implications of Aristarchus' principle of *numerus versuum* can be explored further by rethinking (and moderating), as Apthorp has done, the extreme formulation of George Melville Bolling.[47] For this particular neo-Aristarchean, the canonical length of the "Π Text," which was the putative "archetype" of our *Iliad* and which supposedly dates from the sixth century BCE, was around 14,600 verses.[48] Over the next couple of centuries—so goes Bolling's theory—the *Iliad* grew in length to around 15,600 verses; supposedly, this was the accretive "A Text" with which Aristarchus was forced to contend and which corresponds roughly to the

44. See above, note 39.
45. More on this passage in Ch.4.
46. Apthorp 1980; see also his articles as listed in the Bibliography.
47. Bolling 1950.1–16.
48. I focus here only on Bolling's reconstruction of the length of this hypothetical "Π Text"; his reconstruction of the actual diction of the text seems to me far less useful.

Iliad that survives by way of the medieval manuscript traditions. In terms of Bolling's theory, Aristarchus reduced the text of the *Iliad* from around 15,600 to around 14,600 verses by way of athetesis (that is, marking a given verse in the left margin with the critical sign known as the obelus, to indicate the editor's doubts about the authenticity of that verse). Such verses were thought to be textual interpolations, the result of "corrupting" accretion.

Bolling's theory of Homeric "interpolations" needs to be refined in terms of two related considerations: (1) the principle of *numerus versuum* and (2) the distinction between the editorial procedures of athetesis and deletion. As Apthorp argues, the Homer edition of Aristarchus became the standard source for subsequent applications of the editorial principle of *numerus versuum*, and literary authorities like Plutarch were well aware of this principle.[49] Apthorp emphasizes that Aristarchus in his Homer edition not only athetizes some verses (that is, marks them with an obelus but keeps them in the text proper): he also deletes ("omits") some other verses altogether. *The criterion for deletion ("omission") was based on manuscript evidence.* To quote Apthorp, "Aristarchus ... omitted only lines which he found very weakly attested."[50] Such lines are "plus verses."[51] Apthorp goes on to argue that "the numerous lines absent from all our mss. which we know to have been pre-Aristarchean but absent from Aristarchus's edition— some cited by the scholia, some present in extant Ptolemaic papyri, some included in ancient quotations or discussions of Homer—stand condemned as interpolations alongside the weakly-attested lines of the mediaeval mss."[52] Whether or not we choose to think of these "plus verses" in terms of "interpolations," the point for now is simply this: Aristarchus' foundational research in determining the editorial principle of *numerus versuum* must have required a large-scale collection and collation of manuscripts—as many and as varied as he could find.[53]

49. Apthorp 1998.187.

50. I use the term "delete" instead of "omit" in order to reinforce Apthorp's emphasis on the deliberateness of the editorial cancellation of such plus verses. See also Ludwich 1885.132–143 ("Athetierte und ausgestossene Verse"), especially p. 142 on the remark ἔνιοι ὑποτάσσουσι 'some put into a subordinate category' [followed by the quotation of a plus verse] in the scholia at *Iliad* I 140 and 159. West's comment on both these lines, "add. quidam ante Ar" (cf. Monro-Allen, "quidam ant."), does not convey the editorial implications of the expression ἔνιοι ὑποτάσσουσι.

51. Apthorp 1980.xv. Unlike predecessors like Bolling, Apthorp avoids using the term "plus verse" with reference to verses athetized but not deleted ("omitted") by the Alexandrian editors. More on "plus verses" in Ch.2 above.

52. Apthorp 1980.xvi.

53. For more on "plus verses," see especially Apthorp 1998 on *Iliad* I 458–461, with new papyrus evidence for deletion ("omission"); cf. my discussion in *PP* 139n135, where

The question of an "original" Homeric *numerus versuum* now brings us to an essential point that we have not yet considered about Homeric textual variants. In fact, there were not one but two dimensions of variation in the history of Homeric textual transmission. Until this point, I have been speaking exclusively in terms of "horizontal" variants, that is, where the ancient editor had to choose between different wordings that make up a single line of Homeric poetry. But now that I am speaking of a *numerus versuum*, we can see that the ancient editor also had to contend with "vertical" variants, where he had to choose between fewer or more lines that make up a given sequence of lines.[54]

The vertical dimension of textual variation can best be understood by coming to terms with one of the most basic—and elusive—concepts in the history of Homeric scholarship, the so-called Homeric "vulgate." Earlier, I examined this concept by focusing on the Aristarchean usage of the Greek term *koinē* in the combined sense of a 'standard' and a 'common' text of Homer; this combined sense, I argued, corresponds to Jerome's usage of the term *vulgata*.[55] I confine myself here to stressing a single point in my earlier argumentation: modern editors of Homer tend to skew the meaning of the term "vulgate" by overemphasizing the sense of 'common' and underemphasizing the sense of 'standard', so that the expression "Homeric vulgate" is commonly understood to mean nothing more than the default text of Homer. The usage of West is illustrative: he highlights the readings of Aristarchus, as reported by Didymus, against the backdrop of the "vulgata traditio."[56]

As I have already argued, the Aristarchean mentions of the *koinē* or *koinai* texts refer to a standard Athenian version of Homer.[57] What needs to be stressed now is simply that the concept of a Homeric vulgate can be applied systematically to the study of Homeric variants, and that the vertical variations in the history of the Homeric text provide a particularly rich source for such systematic study. This point is linked to my ongoing argument that Aristarchus' editorial policy concerning vertical variants reveals his active interest in the collecting and collating of manuscripts.

"a papyrus" should have been specified as P.Ant. III.158. Apthorp adduces P.Ant. III.158, P.Ant. III.160, and the Leiden glossary. West's apparatus does not mention P.Ant. III.160; but it adduces a new Oxyrhynchus papyrus, "1139" (West's apparatus indicates that the plus verses are omitted here as well).

54. *PP* 139–140.
55. N 1997d.118–122, rewritten in Ch.1 above.
56. West 1998b.vii.
57. *PP* 117, 133–134, 152–156, 185–190, 193–195.

In order to test the concept of a Homeric vulgate, let us turn to the editorial criteria of a neo-Aristarchean like Ludwich, who systematically distinguished between the vulgate and the Aristarchean versions of Homer. For this editor, the vulgate Homer was both pre-Aristarchean and post-Aristarchean.[58] If we apply Ludwich's distinction between vulgate and Aristarchean readings to the vertical dimension of textual variation, then we can say that the pre-Aristarchean vulgate represents an accretive text that exceeded the length of the putative Homeric "original." We can also say that the work of the Alexandrian editors, especially Aristarchus, helped re-establish the "original" *numerus versuum* by way of deleting ("omitting") the accretive verses. We can even say, finally, that the post-Aristarchean vulgate represents a newly accretive textual tradition that unsystematically re-absorbed accretive verses deleted by Aristarchus.

As the discussion proceeds, it will be evident that I do not agree with Ludwich's views concerning the inherent superiority of Aristarchean readings over their vulgate counterparts. I focus here simply on his systematic application of the actual distinction between Aristarchean and vulgate readings. This distinction continues to be most useful, as we will see, for studying the phenomenon of vertical—and horizontal—variation in the history of the Homeric textual tradition.

In this context, it is instructive to contrast Ludwich's (1898) neo-Aristarchean view of the "vulgate" with such anti-Alexandrian views as represented by Marchinus van der Valk, for whom a pre-Aristarchean "vulgate" had "preserved the authentic text," and this text "was also transmitted by the vulgate of the medieval manuscripts."[59] The contrast has to do with the validity or invalidity of the Alexandrian editions of Homer.

Here I repeat my earlier formulation.[60] For both Ludwich and van der Valk, the "vulgate" is distinct from the Homer "editions" of the Alexandrians, especially that of Aristarchus. For van der Valk, however, the readings of the "vulgate" are generally more authentic than the variant readings attributed by the Homer scholia to scholars like Aristarchus, which he generally takes to be "conjectures"; for Ludwich, by contrast, such variants are not "conjectures" but authentic readings preserved by the scholia from the Alexandrian editions of Aristarchus and others.[61] For Ludwich, the Alexandrian "edition" of Aristarchus represents a quantum leap beyond the pre-Alexandrian "vulgate"; for van der Valk, by contrast, the pre- and post-

---

58. Ludwich 1885.192–199 ("Aristarch und die Vulgata").
59. Van der Valk 1963.609.
60. N 1997d.114–115, rewritten in Ch.1 above.
61. Cf. *PP* 185.

Alexandrian "vulgate" text is relatively superior to the Alexandrian "edition" of Aristarchus, which may not even be deserving of the term "edition."

The negative position of van der Valk in questioning the validity of the Alexandrian editions has been influential in shaping the views of Homerists about the variants reported by Aristarchus.[62] Haslam remarks: "A newly fashionable attitude, owed to van der Valk, is to revere the vulgate and condemn the Alexandrians for tampering with it."[63] A prominent defender of van der Valk's anti-Alexandrian position has been Richard Janko.[64] I should stress, however, that Janko's own negative position applies mainly to Aristarchus' treatment of what I call horizontal variants. When it comes to vertical variants, Janko's position shifts, at least in part: like the neo-Aristarcheans, he seems to approve whenever Aristarchus deletes ("omits") plus verses on the grounds that they are interpolations,[65] though he tends to disapprove whenever Aristarchus athetizes.[66] I think that Janko is applying a double standard here. Further, as we will see later, I generally think that there is no need to decide whether the vertical—and horizontal—variants transmitted by Aristarchus are inferior or superior to those transmitted by the vulgate. For the moment, though, I simply note the importance of the variations themselves, and the conflicting inferences they inspire.

There are important precedents for van der Valk's and Janko's negative positions about the Alexandrian editions. A most notable example is the work of Hartmut Erbse.[67] Some have interpreted Erbse's negativity about the Alexandrian editions as a revolution against neo-Aristarcheans like Lehrs and Ludwich, who in turn had revolted against the 1795 *Prolegomena* of Wolf. I return here to the words of Rudolf Pfeiffer, as I quoted him in Chapter One: "it looks to me as if by a sort of unconscious counter-revolution Wolf has now been put back on the throne from which Lehrs had driven him."[68] For now I leave aside the question whether the work of Lehrs and Ludwich represents a revolution—or a counter-revolution, from the standpoint of those for whom Wolf's work was the real revolution in the first place. Instead, I continue to focus on the far-reaching consequences of choosing either an Aristarchean or a "Wolfian vulgate" model in the editing of Homer.[69] Pfeiffer's formulation may conceivably apply to the *Odyssey*

62. *PP* 136–137.
63. Haslam 1997.87.
64. Janko 1992.21n6; cf. *PP* 137.
65. Janko 1992.21n6; cf. *PP* 139–140.
66. Janko 1992.27.
67. Erbse 1959.
68. Pfeiffer 1968.215.
69. For a critical look at the term "Wolfian vulgate," see Ch.1 above.

and *Iliad* of van Thiel (1991, 1996), but surely not to the *Iliad* of West, who generally bypasses Wolf and the model of the "Wolfian vulgate." More important for now, we have seen that West generally bypasses the model of the neo-Aristarchean editors as well. Most important of all, he even bypasses the editorial method of Aristarchus himself.

For West, there is no need to go back to the edition of Aristarchus in order to recover the text of Homer. He thinks that the closest thing to an original *Iliad* is his own reconstruction of the text composed by the "primus poeta." West's belief that the poet of the *Iliad* produced a written composition helps explain this editor's optimism about reconstructing the *ipsissima verba* of a prototypical poet. Aristarchus' own belief was probably similar to West's, to the extent that he too posited a written text produced by the prototypical poet. He too aimed to reconstruct the poet's *ipsissima verba*, relying on the external evidence of available manuscripts as well as the internal evidence of the composition and the diction. West relies on the same two kinds of evidence, but he differs from Aristarchus in how he uses that evidence. Further, he differs from Aristarchus (and the neo-Aristarcheans) in how he responds to this basic question confronting an editor of Homeric poetry: how is one to judge the variants of the overall manuscript tradition? In general, West's version of the *Iliad* shows less flexibility in allowing for variation, while that of Aristarchus shows relatively more. It comes as no surprise, then, that West's version of the master poet's *ipsissima verba* frequently differs from the version of Aristarchus.

I submit that Aristarchus' ancient edition of the *Iliad*, if it had survived complete in the format designed by him, would in many ways surpass West's present edition. It would be a more useful—and more accurate—way to contemplate the *Iliad* in its full multiformity.

The multiformity of Homeric poetry is an aspect of its prehistory as an oral tradition.[70] This essential observation emerges, as we have seen, from the research of Milman Parry and Albert Lord, who explained Homeric poetry as a system derived from oral poetic traditions of composition-in-performance.[71] Their explanation is validated by the editorial work of Aristarchus. Although this ancient editor hardly thought of Homer in terms of oral traditions, his objective study of the Homeric texts provides crucial evidence for an inherent multiformity, which is indeed typical of oral poetic traditions. As Parry asks, in criticizing the "neo-unitarian" Homerists of his day (1930): "How have they explained the unique number of *good* variant

---

70. See Ch.2.

71. Parry 1971 (collected papers = *MHV*) and Lord 1960, 1991, 1995. See Ch.2. See also Dué 2001.

readings in our text of Homer, and the need for the laborious editions of Aristarchus and of the other grammarians, and the extra lines, which grow in number as new papyri are found?"[72] In the *Praefatio* to his *Iliad*, West ignores altogether the work of Parry and Lord. Throughout his edition, moreover, there is a noticeable lack of engagement with oral poetics. West believes that the master poet wrote the *Iliad*, and that is all there is to it.

In the Homeric textual transmission, we can find many signs of oral poetry, but West consistently prefers to explain such signs in terms of written poetry. For example, with reference to the mechanics of "movable ν (nu)" in the Homeric text, West adduces the evidence of the mid-seventh-century Nikandre inscription (*CEG* 403): the poetry of this inscription, composed in the Ionic dialect, shows that movable ν was already being used in this early period for the sake of preventing hiatus caused by the loss of digamma in this dialect. There is evidence for arguing that the technology of writing in such early inscriptions was used not for the actual composition but only for the recording of poetry.[73] West ignores such arguments, assuming that the use of movable ν in such an early poetic inscription is proof that the analogous use of movable ν in Homeric diction was likewise a matter of written poetry:

> This [= the use of "movable ν (nu)" in the Nikandre inscription] shows that by that time Ionian poets were already using movable nu to cure digamma hiatus. If one believes, as I do, that the *Iliad* was composed and written down at about the same period, one will take this as adequate justification for leaving such nus in the text. It is not unreasonable to suppose that the insertion of particles such as γε, κε, τε, or ῥα for the same purpose began as early as the addition of the nu.[74]

West assumes that the Nikandre inscription is a case of written rather than oral poetics, and he implies that the dating of the Nikandre inscription therefore gives him a *terminus ante quem* for the writing down of the *Iliad*. I disagree. The justification for leaving such ν forms in the text is to be found in the internal and comparative evidence of oral poetics, not in the fact that we can find such ν forms in a poetic inscription that West thinks is contemporaneous with the composition of the *Iliad*. It can be argued that the

---

72. *MHV* 268. When Parry says "unique" in this context, I interpret it to mean "uniquely characteristic of oral poetics." For a fuller application of this quotation, with more context, see Ch.5 below. For another application of this same quotation, see the important discussion of Apthorp 1980.110n67.

73. *HQ* 34–37.

74. West 1998a.101.

"insertions" of such particles and of morphophonemic elements like movable ν are part of an overall formulaic system and have nothing to do with the technology of writing. For parallels to be found in the living traditions of South Slavic oral poetry as recorded by Parry and Lord, I refer to an interesting discussion of hiatus-breakers (= "bridging consonants") that prevent the occurrence of glottal stops.[75]

West's lack of engagement with oral poetics has a direct effect on the actual text of his *Iliad* edition, especially with respect to his judgments about horizontal and vertical variants in the textual evidence. Conversely, the factor of oral poetics has its own direct effect on the actual editing of Homeric poetry, as I have argued in my previous publications.[76] None of these is cited in West's *Praefatio*.

In terms of oral poetics, there is an important reason for keeping track of all horizontal and vertical variations in the Homeric textual transmission as attested in the medieval manuscripts, the ancient quotations, and the papyrus fragments. The reason is simple: in principle, any surviving variant in the Homeric textual transmission may represent an authentic form generated by Homeric poetry.

From the standpoint of oral poetics, Homeric poetry is a system that generates the forms that survive in the texts that we know as the Homeric poems. Homeric poetry is not the same thing as the Homeric texts that survived in the medieval manuscripts, the ancient quotations, and the papyrus fragments. Still, the Homeric textual tradition stems from the performance tradition of Homeric poetry. It can be shown, by way of formula analysis, that many of the variants we find in the Homeric texts result directly from the variability inherent in the poetic system itself.[77] In other words, the textual variants in the Homeric poems stem from formulaic variations in Homeric poetry.

Even from the standpoint of West's theory of a written text produced by the "primus poeta," there is an important reason for keeping track of all vertical and horizontal variations in the Homeric textual transmission as attested in the medieval manuscripts, the ancient quotations, and the papyrus fragments. Again, the reason is simple, and I formulate it in West's terms: in principle, any surviving variant in the Homeric textual transmission may represent *the* authentic form that goes back to *the* prototypical text of *the* prototypical poet. In terms of West's editorial stance, there can be ultimately only one authentic form in each case of variation, that is, the form that goes

75. Foley 1999.73–74, 85, 88, 293n28.
76. Especially *PP* and *HQ*.
77. N 1998b, rewritten as Ch.5 below.

back to the "primus poeta." For West, the horizontal and vertical variants in Homeric textual transmission are important only insofar as one given variant in each case may be the right form, while all other variants would have to be wrong forms. Even where West is not sure whether a given variant is right or wrong, he is forced to take a stand on whether it has a better or worse chance of being the right reading: for him there can exist better or worse variants even where the difference between right and wrong variants cannot be determined.

Obviously, such an editorial stance is necessary for those like West who espouse the theory of an original written *Iliad* and *Odyssey* by an original poet. As West says, "We may assume that there existed a complete and coherent *Urtext* of each epic, the result of the first writing down."[78] Maybe less obviously, such an editorial stance is also necessary for Richard Janko, even though he espouses the theory of an orally composed *Iliad* and *Odyssey*. Janko actively uses the criteria of right or wrong, better or worse, in judging the variants surviving in the Homeric textual tradition.[79] Like West, Janko needs these editorial criteria because he too needs to assume original texts from which our *Iliad* and *Odyssey* can be derived. These poems, he thinks, were written down from dictations made by Homer himself, sometime in the eighth century BCE.[80] Thus, in terms of Janko's dictation theory, the "original" *Iliad* and *Odyssey* are not only oral compositions but also, at the same time, textual archetypes.

In a review of West's edition of the *Iliad*, Janko expresses general agreement with West's construct of an original text of the *Iliad*, and most of his disagreements are limited to specifics, except for the general distinction between a writing poet (so West) and a dictating poet (so Janko).[81] In a review of my work, Janko complains about my resisting his theory about the origins of Homeric texts.[82] At the conclusion of his review of West, Janko recalls this complaint of his: "Given that it has been claimed, by some who would have us know less than we used to, that there *was* no original text of Homer,[83] these disagreements [with West] are minor."[84]

I would never want to say it that way—that there *was* no original text of Homer. Obviously, at some point in history, there had to be a first time for textually recording what we know as the *Iliad* and *Odyssey*. But the basic

---

78. West 1998a.95.
79. Janko 1992.26.
80. See especially Janko 1992.22, 26.
81. Janko 2000.
82. Janko 1998a, reviewing N 1996a.
83. Here Janko refers to his review, Janko 1998a, of *PP*.
84. Janko 2000.4.

problem remains: such an *Iliad* and *Odyssey* were not the same texts that we know as our *Iliad* and *Odyssey*.

Instead, I prefer to say it this way: there is no original text of the *Iliad* and *Odyssey* that Janko or West or anyone else can reconstruct on the basis of the existing textual tradition. The variations that survive in this textual tradition, many of which are transmitted by Aristarchus, prevent such a uniform reconstruction. The significance of these textual variations has been dismissed by Janko, who follows van der Valk in claiming that most Aristarchean readings, especially those that are weakly attested in the surviving manuscript traditions, are "conjectures" and should be rejected.[85] In his review of West's *Iliad*, Janko commends him for following this same editorial stance: "Following van der Valk, he [West] holds that Zenodotus was arbitrary and the majority of Aristarchus' unique readings are wrong."[86] In a follow-up article, I called into question Janko's editorial stance by critically re-examining each one of his entries in his sample list of some thirty-three cases of Aristarchean "conjectures" in the *Iliad*.[87]

In general, I have also called into question the overall editorial stance of judging variants in terms of a hypothetical Homeric archetype. As I have argued in an earlier work, "we cannot simplistically apply the criteria of right or wrong, better or worse, original or altered, in the editorial process of sorting out the Homeric variants transmitted by Aristarchus or by earlier sources"; instead, we can ask "whether a variant is authentic or not— provided we understand 'authentic' to mean *in conformity with traditional oral epic diction*."[88] If indeed Homeric poetry, as a system, derives from traditional oral epic diction, then we can expect such a system to be capable of generating multiform rather than uniform versions, and no single version can be privileged as superior in and of itself whenever we apply the empirical methods of comparative philology and the study of oral tradition.[89]

In terms of oral poetics, the multiformity of variations applies to vertical as well as horizontal variants in the textual history of the Homeric poems. With specific reference to vertical variations, it needs to be emphasized that whatever appears to be an interpolation or an omission of a verse in terms of

---

85. Janko 1998a.

86. Janko 2000.1. On both points, Janko refers to West p. vii. In a separate work, I hope to dispute West's general dismissal of Zenodotus, as he phrases it on this page. On the value of variant readings that go back to Zenodotus, in terms of oral poetics, see *PP* 133–138; see also *PP* 144n160 on Aristophanes of Byzantium (with a discussion of the *numerus versuum* of Aristophanes' Homer edition, on which see also Apthorp 1980.3).

87. N 1998a, rewritten as Ch.5 below.

88. *PP* 153.

89. *PP* 117–118.

Homeric textual history may in fact be a matter of expansion or compression respectively in terms of oral poetics.[90]

In terms of oral poetics, moreover, the compositional phenomena of expansion and compression correspond respectively to the lengthening and shortening of the number of verses in expressing a given essential idea. In terms of textual history, such cases of lengthening and shortening could be reinterpreted as corresponding respectively to the scribal phenomena of interpolation and omission. From a diachronic point of view, however, the actual adding or subtracting of verses is basically a matter of variation, and we may think of the longer and shorter versions as vertical variants.

Thus the textual phenomena of (1) interpolation / omission and (2) *varia lectio* are comparable to the oral poetic phenomena of (1) expansion / compression and (2) intralinear formulaic variation. In terms of oral poetics, we can even expect situations where the two textual phenomena are found together. In terms of textual criticism, we actually have an Aristarchean formulation for just such a co-occurrence. In the course of his correspondences with me, Apthorp has highlighted this Aristarchean editorial criterion, as mediated by Didymus: 'an indication of interpolation is the fact that the given line is also transmitted differently' (scholia A at T 327: τεκμήριον δὲ τῆς διασκευῆς τὸ καὶ ἑτέρως φέρεσθαι τὸν στίχον, "εἴ που ἔτι ζώει γε Πυρῆς ἐμός, ὃν κατέλειπον").[91] In terms of textual criticism, I offer this restatement: *cases of vertical variation typically coincide with cases of horizontal variation.* In terms of oral poetics, the *varia lectio* at Iliad T 327, εἴ που ἔτι ζώει γε Πυρῆς ἐμός, ὃν κατέλειπον, is an intralinear formulaic variant of the "vulgate" reading εἴ που ἔτι ζώει γε Νεοπτόλεμος θεοειδής.[92]

In this light, I offer a reformulation of Bolling's formulation concerning Aristarchus' editorial work on the text of Homer. According to Bolling, as we have seen, Aristarchus narrowed down the so-called "A Text" of the *Iliad*, which consists of around15,600 lines, to a supposedly prototypical "Π text," which consists of around 14,600 lines, by condemning approximately a thousand lines that were supposedly non-Homeric.[93] The fundamental problem with the methodology of Bolling is that he allows only for expansion, never for compression, in the history and prehistory of Homeric poetry. If we apply the perspective of diachronic studies in oral poetics,

90. On the mechanics of expansion and compression in oral poetics, see *PP* 76–77.

91. Apthorp *per litteras* 1/26/1999. I translate the Homeric variant adduced here: 'if my Purēs [= Pyrrhos = Neoptolemos] still lives, the one I left behind'.

92. I translate this variant: 'if godlike Neoptolemos still lives'.

93. Bolling 1950.1–16.

Bolling's assumptions about a tradition that can only add, never subtract, are unjustified.[94]

Pursuing further the phenomenon of vertical variation, I stress again the fact that Aristarchus not only athetized verses he also deleted ("omitted") verses. And it was only when a verse was weakly attested in the manuscripts known to Aristarchus that he would actually consider the deletion ("omission") of such a verse from his edition.[95]

The distinction between athetized and deleted ("omitted") is relevant to my resisting West's theory that it was Didymus, not Aristarchus, who collected and collated the Homer manuscripts that yielded the variant horizontal readings tagged as "novit Didymus" in the apparatus criticus of West's *Iliad*. Aristarchus' procedure concerning deleted ("omitted") verses, as distinct from athetized verses, was not subjective: it depended on external evidence, and on the application of formal criteria to that external evidence. As we have just seen from my brief review of Apthorp's findings, Aristarchus systematically contrasted the stronger and weaker attestations of textual variants. In other words, the editorial criteria of Aristarchus must have required an active policy of collecting and collating manuscripts. An editorial practice of distinguishing between athetesis and deletion ("omission") simply could not work without such a policy. I submit, then, that the cumulative testimony of the scholia concerning Aristarchus' editing of vertical variations provides additional evidence in favor of resisting West's "novit Didymus" theory—and editorial practice.[96]

What I have just argued about Aristarchus' editorial policy on vertical variants applies also to his policy on horizontal variants. His evaluation of these variants must have required the collecting and collating of manuscripts. In this case, however, it is more difficult for us to intuit the degree of variation, from manuscript to manuscript, since any discussion of variants emerging from Aristarchus' study of the manuscript evidence would have been reserved for his *hupomnēmata* 'commentaries'. Such Aristarchean discussions of horizontal variants, abridged by Didymus and further abridged by the Homer scholia, have reached us in a most unsatisfactory state of incompleteness. The testimony of the scholia at *Iliad* A 423–424, which we have considered earlier, is exceptional in showing a relatively less

94. N 1997d.116n48.

95. Cf. again Apthorp 1980.xv.

96. This is not to say that Didymus did not collate Homer manuscripts in his own right or that Aristarchus was the only collator (cf. Bolling 1925.39, who argues for a post-Aristarchean dating of the *Krētikē*). It is only to say that the primary collator of Homer

abridged version of Aristarchean commentary. Moreover, the actual forms of the horizontal variants, as mentioned in the Aristarchean *hupomnēmata*, could easily be ignored by copyists if their primary task was simply to transcribe the *ipsissima verba* featured in the text proper of the Aristarchean edition. From the standpoint of copyists who had no stake in the complete Aristarchean editorial legacy, *hupomnēmata* and all, vertical variation would have mattered far more than horizontal variation: there was far greater or less labor involved in the copying of more or fewer verses.[97]

Throughout this discussion, we have seen how the testimony of the Homer scholia concerning Aristarchus' editorial policy on vertical variants helps us better understand his corresponding policy on horizontal variants. To summarize both editorial policies, I offer the following template:

1 Vertical variations
   1a Aristarchus kept in his base text the "vulgate" variant verses that he athetized, while he reserved his judgment of the wrongness of these verses for discussion in his *hupomnēmata* (marginal marks in the text proper would signal such a discussion).
   1b It was only when the manuscript attestation for a given verse was weak that he could delete ("omit") it rather than athetize it in his base text, perhaps justifying the deletion in his *hupomnēmata*.
2 Horizontal variations
   2a Aristarchus kept in his base text the "vulgate" wording, while he reserved his judgment on the rightness or wrongness of corresponding non-"vulgate" variant wordings (derived from the 'more elegant' manuscripts, the *khariesterai*) for discussion in his *hupomnēmata*.[98] Marginal marks in the base text would signal such a discussion.
   2b Only when the manuscript attestation for a given "vulgate" wording was unstable—that is, when more than one "vulgate" wording was available and no single wording was clearly preferable—did Aristarchus make a choice about what to write in the base text, justifying the choice in his *hupomnēmata*.[99]

---

manuscripts was Aristarchus himself and that Didymus did not have access to all the sources still available to Aristarchus (cf. again Bolling, ibid.).

97. Cf. Apthorp 1980.9–10.

98. For more on the Aristarchean concept of Homeric texts that are *khariesterai* (χαριέστεραι) 'more elegant', see Ch.4 below. See also *PP* 116, 122–124, 188.

99. This formulation modifies slightly the formulation in N 2000a. The modification is meant to accommodate rare situations where the two *ekdoseis* 'editions' of Aristarchus (as tracked by Didymus) reflect two different wordings in the base text. In such situations, as we can see from further discussion in Ch.4 below, it seems that the two 'editions' (as produced by Aristarchus or, more likely, by later Aristarcheans) indicate different choices

In terms of this posited template, with specific reference to horizontal variations, let us take another look at *Iliad* I 394, where West chooses for his own base text the Aristarchean reading γε μάσσεται instead of the "vulgate" reading γαμέσσεται. As I have remarked earlier, such a choice is exceptional for West. In most other cases where Aristarchean variants are reported, he tends to choose a variant reading that is non-Aristarchean if the corresponding Aristarchean variant is only weakly or not at all attested in the medieval manuscripts and in the papyri (as at *Iliad* Γ 406).[100] He is likely to opt for an Aristarchean variant only if he finds it strongly attested in the medieval manuscripts and in the papyri.

Here we have an opportunity to compare West's general editorial stance with that of Aristarchus as I have just outlined it. Ironically, West comes closest to an Aristarchean editorial principle precisely in those situations where he has to make a choice between an Aristarchean and a non-Aristarchean variant. In other words, he resorts to Aristarchean methodology in order to reject Aristarchean variants. When he is forced to choose between an Aristarchean and a non-Aristarchean variant, he tends to rely more than usual on the external evidence—and less than usual on the internal. In other words, in such situations he is more likely to allow the relative strength or weakness of manuscript attestation to influence his choice. If the Aristarchean variant is weakly attested, he tends to reject it. If it is strongly attested, he tends to adopt it. That is because, for West, an Aristarchean variant is like any other variant.

By contrast, if we follow the neo-Aristarcheans, then any variant reported by Aristarchus has a special status, because it may indeed come from ancient manuscripts or manuscript traditions that were known to Aristarchus and are no longer known to us. In those ancient traditions, the relative strength or weakness of manuscript attestations may indeed have been markedly different from what is available to modern editors like West.

I should emphasize that West in these special situations merely *tends* to make choices on the basis of external evidence. Even here, as elsewhere, he is not systematic in applying the criterion of stronger vs. weaker attestation. Confronted with a choice between a weakly attested Aristarchean variant and a strongly attested non-Aristarchean counterpart, he does not always opt for the second alternative. Again I point to such salient exceptions as his choice of the Aristarchean reading γε μάσσεται instead of the "vulgate" reading γαμέσσεται at IX 394. Exceptions like this help account for the

---

to be made, as when more than one "vulgate" variant emerged from a comparison of "vulgate" texts.

100. See my earlier discussion of the scholia at Γ 406.

qualification built into the wording of Janko: "[West] holds that ... the majority of Aristarchus' unique readings are wrong."[101]

With regard to choices to be made between Aristarchean and non-Aristarchean variants, Ludwich's editorial principle is more straightforward than West's: he generally sides with Aristarchus wherever a choice is available on the basis of available manuscript evidence, that is, wherever Aristarchus' own choice between variants is backed up by manuscript evidence available to Ludwich. In the apparatus criticus of Ludwich's *Iliad*, the most striking illustration of this principle is the ubiquitous formula "Aristarchus + Ω," that is, where the choice of Aristarchus is backed up by "Ω," designating a relatively strong attestation in the medieval manuscript tradition. West has adopted Ludwich's "Aristarchus + Ω" formula in the apparatus criticus of his own *Iliad*, and we find it applied with the greatest frequency.[102] On the surface, then, it seems as if Ludwich and West are applying the same criterion in such situations. Underneath the surface, however, the criteria differ: for Ludwich, the "Aristarchus" component of the "Aristarchus + Ω" formula has special status, but for West it has merely equal status. Correspondingly, whenever the "Ω" drops out, that is, whenever the manuscript support is lacking or weak, the Aristarchean variant tends to be kept by Ludwich but dropped by West. To repeat, West's adoption of γε μάσσεται instead of γαμέσσεται at *Iliad* I 394 is for him exceptional.

From the standpoint of oral poetics, I should emphasize, such choices do not have to be made. In the case of the two variants γε μάσσεται and γαμέσσεται, for example, both actually fit the formulaic system of Homeric diction, as we will see later.[103] In other words, the internal evidence indicates that both forms are functional variants in the formulaic system of Homeric poetry. The external evidence gives further support, if we agree with Ludwich that γε μάσσεται is a variant that Aristarchus had authenticated on the basis of manuscript evidence known to him, just as γαμέσσεται is a variant authenticated on the basis of manuscript evidence known to us.

Although West has a generally negative policy about Aristarchus' reliability concerning horizontal variants, he is more positive about the vertical variants. He tends to approve whenever Aristarchus athetizes or deletes ("omits") verses on the grounds that they are interpolations (as in the scholia at Γ 144a).[104] Such a double standard toward vertical and horizontal

101. Janko 2000.1.
102. I should note one important difference between West's and Ludwich's usage: for West (see his p. xiii), but not for Ludwich, readings from "Ω" are regularly to be contrasted with readings from "Z" (= Ve1 Allen).
103. Ch.5, rewritten from N 1998a.
104. Cf. West 1999a.186–187.

variations as mediated by Aristarchus is also evident, as I have noted earlier, in the work of Janko.[105] For West's *Iliad*, in any case, the final judgment on both vertical and horizontal variations does not depend on the external evidence of manuscript attestations. Whatever this evidence may have been in the time of Aristarchus, and whatever it is now as we contemplate the texts and quotations that do survive into our time, the ultimate criterion for West is whether a given variant does or does not fit the model built on his assumption that our *Iliad* and *Odyssey* go back to "originals" written around the middle of the seventh century BCE. I have already quoted him as saying: "We may assume that there existed a complete and coherent *Urtext* of each epic, the result of the first writing down."[106] But can we actually restore this *Urtext*?

West's answer is no: "we are not in the position to restore the original version." He goes on to ask: "Should we then be aiming to recover the Athenian text of the epics, as they were recited at the Panathenaea after Hipparchus, or at any rate as they were known to Thucydides, the orators, and Plato?" The answer, again, is no: "the text at this period was in a far from settled state." West explains that "there was no single 'Athenian text.'" And "the text" becomes only more unsettled thereafter, in the era of the early Ptolemaic papyri: now it is "characterized by so-called 'wild' variants (think of wild flowers rather than wild poets, perhaps), diverging from the medieval vulgate not in narrative substance but with substitution of formulae, inorganic additional lines, and so forth." So, finally, we have come all the way down to the Alexandrian editors. West now asks the inevitable follow-up question: "Should our aim, then, be to reconstruct the Alexandrian text?" One last time, the answer is no: "But again, there is no single Alexandrian text, even if some agreement was reached in terms of

105. Janko 1992.21n6; cf. *PP* 139–140. For more on Aristarchus' editorial methodology in using external manuscript evidence for determining whether or not to apply athetesis, see the extended discussion in *PP* 146–147n169. Janko 1998c.147 has asserted about my discussion: "N. also believes (146, n. 149 [his reference should be corrected to 169]) that the Alexandrians athetised suspect verses because of ms evidence, whereas in fact they athetised such verses, rather than omitted them, only when they *lacked* external evidence against them." This assertion is criticized by Apthorp 1999.19n22: "As M. Haslam correctly states, 'It is ... clear that Aristarchus did at least on occasion have manuscript authority for his atheteses' [1997.76]. The evidence for this is assembled in [Apthorp 1980] pp. 49–53, with notes on pp. 102–9. R. Janko is misleading when he writes that 'the Alexandrians athetised suspect verses,... rather than omitted them, only when they *lacked* external evidence against them' [1998c.207, in Janko's review of *PP*]. Elsewhere, Janko tones down his assertion by inserting the qualification 'largely' [1992.28]: 'for him [Aristarchus], athetesis was largely based on *internal* evidence.'"

106. West 1998a.95. The following quotations from West in this paragraph all come from this same location.

Versbestand." West explains: "We know of many variant readings current in the Alexandrian period, from which we must make our choice." So it seems that there has never been any single text, not since the *Urtext*. In the face of all this multiformity sketched by West in his survey of Homeric textual history, we may well ask: how and even why must we "make our choice"? What kind of uniformity should an editor try to reconstruct? West's answer is guarded:

> The answer must be some kind of compromise. Let us state our aim to be the establishment, so far as our means allow, of the pristine text of the poems in the form they attained following the last phase of creative effort. We must concede that, as the tradition passed through several centuries of "wildness," it may be impossible to establish exactly what lies on the far side. But let that be our objective.[107]

West is eager to cross the fence and move on to that far side, where the wild flowers grow—and far beyond that, far beyond the horizon. He leaves behind whatever we can still see on this side of the fence, the ruins of gardens once teeming with cultivated flowers tended by the Alexandrian editors. As we have already noted, West has not much use for Aristarchus, and even less for Aristophanes of Byzantium; as for Zenodotus of Ephesus, that Alexandrian editor is practically of no use at all.[108] West asks: "why limit our ambition to reconstructing an Alexandrian text, stopping five hundred years short of the originals, when we have at least a modicum of evidence that takes us further back?"[109]

The problem is, trying to go further back to "the originals," to a single text, is an impossible task, when all you have is a "modicum of evidence." To wander off on such a quest is to leave untended the evidence that is closer at hand, available from the Alexandrians. In terms of West's own reconstruction, as we have seen, there is no evidence for a "single text." For him, the last time there was any single text was the time of the hypothetical *Urtext*. Similarly for Janko, we need to go back to an *Urtext*—this time, by way of a prototypical dictation, in terms of his own theory.

West envisions his Homeric *Urtext*, once it took shape in the seventh century BCE, as a dead thing. He makes this vision evident in another work, where he surveys West Asiatic influences on Homeric poetry.[110] Tracing these influences back to the seventh century BCE, West treats his dating

107. West 1998a.95.
108. West 1998b.vi–vii, though there are a few exceptions listed at his n6. On Zenodotus, I refer again to my defense of his editorial methods in *PP* 133–138.
109. West 1998a.95.
110. West 2000c.587, 627–630.

as a terminus for the life of Homeric poetry and of early Greek poetry in general: "In the final reckoning,... the argument for pervasive West Asiatic influence on early Greek poetry does not stand or fall with explanations of how it came about. A corpse suffices to prove a death, even if the inquest is inconclusive."[111] West seems to be saying that Homeric poetry after the seventh century BCE is no longer a living corpus. Rather, it has become a dead thing, a corpse.[112] And yet, I see no proof for the notion that Homeric poetry—let alone early Greek poetry in general—was already a "corpse" after the seventh century.[113]

As we come back to the realities of multiformity described by West in his sketch of Homeric textual history, I must repeat my question: what kind of uniformity should an editor try to reconstruct? The answer, I submit, is that the evidence of textual multiformity precludes a uniform reconstruction, a "unitext" edition of Homer. Instead, the editor of Homer needs to keep coming back, I submit, to the facts of textual multiformity. The basic source for these facts, however incompletely preserved they may be, remains Aristarchus. *Revenons à cultiver notre jardin.*

We cannot afford to lose sight of the facts known to Aristarchus and no longer known (or known as well) to us, even if we think that his editorial judgment was impaired because he in turn did not know some other facts that we do indeed know. In comparing our own cumulative knowledge with that of Aristarchus, it is tempting for some to feel superior to him, as we see from the explanation given by Janko for his general disapproval of Aristarchean atheteses: "The ethical and probabilistic criteria he [= Aristarchus] applies are not those of Homer's society; his knowledge of epic usage is less complete than ours (based on sophisticated indices and concordances); he was unaware of Indo-European and Near Eastern philology, archaeology, oral poetry, ring-composition and Linear B; and, as for literary insight, he is often outshone by the later scholarship seen in [scholia] bT."[114] So also in the *Iliad* of West, as we have seen, the editorial judgments of Aristarchus are often overruled on the basis of considerations derived from current Homeric scholarship, much as they are being described

---

111. West 2000c.630.

112. In West 2003.13–14, he elaborates: after the *Iliad* became a fixed text, the "creativity" of rhapsodes "was able to express itself in novel ways"—by way of manipulating existing texts. He dates this period of literary "creativity" between 620 and 520 BCE, adding (p. 14): "Once we shake the oralists off our backs and recognize the status of written texts in this period and the use made of them, we begin to gain insights into their interrelationships and chronology, and a nebulous process of development begins to take on sharper outlines."

113. This paragraph has been added to the original version of my review.

114. Janko 1992.27.

by Janko. Still, there remain three fundamental facts that remain unaffected by such considerations.

One, Aristarchus knew far more about the ancient manuscript evidence than we do.

Two, on the basis of all his manuscript evidence, Aristarchus could not and would not produce a single unified text of Homer. He left room for choices among variants—both horizontal and vertical—in his *hupomnēmata*.

Three, on the basis of all the manuscript evidence available to us, which I think is less informative than the manuscript evidence available to Aristarchus, editors like West are forced to admit that they cannot produce a single unified text of Homer. The unity of their "unitext" editions is achieved by way of reconstructions and conjectures based on considerations of chronology, dialect, historical provenance, and so forth.

In light of these three facts, I propose an alternative to the concept of a "unitext" edition of Homer. Instead, I advocate the concept of a *multitext edition*. Such an edition needs to account for Homeric multiforms attested as textual variants, recovered mostly through the research of the Alexandrian editors, especially Aristarchus.[115]

In introducing this concept of a multitext edition, I stress again the textual multiformity of the Homeric poems, which as I have argued indicates a heritage of oral poetics. Although the Alexandrians did not think in terms of oral poetics, their editorial work on textual variants provides evidence of this heritage:

> Even though Aristarchus, following the thought-patterns of myth, posited a Homeric original, he nevertheless accepted and in fact respected the reality of textual variants. He respected variants because, in terms of his own working theory, it seems that any one of them could have been the very one that Homer wrote.... That is why he makes the effort of knowing the many different readings of so many manuscripts. He is in fact far more cautious in methodology than some contemporary investigators of Homer who may be quicker to say which is the right reading and which are the wrong ones. Aristarchus may strike us as naive in reconstructing an Athenian Homer who "wrote" around 1000 [BCE], but that kind of construct enables him to be more rigorous in making choices among variants.... What, then, would Aristarchus have lost, and what would we stand to lose, if it really is true that the variants of Homeric textual tradition reflect for the most part the multiforms of a performance tradition? If you accept the reality of multiforms, you forfeit the elusive certainty of finding the original composition of Homer but you gain, and

115. Cf. Bird 1994.

I think this is an important gain, another certainty, an unexpected one but one that may turn out to be much more valuable: you recover a significant portion of the Homeric repertoire. In addition, you recover a sense of the diachrony.[116]

My concluding sentences here about diachrony were used already earlier, in Chapter Two, where I was making the point that Homeric multiformity needs to be viewed diachronically as well as synchronically. The need for a diachronic perspective in analyzing Homeric poetry was the impetus for my developing an evolutionary model for the making of this poetry. As I said in Chapter Two, this model was designed to account for all variations that stem from the performance traditions of Homeric poetry.

The multiformity of variations in the oral poetic context of composition-in-performance cannot be viewed exclusively from a synchronic perspective.[117] A multitext edition of Homer is needed to provide a diachronic perspective on this multiformity. Ideally, a multitext edition of Homer should be formatted to display most clearly all the surviving textual variants, both vertical and horizontal. It should have a base text (*texte de base*) that is free of arbitrary judgments, such as the choosing of one variant over another on the basis of the editor's personal sense of what is right or wrong, better or worse. In other words, the base text needs to be formatted to show all locations where variants are attested, and all the variants that can be slotted into those locations—without privileging any of these variants. Working within the framework of "*hupomnēmata*," editors of the base text may then proceed to analyze the variants from a diachronic perspective, making their own considered judgments about differences in the chronology, dialect, historical provenance, and so forth. For such a multitext edition, the most convenient base text would be the relatively most standard and common manuscript tradition. For Aristarchus, that base text was essentially the *koinē* version of Homer—what neo-Aristarcheans call the "vulgate."[118] As of this writing, the closest thing to such a base text is the Homer of van Thiel.[119] Something much closer to an ideal, however, would be the edition of Aristarchus, if only it had survived. In fact, Aristarchus' edition of Homer would have been the closest thing to what I am describing here as an ideal multitext edition.

If van Thiel's Homer were chosen as the most convenient base text for a modern multitext edition, where could we go from there? What models could we find for the "*hupomnēmata*" to accompany such a base text? The

116. *PP* 151–152.
117. *PR* 3–5.
118. Cf. Ludwich 1884.11–16 ("Die alte Vulgata").
119. van Thiel 1991, 1996.

apparatus criticus of West's Homer seems a most elegant model, at least as a starting point. But there are problems, as we see from the interplay of his apparatus criticus with his testimonia, that is, with his display of the ancient quotations of Homer.

The testimonia take up a separate middle band on each page of West's *Iliad* (his edited text is of course in the upper band, while his apparatus criticus is in the lower band). This middle band turns out to be of limited value to the editor—let alone the editor's readers. After all, West thinks that most ancient quotations are of limited value in the first place.[120] In his 1898 book, *Die Homervulgata als voralexandrinisch erwiesen*, Ludwich had already published an exhaustive collection of ancient quotations, down to the Augustan period. Ludwich's mass of cross-references, now further supplemented, has been assimilated by West into the middle band of his *Iliad*.[121] Ludwich's original motive—and premise—in making his 1898 collection had been simple: he thought that these ancient quotations would help further recover the pre-Alexandrian vulgate. Since West does not operate on this premise, his updating of Ludwich's repertoire merely exemplifies the law of diminishing returns. The ubiquitous references to "t" and "tt" ("testimonium" and "testimonia") in the lower band containing the apparatus criticus, drawing our attention upward into the middle band containing the testimonia, hardly make a difference whenever it comes to the question of what reading is finally chosen by West in the upper band containing the edited text proper. Typically, "t" or "tt" simply join the chorus of "Ω" readings in privileging the vulgate version of Homer. For West, they seldom make a difference.[122] By contrast, wherever an ancient quotation does make a difference in Ludwich's *Iliad*, that editor simply confronts it directly in his apparatus criticus (his *Iliad* does not feature a separate middle band of testimonia, which he published separately, as we have seen, in 1898). In this respect, Ludwich's policy seems more economical—and elegant.

Although the "lower band" of West's three-band *Iliad*, his apparatus criticus, is a most valuable contribution to our knowledge of the Homeric textual tradition, the "upper band," his base text, is of questionable value. The text of West's *Iliad* contains many editorial judgments that go beyond the manuscript evidence and that flatten out the textual history of Homer. Here is where his "unitext" edition differs most radically from a multitext edition.

120. West 1998b.x.
121. Cf. West 1998a.97.
122. West 1998b.x n14 lists a handful of exceptions; see also West 1998a.97.

A salient example of differences between "unitext" and multitext editorial approaches to Homer is the case of Athenian forms and themes that we find embedded in the Homeric textual tradition. From a diachronic point of view, we may expect a multitext edition of Homer to accommodate even those textual variants that are dated as late as the sixth through the fourth centuries BCE, the era of Athenian performance traditions.[123] In fact, there are numerous Homeric textual variants that reflect Athenian accretions in both form and content.[124] For a "unitext" Homer edition like West's, however, the goal is to reconstruct the prototypical text of the prototypical poet. Accordingly, for all practical purposes, West's *Iliad* has screened out all the textual variants of Athenian provenance. In the case of horizontal variants, West consistently chooses the non-Athenian form over the corresponding Athenian one (Ionic τεσσερ- vs. "Attic" τεσσαρ-, *passim*).[125] Wherever an Athenian form occurs without the attestation of a non-Athenian textual variant, he will simply emend the transmitted Athenian form and conjecture a corresponding non-Athenian form. In the case of vertical variants, he will bracket or simply omit from his text any line that suggests any kind of Athenian cultural agenda stemming from the sixth century or thereafter (a prime example is *Iliad* B 547–551).

At one extreme, then, West's edition tends to underestimate the chronological diversity of the Homeric tradition. At the other extreme, however, it occasionally lapses into overestimations that defy credibility. In particular, the relatively older forms tend to be treated without sufficient regard for the operative system of Homeric diction. For example, West claims that the Luvian particle *tar* (which he translates as "usquam") is a cognate of the Homeric particle ταρ, and that the Luvian usage of *tar* is key to understanding the Greek usage of ταρ in the *Iliad*, as at A 8, 65, 123, and so forth.[126] In printing ταρ instead of τἄρ in these contexts, West is following the testimony of Apollonius and Herodian, according to whom the particle ταρ counts as one word, by contrast with τἄρ. The particle τἄρ counts as two words, τ' (from τε) plus ἄρ. If Homeric ταρ is really cognate with Luvian *tar*, then it cannot be related etymologically to Homeric τἄρ. And yet, I see no convincing way of separating completely the Homeric contexts of this ταρ from Homeric contexts of τἄρ where the constituents τ' (from τε) plus ἄρ

123. N 1999b.271–272 (see now *HR* 69–70).

124. West 1998b.vi; cf. N 1998b, rewritten as Ch.5.

125. West 1998b.xxxv.

126. West 1998b.xxix; here he is following Watkins 1995.150, who refers at p. 151 to an unpublished 1994 work of Joshua Katz on Homeric formulas beginning αὐτὰρ ἐπεί (for an abstract, see Katz 1998).

are transparently functional, as at *Iliad* A 93, Γ 398, and so forth. Moreover, the etymology of γάρ, another particle that counts as one word, can serve as evidence against the etymological separation of ταρ from τἄρ: in the case of γάρ, the constituents are transparently γ' (from γε) plus ἄρ.[127] Just as some usages of γάρ preserve the syntax of the constituent γε (as in the case of ὁ γάρ via ὅγε plus ἄρ),[128] so also some usages of τἄρ preserve the syntax of the constituent τε (as in the case of τἄρ at Γ 398).[129] Further, just as other usages of γάρ no longer preserve the syntax of the constituent γε, so also it is possible that other usages of τἄρ no longer preserve the syntax of the constituent τε; whence the special status of Homeric ταρ.[130] Here and elsewhere, there are problems with West's application of linguistics in the process of rewriting the received text of the *Iliad*.[131]

Concluding, I should stress that my criticisms of West's *Iliad* are not meant to detract from the praise he deserves. I gratefully acknowledge all his valuable contributions to Homeric scholarship. Even the size of this review-essay can be taken as a tribute to the editor's industry and learning. West's *Iliad* is a most useful and important edition. Still, it cannot be considered an authoritative replacement of previous editions of the *Iliad*. Many of those—including the 1902 Teubner text of Ludwich and the 1920 Oxford Classical Text of Monro/Allen—will continue to have their uses.

127. Chantraine *DELG* p. 210.

128. See Schywzer/Debrunner 1966.560.

129. In this case, West's apparatus shows a syntactically analogous textual variant δ' ἄρ actually attested in the papyri.

130. If indeed Homeric ταρ is derived from τ' (from τε) plus ἄρ just as γάρ is derived from γ' (from γε) plus ἄρ, we still need to account for the enclitic status of ταρ in some Homeric contexts and the non-enclitic status of τἄρ in others. It may be relevant that γάρ is fully lexicalized in all its attestations, that is, it has become a single word, whereas neither ταρ nor ἄρ / ρα (vs. ἄρα) have achieved that status in Attic/Ionic, outside of poetic diction. With reference to the arguments of Katz 1998, I see further evidence for counter-arguments. For example, not only are αὐτάρ and ἀτάρ syntactically parallel in a variety of Homeric contexts: so also are ἀτάρ and (δ') αὖ / (δ') αὖτ(ε). Note too the collocations αὐτὰρ ἄρα at B 103 and αὐτὰρ ὁ αὖτε at B 105, 107.

131. For examples of questionable rewritings in West's *Iliad*, see also the criticisms of Janko 2000.1. I hope to discuss further examples in a separate project.

Editing the Homeric Text: Different Methods, Ancient and Modern

Martin West published in 2001 a book that supplements his 1998 / 2000 edition of the Homeric *Iliad*.[1] It serves as a vehicle for explaining (1) his overall editorial stance and (2) the differences between his edition and those of his predecessors. My essay here concentrates on debating those two aspects of the book.[2] Such debate serves as a point of re-entry into an ongoing question, basic to Homeric studies: how was the text of Homer edited in the ancient world, especially in Alexandria, and how were the editing methods of the ancients different from those of the moderns?

West thinks of his own text of the *Iliad* as the "version" produced by Homer himself—or, in West's terms, by the poet of the *Iliad* (as we saw

---

* The original version of this essay is N 2003b, reviewing West 2001b. The present version is supplemented with references to the insights of Rengakos 2002, author of another review of West 2001b. Rengakos and I had read pre-published drafts of each other's essays, and I acknowledge gratefully his advice, as also the advice of Michael Apthorp, who read a draft of my essay in July 2002.

1. West 2001b, supplementing West 1998b/2000c.

2. Other aspects of the book are (1) new information on Homeric papyri, pp. 86–138; (2) a reassessment of the interrelationships among the early medieval manuscripts, pp. 139–157; (3) "Notes on Individual Passages," pp. 173–285. In the discussion that follows, I will comment selectively on these aspects as well. Mistakes in the book are rare (at p. 277 line 8, read "Achilles" not "Hector").

earlier, he denies that the poet's name was Homer): "We have to choose one version that we are aiming to establish, and clearly it should be the poet's last version."[3] I focus on a detail in this statement. West's assumption, and his wording makes it clear, is that he is working with something other than oral poetry.

There is a serious problem with this assumption. West is claiming that he can isolate one distinct and integral "version" of the *Iliad*, sorting it out from a mass of multiple versions contained in the Homeric textual tradition. He claims further that this "version" was produced by a single poet. Even further, he claims that he can distinguish between earlier and later "versions" stemming from this same poet.

As I have been arguing all along, the study of living oral poetic traditions shows that different available versions cannot be reduced to a single basic version from which all versions are to be derived. For West's editorial method to succeed, it must be assumed, as a starting point, that the *Iliad* is not a matter of oral poetry.[4]

Whether or not it is true that the *Iliad* is oral poetry, one thing is for sure: West has simply bypassed the available comparative evidence provided by the study of oral poetics. Especially valuable, for comparison with Homeric poetry, is the evidence of oral poetry as attested in literate—not illiterate—societies. There are many examples from over the world, but the textual traditions of medieval vernacular poetry in Western Europe offer perhaps the most relevant and telling points of comparison. Detailed descriptions can be found in the work of medievalists like Paul Zumthor, whose descriptive model of *mouvance* is most useful to Homerists, as I have argued elsewhere.[5] Also useful is Bernard Cerquiglini's alternative model of *variance*.[6] West chooses not to engage with any such models.

A basic lesson to be learned from studies of oral poetry as transmitted through texts has to do with the actual variation that we find in such texts. Such variation, in and of itself, reveals the workings of oral poetry. So long as oral poetry persists in a given literate society, each written instance of a "version" will be different from each succeeding instance—even in traditions where the audience at large assumes that each new instance is simply a repetition of previous instances. The degree of variation is itself a variable.

3. West 2001b.158–159.

4. In another publication, West (2000c.630) assumes that Homeric poetry died after the Homeric poems become established as some kind of *Urtext*, which is imagined as a "corpse" (see p. 69 above).

5. Zumthor 1972. Cf. *PP* 7–38.

6. Cerquiglini 1989.

Studies of oral poetry as transmitted though texts have made it clear that the degree of variation—and even the audiences' awareness of it—will itself vary from culture to culture, or even from phase to phase in any one culture.[7] The actual fact of variation, however, remains a constant. Variation is an essential feature of oral poetry, which is a process of composition-in-performance, and this feature is reflected—in varying degrees—by the written records of oral poetry. In terms of ancient Greek, a word that approximates such a model of variation is *poikilia* (ποικιλία) 'variation, variety'.[8]

Beyond the work of Zumthor and others on oral traditions in literate societies, it is essential to keep in mind the more fundamental work of Milman Parry and Albert Lord on oral traditions in general.[9] In terms of Lord's analysis, a suitable word for describing the variation to be found in Homeric poetry is *multiformity*.[10] West not only bypasses this concept: he ignores altogether the work of Parry and Lord. In West's 2001 book, as also in the introduction to his 1998 / 2000 edition of the *Iliad*, he does not even mention the names of Parry and Lord anywhere.[11]

When West dismisses various arguments about the multiformity of Homeric poetry as a sign of its oral poetic heritage, he backs up his dismissal by citing an article that purports to show how the *Iliad* is not multiform but "uniform."[12] Unfortunately, this whole article is based on a misunderstanding of Lord's concept of multiformity in oral poetry.[13] West's citation of the article is not only derivative—since he ignores Lord's concept of multiformity—but also inadequate.

In this context, West also dismisses a related concept, "multitext."[14] The model of a multitext edition of Homer, developed for the purpose of addressing the multiformity of oral poetry and of Homeric poetry in particular, is designed as an alternative to West's hypothesis of recovering an "original" version of Homer.[15] A multitext edition offers an alternative to

7. *HQ* 29–63.

8. *PP* 7–38.

9. Parry 1971; Lord 1960. See Ch.2 above.

10. Lord 1995.23. See Ch.2 above.

11. West 2001b, in his reply to N 2000a, mentions Parry and Lord—but only to say that their work is not relevant to his edition of the *Iliad*.

12. West 2001b.159n1, citing Finkelberg 2000. At p. 9 Finkelberg cites the model of multiformity as outlined by Lord 1960; not cited is Lord 1995. See again Ch.2 above.

13. The misreading by Finkelberg 2000 is analyzed in Ch.2, a rewritten version of N 2001a; see also Dué 2001.

14. For a discussion of the concept of "multitext," see Ch.3 above, a rewritten version of N 2000a.

15. See again Ch.3.

West's reconstructing a single "version" as the basis for his explanations of all other "versions." West misreads the concept of multitext when he claims that a multitext edition of Homer promotes an attitude of indifference toward the critical evaluation of variant readings in the history of the Homeric textual tradition. Contrary to West's claim, a multitext edition of Homer does indeed allow for the privileging of one variant over others—but only in relative terms, since the editor may find that different variants became dominant in different phases of the Homeric tradition. In terms of a multitext edition, the editor of Homer needs to adopt a diachronic perspective—as an alternative to a pseudo-synchronic perspective. The term "pseudo-synchronic" will be explained further below.

From a diachronic and even historical point of view, it is indeed possible to think of a single given variant as the definitive variant at a single given time and a single given place. But the privileging of any given variant by any given audience is itself a matter of variation, and a diachronic perspective makes it clear that different variants were perceived as the "right" version at different points in the history of the Homeric tradition.

It is not that a diachronic perspective avoids "passing any value judg-ments," as West claims.[16] The point is, rather, that the modern value judgments of the editor need to be responsive to changes in the ancient value judgments about Homeric poetry throughout the historical continuum of the Homeric tradition. West applies the term "value judgments" only to the critical stances of modern editors and their readers. But what about the "value judgments" of the ancient world? In this case, a more suitable term is "reception." The problem is, West does not take into account the history of Homeric reception. If indeed Homeric poetry—as recorded by the Homeric textual tradition—reflects a system derived from oral poetry, then the value judgments of an editor need to be responsive to the multiple value judgments represented by that system as it evolves through time. An empirical analysis of the textual evidence reveals an underlying system capable of generating a multiplicity of versions, and it is methodologically unsound for an editor to assume that only one of these extant versions was basic while the others were derivative. Such an assumption exemplifies what I call a "pseudo-synchronic" point of view. I define such a point of view as one that treats irregularities within a given traditional system as if they could never have been regularities in other phases of that same system.

A related problem is West's uncritical usage of the term "original." In terms of such an absolutizing concept, any attested variant that happens to

16. West 2001b.159n2; also his p. 3.

be different from the "original" variant will be dismissed as not genuine, not authentic, not worthy of the "original" author, and so on. If the "original" version involves fewer verses than other versions, the additional verses in the other versions will be judged to be a textual interpolation. If the "original" involves more verses, then the absence of these verses in the other versions will be judged to be a textual lacuna.[17] Such an approach, looking at Homeric texts without considering the system that produced these texts, loses sight of what we know about the workings of oral poetry. If indeed Homeric poetry is at least derived from oral poetry—and even West concedes such a derivation—then the privileging of any one Homeric variant is merely a hypothesis, and the rejection of other variants depends on that hypothesis.[18] Then the judgments of privileging or rejecting one or another variant can be exposed for what they are—the product of an exercise in circular reasoning.

Even in terms of this circular reasoning, West's book is inconsistent. On the one hand, he is certain that the poet of the *Iliad* had his own "version," on the grounds that there must have been an "original text." On the other hand, West is also certain that this text was original on the grounds that it must have been the only truly "oral" version, while the other versions were somehow "non-oral" on the grounds that they stem from *rhapsōidoi* (ῥαψῳδοί) 'rhapsodes'. West wants to have it both ways—not only an original text but also a truly oral version. The problem is, these two concepts are mutually exclusive. There is a further problem with his model of the "oral" version: West's distinction between Homer (or West's "*Iliad* poet") and the "rhapsodes," representing respectively "oral" and "non-oral" traditions, is merely an assumption. Several works, applying the "diachronic perspective" that West rejects, have demonstrated the arbitrariness and artificiality of this distinction, but West does not engage with any of these works.[19]

Sometimes a model, even if it happens to be flawed, turns out to be a useful approximation of reality. Let us assume, for the moment, that West's model is the closest thing to reality. Even if that were so, it is unjustifiable for him to claim from the very start that his explanation is the absolute truth. Such a claim is evident from this statement of his:

> Nagy fails to see the difference between a genuine creative oral tradition
> and the reproductive tradition of the Homeric rhapsodes, whose business

17. Examples in West 1998 are cited in N 2000a, rewritten here as Ch.3.

18. For an example of a discussion where at least the derivation of Homeric poetry from oral poetry is conceded, see West 2001b.159n2.

19. For discussion and further references, see *HQ* 82–94.

was to perform excerpts from specific poems conceived as fixed entities. Of course their interpolations and "oral"[20] variants are valid and interesting as manifestations of their art, but they have a quite different and inferior status to the *original*, normative *text* that the rhapsodes were supposed to be presenting. My edition is for those whose greater interest is in that *original text*.[21]

A casual reader may be led to think that West's "original text" is some kind of established reality. It is not. Nor can it be asserted as a fact that the business of rhapsodes was to perform "excerpts" from "specific poems." Such an assertion assumes not only an "original text" but also a textual procedure of "excerpting" parts from a totality. While asserting this assumption, West ignores alternative arguments, including my argument for rhapsodic "relay mnemonics," a performative procedure of sequencing a totality from start to finish.[22]

In West's "Notes on Individual Passages," he consistently makes a distinction between the "original" poet and the "interpolating" rhapsodes.[23] Here are examples from the first half of the *Iliad*, and in each case I will highlight the words "original," "interpolate," and "rhapsode." At B 258, "<u>rhapsodes</u> had difficulty in remembering this unusual phrase (νύ περ [at] β 320 v.l.; not elsewhere, at least in Homer), and improvised substitutes."[24] The verses at B 491–492 "must have been added by a <u>rhapsode</u> who misinterpreted πληθύν in 488, not realizing that the mass of the army was being distinguished from the leaders."[25] On B 535: "perhaps it was added by a <u>rhapsode</u> who thought ... East Locrians should be unequivocally distinguished from the Ozolian Locrians."[26] On B 547–551: "I have therefore bracketed these five lines, assuming them to have replaced the <u>original</u> list of towns."[27] On Γ 41: "but it [= an idiomatic usage containing an implicit comparative] may have prompted a later <u>rhapsode</u> to <u>interpolate</u> a line

20. The scare-quotes are West's.

21. West 2001b.159n1. The italics are mine.

22. *PR* 10–17.

23. West 2001b.173–285.

24. West 2001b.175.

25. West 2001b.178; cf. also p. 221. His assumption of such a distinction here in the Catalogue of *Iliad* B does not take into account the variable usages of inclusion and exclusion involving πληθύς (examples of inclusive contexts: B 278, I 641, O 305). One assumption leads to another: West p. 178 claims that Ibycus in the "ode" to Polycrates (S 151.23 and following) "seems already to have known" the Iliadic passage "in its interpolated form."

26. West 2001b.179.

27. West 2001b.180.

containing the explicit comparative."[28] On Γ 144: this verse "was added by someone who knew the Aithra story."[29] On Δ 177: "This verse may be a <u>rhapsode's</u> addition. It adds a gratuitous crudity to a sentence which is perfect without it."[30] On E 313: "this inorganic line ... may be a <u>rhapsode's</u> addition."[31] On E 398–402: "Hades' withdrawal to Olympus ... cannot have been an essential part of the <u>original</u> myth."[32] On E 778: τώ not αἵ "is the <u>original</u>, guaranteed by the principle 'utrum in alterum abiturum erat?'"[33] On E 820–821: "Mechanical repetition is not foreign to Homeric technique, but it may also result from a <u>rhapsode's</u> or copyist's zeal."[34] On Z 354, in conjunction with Γ 100 and Ω 28, with reference to the variants ἀρχῆς and ἄτης in all three passages: "The explanation is probably that each noun is <u>original</u> in one or two of the three passages and was then introduced in the remainder by contamination in some sources."[35] On Z 388: "the <u>interpolator</u> presumably felt that a nearer main verb [= nearer than the one at Z 386] should be provided."[36] On H 135 as an "interpolation": "It might have been due to a <u>rhapsode</u> who had some particular interest in Pheia, or in pleasing an audience in Pheia (cf. ο 297?)."[37] On Θ 359: "suspicion of a <u>rhapsodic interpolation</u> may well be founded. Not only is the line otiose as a whole, but ἐν πατρίδι γαίῃ is especially feeble and irrelevant."[38] On I 320: "The <u>rhapsode</u> responsible failed to follow the tenor of the argument."[39] On I 523: this verse "better fits the logic" of the context of χ 59 and is "surely a <u>rhapsode's</u> addition."[40] On Λ 662: "It is an ill-considered <u>interpolation</u> from Π 27" (similarly on Λ 830).[41] On M 175–180: "But it is hard to see why a <u>rhapsode</u> should have <u>interpolated</u> lines that seem so at variance with the situation. I suspect that we have here a fragment of composition originally

28. West 2001b.185.

29. West 2001b.186.

30. West 2001b.189.

31. West 2001b.191.

32. West 2001b.192.

33. West 2001b.194. I would agree with his statement here if he had simply said "earlier" not "original."

34. West 2001b.195.

35. West 2001b.198.

36. West 2001b.198.

37. West 2001b.200.

38. West 2001b.202.

39. West 2001b.207.

40. West 2001b.209.

41. West 2001b.214.

meant for another setting."[42] M 372 "seems to be an Attic <u>interpolation</u>" and M 426 is "surely a gloss by a <u>rhapsode</u>,"[43] while M 449 "was <u>interpolated</u> by a <u>rhapsode</u> who missed the point."[44]

Here are further examples, from the second half of the *Iliad*. O 551 is a "concordance-<u>interpolation</u>."[45] Σ 39–49 may be a "casual omission by a <u>rhapsode</u>."[46] On T 76, with reference to a variant adduced by Zenodotus: "if this were the <u>original</u> text, it would be difficult to understand the logic of 79–82."[47] On Ψ 870–871, I refer to my extended comments further below.[48] On Ω 616: "Some later <u>rhapsodes</u> or scribes, being unfamiliar with the name [Ἀκελήσιος], assimilated it to the well known [Ἀχελώιος]."[49]

I have gone to all the trouble of collecting these examples because they show the pervasiveness of West's attitude. They give a valuable insight into his overall approach in establishing the text of the *Iliad*. There is no reason, of course, to question West's attempts to pass editorial judgment on variations in the Homeric textual tradition. But there is indeed reason to question his setting up an arbitrary dichotomy between "original" poet and rhapsodes, "original" text and interpolation. Such a dichotomy flattens the history of Homeric reception. I see here a "unitext" explanatory model of Homeric poetry, based on the pseudo-synchronic perspective of imagining an "original" poet. Such a model requires, ideally, the editorial elimination of all variants from a once-uniform text. But the textual variations noted by West—and he could have adduced hundreds and even thousands of further examples from the *Iliad*—have a history of their own, which cannot be extricated from the compositional variations inherent in Homeric poetry itself. This history—which is the history of Homeric reception—can be studied systematically by applying what I have described as a multitext model of Homeric poetry. Such a model allows an editorial evaluation of variants from a diachronic perspective encompassing the entire history of Homeric performance traditions.

In a few isolated cases, West's response to textual variants goes beyond his simple distinction between "original" poet and "interpolating" rhapsodes. It is in such cases that I see a better chance for establishing a scholarly

---

42. West 2001b.218. In terms of his reasoning, such a "fragment" is somehow more than an "interpolation."
43. West 2001b.220.
44. West 2001b.221.
45. West 2001b.233.
46. West 2001b.245.
47. West 2001b.253. On the logic of T 79–82, see *PR* 19–22.
48. See p. 97. My interpretation, as we will see, differs from that of West 2001b.275.
49. West 2001b.280.

dialogue that could lead to making more complex distinctions between relatively earlier and later phases of a tradition that drew its life from public performance. A prime example is *Iliad* O 64–71: these verses, says West, were composed:

> … as the conclusion of a Διὸς ἀπάτη recited as a self-contained lay. The <u>rhapsode</u> responsible rounded off his tale with a brief prospectus of the principal military events of the rest of the *Iliad*, and a more distant sight (changing into the optative) of the *Iliou Persis*. From his manuscript of the Διὸς ἀπάτη someone copied the extra lines into a manuscript of the whole *Iliad*.[50]

We can see in this formulation, if we subtract from it West's speculation about textual tampering, the bare outlines of distinct phases in the development of the *Iliad* as a composition subject to ongoing recomposition-in-performance.

I offer some further examples. On O 263–268, "repeated from" Z 506–511, West remarks: "There is no reason why the poet should not have repeated at least a part of the simile in Z. But the truism that 'repetition inheres in the oral style' (Janko ad loc.) should not be used as a defence of the whole passage, since it is equally true that repetition from other contexts is typical of <u>interpolations</u>."[51] At least we see here a concession about the realities of "oral style." Then there is Τ365–368, which is parallel to verse 164 of the Hesiodic *Shield of Herakles*; this parallelism, says West, "puts the author in bad company, and it may be suspected that he was a <u>rhapsode</u> of the same period (early sixth century) who saw fit to add what he thought was a dramatic touch to the account of Achilles' arming."[52] A more positive way of looking at this parallelism is to investigate further the implications of the relative dating to the sixth century. On Υ 213–241: "The genealogy … looks like an addition to the <u>original</u> speech, hardly anticipated in 203–9. But it may be an addition by the first poet, after he received the impulse to honour the [Aineiadai] as the latter-day royalty of Troy."[53] West's category of "first poet" is a roundabout way of admitting that the wording of the "interpolation" rivals in importance the wording of the "original." On Υ 485–499: "Andromache's lament is one of the emotional high points of the *Iliad*. We are in the presence of great poetry here, but also of a passage irreconcilable with the view that our text is the product of a straightforward

---

50. West 2001b.231. The highlighting is mine.
51. West 2001b.231–232.
52. West 2001b.254.
53. West 2001b.256.

process of dictation by an oral poet who never altered or added to his primary effusions."[54] The "dictating oral poet" seems to me a "straw man"; what is of primary importance, rather, is West's concession about the "great poetry." On Ω 662–663: these verses are "genuine lines, but not part of the passage as <u>originally</u> composed. They were inserted later by the poet, after he had related the domestic laments for Hector (723–76) and found himself with nine days still to fill."[55] Once again, West's speculation about textual tampering can be reinterpreted in terms of distinct phases in the history of the *Iliad* as a composition subject to ongoing recomposition-in-performance.

We have by now seen in some detail how West's notion of an "original text" of the *Iliad* pervades his editorial treatment of surviving textual variants in general. These variants fall into the following categories of transmission: the medieval textual tradition,[56] ancient quotations,[57] papyri,[58] and ancient editions.[59] Of special relevance is West's treatment of the variants reported by the three major editors of Homer in Hellenistic Alexandria—Aristarchus of Samothrace, Aristophanes of Byzantium, and Zenodotus of Ephesus.

54. West 2001b.265. For more on his debate with Janko over Janko's "dictation theory," see West 2000b.

55. West 2001b.281.

56. See Part I section 5, West 2001b.139–157. In the medieval textual tradition, a most interesting pattern of variation is the distinctness of variants in manuscript Z from those of all other medieval manuscripts labeled Ω by West pp. 143–144. (West p. 144 now speaks of Ω as a "notional entity"; his clarification at p. 144 n. 5 concerning his use of Ω vs. *Ω in the apparatus criticus of his *Iliad* edition may be a response to my criticism in N 2000a.) An illuminating example is the variation at Γ 212, as discussed by West p. 187, where Z shows ἔφαινον vs. ὕφαινον in Ω. The reading preferred by Callimachus was evidently ὕφαινον (Rengakos 1993.130). I suggest the possibility of reconstructing a variation φαῖνε / *ὕφαινε at θ 499, but I postpone the discussion for another occasion.

57. West's book offers no special section on this aspect of the Homeric paradosis. For an illustration of the importance of the evidence available in Homeric quotations by ancient authors, see Dué 2001.

58. See Part I section 4, West 2001b.86–138, which gives an inventory. An update is needed for West's reference at p. 86 n. 4 to the online inventory of the founding editor of *Homer and the Papyri*, D. F. Sutton (his editorship extended from 1992 to 2001). The new online address of *Homer and the Papyri* is http://chs.harvard.edu/homer_papyri.htm; this website includes information about the current editorial board. Following the general procedures developed by the founding editor, the present editors of *Homer and the Papyri* are committed to online re-publications of the texts of new Homer papyri as soon as the relevant publications appear in print or in electronic form. The numbering of the papyri after Papyrus 704a will normally follow the order of the appearance of these publications. Any alternative numbers assigned to these papyri before their publication, such as those assigned by West 2001b, will be tracked by way of a *comparatio numerorum* (West had generously provided the editors with a preview copy of his list).

59. See Part I sections 2–3, West 2001b.33–85.

For background, it is important for me to review here the essence of my discussion in the first chapter, where we examined what we can learn from the Homeric scholia about the actual procedures of ancient editorial work on the text of Homer. My general term "editorial work" is meant to encompass a wide range of different methods employed by ancient scholars, especially by the Alexandrians. I use this term to accommodate the meaning of Greek *diorthōsis* (διόρθωσις), for which I have developed the working translation 'corrective editing'.[60] Two other Greek words are most relevant: *ekdosis* (ἔκδοσις) and *hupomnēma* (ὑπόμνημα), corresponding respectively to the modern concepts of 'edition' and 'commentary'.

The semantic overlaps and distinctions between *ekdosis* (ἔκδοσις) and *diorthōsis* (διόρθωσις) in the reportage of the Homeric scholia concerning the editorial work of Aristarchus can be clarified in light of the observations made by Franco Montanari concerning the history of Aristarchus' Homeric *hupomnēmata* (ὑπομνήματα) 'commentaries, annotations'.[61]

Montanari points out that Aristarchus' first publication of commentaries or *hupomnēmata* to the text of Homer was keyed to the text established by his predecessor, Aristophanes, as we see from the wording in scholia A at *Iliad* B 133a, where Didymus says: ἐν τοῖς κατ' Ἀριστοφάνην ὑπομνήμασιν Ἀριστάρχου 'in the commentaries [*hupomnēmata*] of Aristarchus according to the text of Aristophanes'. After that, there was an *ekdosis*—that is, a 'publication'—of Aristarchus' own *diorthōsis* 'corrective editing' of Homer. After that, according to Montanari, there followed a new set of *hupomnēmata* that were keyed to the editorial work of Aristarchus himself. Relevant are the titles of two monographs produced by Aristarchus' direct successor, Ammonius: (1) περὶ τοῦ μὴ γεγονέναι πλείονας ἐκδόσεις τῆς Ἀρισταρχείου διορθώσεως 'About the fact that there did not exist more *ekdoseis* of the Aristarchean *diorthōsis*' (via Didymus in scholia A at *Iliad* K 397–399a) and (2) περὶ τῆς ἐπεκδοθείσης διορθώσεως 'about the re-edited *diorthōsis*' (via Didymus in scholia A at *Iliad* T 365–368a). Montanari argues persuasively that the two titles are not mutually contradictory. The *ekdosis* or 'edition' of Aristarchus can be viewed as an ongoing process of *diorthōsis*, which, to repeat, I have been translating as 'corrective editing'. Such is the idea in the first of the two titles of monographs attributed to Ammonius, where this Aristarchean scholar refers to a single *ekdosis* (ἔκδοσις) or 'edition' of Homer as opposed to more than one edition; the same idea accounts for

60. Ch.1, p. 22.

61. Montanari 1998.11–20. In N 2000a, reviewing West 1998b, I summarized the relevance of the observations made by Montanari. That summary was located at a point that corresponds to p. 48n31 in Ch.3, the rewritten version of that review. In what follows, I offer a rewritten version of that summary, relocated to this point in the overall argumentation.

Ammonius' reference in the second title to a 're-edition', as expressed by the wording ἐπεκδοθείσης. It seems that Ammonius preferred to think of two distinct phases in the history of Aristarchus' editing of Homer, while others thought—wrongly, according to Ammonius—that there were two distinct editions.[62]

In the Homer scholia, we see that Didymus refers to texts labeled αἱ Ἀριστάρχου 'the texts of Aristarchus' (at *Iliad* B 221, for example, he says ἐν ταῖς Ἀριστάρχου ἐκδόσεσι 'in the editions [*ekdoseis*] of Aristarchus'); elsewhere, he says ἡ ἑτέρα τῶν Ἀριστάρχου 'the other one of the texts of Aristarchus' (as at B 131a, where the wording ἡ ἑτέρα 'the other one' makes it explicit that there were two).[63] Evidently, the stance of Didymus differs from that of Ammonius. For Didymus, there were two *ekdoseis* of Homer by Aristarchus,[64] though there is no reason to think that they were considered autographs of Aristarchus himself.[65]

From the cumulative evidence of the references in the Homeric scholia to the two *ekdoseis* 'editions' attributed by Didymus to Aristarchus, I conclude that these two Aristarchean *ekdoseis* represent a new base text dating from a post-Aristarchean era and featuring the preferred readings of Aristarchus as extrapolated primarily from his commentaries or *hupomnēmata*. This new base text needs to be distinguished from an older and more "standard" *ekdosis*, derived (but distinct) from the *ekdosis* of Aristophanes. It was this more "standard" *ekdosis* that Aristarchus himself had used as the base text for his *hupomnēmata*. Also, the base text of Aristonicus was this older "standard" *ekdosis*, featuring Aristarchean critical signs in its margins.[66]

62. Perhaps the first and the second phases of Aristarchus' *diorthōsis* (= D1 and D2) may be correlated respectively with the first and the second sets of *hupomnēmata* (= H1 and H2). According to the schema of Montanari 1998, the sequence would be H1 D1 H2 D2. But I am not sure that we need to infer, as Montanari does (p. 19), that the contents of D2 were written into the same "copy" that contained the contents of D1.

63. West 2001b.61n44 gives a list of the references by Didymus to two distinct readings in these two *ekdoseis* of Aristarchus. As West p. 61 points out, in scholia A at T 386a Didymus indicates that one *ekdosis* of Aristarchus is earlier than the other, while in the scholia at δ 727 he speaks of one *ekdosis* being 'more elegant' or *khariestera* (χαριεστέρα) than the other. More later on the category of *khariesterai*.

64. In West's apparatus criticus (1998b / 2000a), "Ar ab" is the equivalent of αἱ Ἀριστάρχου 'the editions [*ekdoseis*] of Aristarchus', while "Ar a" *or* "Ar b" are equated with ἡ ἑτέρα τῶν Ἀριστάρχου 'the other of the two editions [*ekdoseis*] of Aristarchus'—and it cannot be specified which one is which.

65. West 2001b.66 says that the two *ekdoseis* 'editions' of Aristarchus "were not claimed [by Didymus] to be the master's autographs and accordingly could not be relied on absolutely."

66. I agree with the observation of West p. 65: "Aristonicus ... assumes a single Aristarchean text and nowhere distinguishes between two recensions."

With this background in place, I proceed to outline West's overall approach to the editions of Homer by Aristarchus and his predecessors. Addressing the editorial work of Aristarchus himself on the textual traditions of Homer, West says that this editor "appears to have been simply unaware of the possible benefits of extensive manuscript collation; or perhaps he realized only too well that it was likely to yield little but a bewildering variety of aberrations."[67] He offers a similar assessment of Aristarchus' predecessor, Aristophanes.[68] As for the earlier editorial work of Zenodotus, West dismisses its credibility altogether, slighting its value as a source for the textual history of Homeric poetry: "As for Zenodotus himself, the text associated with his name is so eccentric that it is impossible to regard it as the product of any rational process of selection of readings from alternative sources—or indeed of any rational thought at all."[69]

Surveying the editorial legacy of Zenodotus, Aristophanes, and Aristarchus, West in the introduction to his edition of the *Iliad* had made the extreme claim that it was Didymus, not Aristarchus, who regularly collated manuscript evidence in search of variants: "Didymus fuit, non Aristarchus, qui exemplaria quam plurima consuluit, ut varias lectiones compararet."[70] In making this claim, West ignored the testimony of scholia A at *Iliad* I 222, where Didymus says of Aristarchus: ἄμεινον οὖν εἶχεν ἄν, φησὶν ὁ Ἀρίσταρχος, [εἰ] ἐγέγραπτο "ἂψ ἐπάσαντο" ἢ "αἶψ' ἐπάσαντο," ... <u>ἀλλ' ὅμως ὑπὸ περιττῆς εὐλαβείας οὐδὲν μετέθηκεν, ἐν πολλαῖς οὕτως εὑρὼν φερομένην τὴν γραφήν</u> 'it would have been better, says Aristarchus, if it had been written "ἂψ ἐπάσαντο" or "αἶψ' ἐπάσαντο"; nevertheless, because of his extreme caution, he changed nothing, <u>having found in many of the texts this attested way of writing it</u> [= "ἐξ ἔρον ἕντο" instead of "ἂψ ἐπάσαντο"]'.

Not only was this testimony ignored in West's 1998 introduction to his edition of the *Iliad*: the most relevant wording—as highlighted here—was

67. West 2001b.37. At p. 62 he makes this distinction between *ekdosis* and *diorthōsis* in the Homer scholia: "Aristarchus' διόρθωσις was the sum of his critical activity on the text, while the ἐκδόσεις were the manuscripts that embodied it." I agree with the first part of his formulation, but I think that the second part needs further qualification: see the previous footnote.

68. West 2001b.59–61.

69. West 2001b.37. He underrates not only Zenodotus but also the foremost work on Zenodotus, that of Nickau 1977. West p. 54 argues (1) that "most of what we know of Zenodotus' text comes from Aristonicus"; also, (2) that Didymus did not have access to the edition of Zenodotus, but Aristarchus did. (I cannot see why West thinks that the second of these two arguments is controversial.) For further criticism of West's position on Zenodotus, see Rengakos 2002, who argues against West's theory that Zenodotus used "an Ionian rhapsodic text."

70. West 1998b.viii.

not even quoted in the apparatus criticus of his 1998 edition of *Iliad* A–M.[71] Then, in his 2001 book, West finally quoted the passage and then backtracked slightly from his earlier claim by saying: "Didymus knew that Aristarchus consulted more than one text, because he cited different scholars' readings on different occasions, but it is just his own assumption that Aristarchus systematically checked 'many' copies before discussing any reading."[72] So, in his 2001 book, West was now more open to the possibility that Aristarchus "checked" some copies, if not "many."

Even in his 2001 book, however, West was still saying: "Not once does he [Aristarchus] appeal to the authority of manuscripts."[73] West justifies this statement by adding in his next sentence: "It is Didymus, not Aristarchus, who makes all the references." At this point, West lists various terms used in the Homeric scholia to designate various manuscript traditions: αἱ πλείους 'the majority [of the *ekdoseis*]', αἱ πᾶσαι 'all', αἱ χαριέστεραι (*khariesterai*) 'the more elegant ones' or αἱ ἀστειότεραι (*asteioterai*) 'the more cultivated ones'. He lists also the antithetical terms ἡ κοινή (*koinē*) or αἱ κοιναί (*koinai*) 'the common one(s)', κοινότεραι (*koinoterai*) 'the more common ones', δημώδεις (*dēmōdeis*) 'the popular ones', εἰκαιότεραι (*eikaioterai*) 'the simpler ones', φαυλότεραι (*phauloterai*) 'the inferior ones'. He thinks that all these terms reflect the usage of Didymus, not of Aristarchus. In addition, he thinks that it was Didymus, not Aristarchus, who "cites the texts" of such early sources as Antimachus of Colophon (late fifth century) and Rhianus of Crete (second half of the third century)—though West immediately appends this qualification: "... even though his [Didymus'] knowledge of some of these sources was indirect."[74] In fact, there is a further qualification implicit in the very fact that West says "cites the texts" here instead of "collates the texts." West is forced to say it this way because, as it turns out, he has no proof that Didymus had direct access to the Homer text of either Antimachus or Rhianus.[75] As we will see later, the question of Didymus' access, especially to the text of Antimachus, is crucial for determining the validity of West's theories about the sources used by Didymus. In what follows, I maintain that these theories are not supported by the evidence of the Homeric scholia.

No doubt, Didymus was a direct source for the information transmitted by the A scholia about variant readings in the Homeric textual tradition. Nor is there any doubt that Didymus spoke with authority about these variant

71. As I pointed out in N 2000a; see Ch.3 above.
72. West 2001b.37n19.
73. West 2001b.37.
74. West 2001b.37.
75. West 2001b.52–54 on Antimachus; pp. 56–58 on Rhianus.

readings. This authority, however, came not from Didymus' searching for variant readings in texts available to him but from Aristarchus himself. Didymus, as a successor of Aristarchus, spoke with the authority of Aristarchus because he situated himself as a continuator of that authority. When Aristarchus said εὕρομεν 'it is our finding', the authority of his finding could be passed on to the latest of Aristarcheans. In this case, that man was Didymus, who flourished over a century after Aristarchus. When Didymus said εὕρομεν 'it is our finding' in his own turn, he too was speaking with the authority of Aristarchus, just as previous Aristarcheans had spoken before him. Such is the dominant mentality of the reportage we read in the scholia of Homer, especially in the Venetus A. My formulation in this paragraph will now be supported by a selection of examples, with commentary.

My premier example is a quotation taken directly from Aristarchus himself, as preserved in scholia A at *Iliad* A 423–424. In my 2000a review of West's 1998 edition of *Iliad* A–M, I had cited this quotation, not mentioned in West's introduction to his edition, as evidence against his theories about Didymus.[76] The quotation, designated as the *lexis* 'wording' of Aristarchus, is introduced this way: λέξις Ἀριστάρχου ἐκ τοῦ Α τῆς Ἰλιάδος ὑπομνήματος 'here is the *lexis* of Aristarchus, from his *hupomnēma* on volume A of the *Iliad*'. The expression λέξις Ἀριστάρχου 'the *lexis* of Aristarchus', as I noted earlier, seems to convey the idea that the *hupomnēmata* of Aristarchus were not only commentaries written down in papyrus scrolls but also, at least notionally, commentaries delivered as lectures by Aristarchus, as if these commentaries were meant to be transcribed by his students.[77] As the quotation proceeds, it is difficult to determine exactly where the words of Aristarchus himself leave off, to be picked up by the words of Didymus.[78] I give the full sequence here, as printed by Erbse:[79]

Scholia A at A 423–424. **Ζεὺς … μετ' ἀμύμονας Αἰθιοπῆας | χθιζὸς ἔβη κατὰ δαῖτα, θεοὶ δ' ἅμα πάντες ἔπονται·** λέξις Ἀριστάρχου ἐκ τοῦ Α τῆς Ἰλιάδος ὑπομνήματος· "τὸ μὲν μετ' ἀμύμονας (423) ἐπ' ἀμύμονας, ὅ ἐστι πρὸς ἀμώμους, ἀγαθούς, τὸ δὲ κατὰ δαῖτα (424) ἀντὶ τοῦ ἐπὶ δαῖτα· οὕτως γὰρ νῦν Ὅμηρος τέθεικεν. ἔνιοι δὲ ποιοῦσι 'μετὰ δαῖτα', ὅπως ᾖ αὐτοῖς αὐτόθεν τὸ μετά ἐπί. χρῶνται δὲ καὶ πλείονες ἄλλοι τῶν ποιητῶν τῇ κατά ἀντὶ τῆς ἐπί. Σοφοκλῆς (F 812 N = 898 P = R)· 'ἐγὼ κατ' αὐτόν, ὡς ὁρᾷς, ἐξέρχομαι'. οὕτως δὲ εὕρομεν καὶ ἐν τῇ Μασσαλιωτικῇ καὶ Σινωπικῇ καὶ

76. N 2000a on West 1998b.

77. In N 2000a, I collected other survivals of quotations of Aristarchus by Didymus, introduced by the tag "*lexis* of Aristarchus." See Ch.3 above, p. 50n39.

78. See Ludwich 1884.194–196.

79. Erbse 1969-1988 I 119–120.

Κυπρίᾳ καὶ Ἀντιμαχείῳ (Φ 132) καὶ Ἀριστοφανείῳ (F 43)." [Erbse places the end of the quotation here.] Καλλίστρατος δὲ ἐν τῷ Πρὸς τὰς ἀθετήσεις (p. 320.36) ὁμοίως, καὶ ὁ Σιδώνιος καὶ ὁ Ἰξίων ἐν τῷ ἕκτῳ Πρὸς τὰς ἐξηγήσεις (F 27).

Scholia A at A 423–424. **Ζεὺς … μετ' ἀμύμονας Αἰθιοπῆας | χθιζὸς ἔβη κατὰ δαῖτα, θεοὶ δ' ἅμα πάντες ἕπονται:** Here is the *lexis* of Aristarchus, from his *hupomnēma* on volume A of the *Iliad*: "The expression μετ' ἀμύμονας [423] is for ἐπ' ἀμύμονας, that is, for πρὸς ἀμώμους, ἀγαθούς. As for the expression κατὰ δαῖτα [424], it is in place of ἐπὶ δαῖτα. For this is the way [= κατὰ δαῖτα] that Homer's usage has it in this passage.[80] Some poets use 'μετὰ δαῖτα', so as to have μετά in the same place as ἐπί. But several others of the poets use the κατά construction instead of the ἐπί construction. Sophocles has 'ἐγὼ κατ' αὐτόν, ὡς ὁρᾷς, ἐξέρχομαι'. This is the way we found it [= κατὰ δαῖτα instead of μετὰ δαῖτα] in the *Massaliōtikē* and the *Sinōpikē* and the *Kupria* and the *Antimakheios* [= text of Antimachus of Colophon] and the *Aristophaneios* [= text of Aristophanes of Byzantium]." [Erbse places the end of the quotation here.] Callistratus in his volume Πρὸς τὰς ἀθετήσεις has it in a similar way; also [Dionysius] Sidonius and [Demetrius] Ixion in the sixth volume of Πρὸς τὰς ἐξηγήσεις.

As I stressed in my 2000a review, the person who is being quoted here, after he expresses his preference for the variant reading κατὰ δαῖτα instead of μετὰ δαῖτα, says the following: οὕτως δὲ εὕρομεν καὶ ἐν τῇ Μασσαλιωτικῇ καὶ Σινωπικῇ καὶ Κυπρίᾳ καὶ Ἀντιμαχείῳ καὶ Ἀριστοφανείῳ 'this is the way we found it in the *Massaliōtikē* and the *Sinōpikē* and the *Kupria* and the *Antimakheios* and the *Aristophaneios*'.[81] I argued that this wording provides evidence against West's claim that Aristarchus did not collate manuscripts. Agreeing with Ludwich,[82] I argued further that the subject of οὕτως … εὕρομεν 'this is the way we found it' is Aristarchus, not Didymus: "the first person of εὕρομεν comes from the direct quotation of words 'spoken' (notionally and I would say perhaps even literally) by the master teacher. In other words, the rhetoric of the quotation is set in the mode of a master's *ipse dixit*."[83]

For confirmation of this way of interpreting οὕτως … εὕρομεν 'this is the way we found it [attested]' in scholia A at *Iliad* A 423–424, I note the wording οὕτως εὑρών 'having found it [attested] this way', applied to Aristarchus

---

80. For νῦν in the sense of 'in this passage', compare the wording in the scholia at *Iliad* B 212b, O 19; see also the scholia at *Odyssey* κ 86 (hypothesis line 34).

81. N 2000a; see Ch.3 above.

82. Ludwich 1884.194–196.

83. N 2000a; see Ch.3 above.

himself by Didymus, in the scholia A at *Iliad* I 222. Didymus says: ἄμεινον οὖν εἶχεν ἄν, φησὶν ὁ Ἀρίσταρχος, [εἰ] ἐγέγραπτο "ἂψ ἐπάσαντο" ἢ "αἶψ᾽ ἐπάσαντο," ... ἀλλ᾽ ὅμως ὑπὸ περιττῆς εὐλαβείας οὐδὲν μετέθηκεν, ἐν πολλαῖς οὕτως εὑρὼν φερομένην τὴν γραφήν 'it would have been better, says Aristarchus, if it had been written "ἂψ ἐπάσαντο" or "αἶψ᾽ ἐπάσαντο"; nevertheless, because of his extreme caution, he changed nothing, having found in many of the texts this attested way of writing it [= "ἐξ ἔρον ἔντο" in place of "ἂψ ἐπάσαντο"]'. I highlighted the pertinent wording, as underlined here, in my 2000a review of West's 1998 edition of *Iliad* A–M.[84] As I noted, the wording is quoted in the apparatus criticus of Ludwich but not in that of West. More important for now, the usage of οὕτως εὑρών 'having found it this way' shows once again that the 'we' of Didymus represents the Aristarchean tradition writ large, of which Didymus considers himself the extension and even culmination—whether or not we agree with this self-assessment. The magisterial οὕτως ... εὕρομεν 'this is the way we found it', as 'spoken' by Aristarchus, is perpetuated by Didymus.[85]

Responding to the criticisms of his theories about Didymus, West in his 2001 book is now forced to reckon with this expression οὕτως ... εὕρομεν 'this is the way we found it' in scholia A at A 423–424. West claims that the subject of οὕτως ... εὕρομεν here must be Didymus, not Aristarchus.[86] To back up his claim, he lists five instances in the Homer scholia where Didymus is the subject of the verb *heuriskein* 'find': scholia at B 131a, B 517a, Δ 3a, O 469–470a, Π 636c.[87]

I note that the first three of these five instances listed by West involve explicit references to what Didymus 'found' in one or the other of the two *ekdoseis* 'editions' that he attributed to Aristarchus himself, which as I argued earlier date from a post-Aristarchean era.[88] To that extent, such instances can even be used as evidence to support my argument that οὕτως ... εὕρομεν 'this is the way we found it' is an Aristarchean usage, faithfully continued by Didymus. As for the last two of the five instances, the fourth and the fifth, we are about to see further indications of Aristarchean usage.[89]

In the fourth instance, the wording suggests that Didymus uses εὕρομεν

---

84. Again, see Ch.3 above.

85. From reading West 2001b.54, one may ask whether Aristonicus was an intermediary for Didymus in any of the contexts signaled by the expression εὕρομεν. In any case, my point remains that the ultimate authority would be Aristarchus.

86. West 2001b.54, 70–72,

87. West 2001b.71.

88. On the two *ekdoseis* 'editions' of Homer attributed by Didymus to Aristarchus, see . Cf. West 2001b.63 on scholia A at *Iliad* E 808, which report that this Iliadic verse is not at all 'found' (εὑρεθῆναι) 'in the editions of Aristarchus' (ἐν ταῖς Ἀριστάρχου).

89. Reacting to what I say in this paragraph and in the paragraphs that follow, West

'we found' in the sense that he is participating in the authoritative report of Aristarchus concerning what variants are attested where:

Scholia A at O 469–470a. **νευρὴν δ' ἐξέρρηξε νεόστροφον, ἣν ἐνέδησα | πρώϊον:** ἀμφότερα γράφεσθαί φησιν ὁ Ἀρίσταρχος, "πρῴην" καὶ **πρώϊον** (470), ‹οὐ› ταὐτὸν δὲ ἐξ ἑκατέρου σημαίνεσθαι. <u>εὕρομεν</u> δὲ καὶ "ἐΰστροφον" (469) γεγραμμένον, καὶ ἔχει τινὰ ἐπί‹σ›τασιν.

Scholia A at O 469–470a. **νευρὴν δ' ἐξέρρηξε νεόστροφον, ἣν ἐνέδησα | πρώϊον:** ('He [= the god] snapped my newly-twisted bowstring, which I strung to my bow this morning'.) Aristarchus says that both ways of writing it are attested, "πρῴην" [= 'just now'] and **πρώϊον** [= 'this morning'] (470), and that the same meaning can<not> be extracted from each of these two forms. And <u>we found</u> it [= νεόστροφον 'newly-twisted'] written also as "ἐΰστροφον" ['well-twisted'] (469), which has some merit.

Aristarchus here is reported by Didymus to be saying that both variants at verse 470, πρῴην 'just now' and πρώϊον 'this morning', are attested or 'written' in the manuscript evidence, γράφεσθαι, and then it is further reported by Didymus that the variant ἐΰστροφον 'well-twisted' is also found to be 'written', γεγραμμένον, alongside the variant νεόστροφον 'newly-twisted' at the previous verse, 469. The train of thought conveys a unified discovery procedure, not a separation of Didymus' authority from that of Aristarchus. The speaker who reports the procedure has just quoted a sequence of Homeric phraseology; this quotation is the *lēmma*, the basis for the speaker's discussion. The speaker then proceeds to discuss the manuscript variants that he finds within the whole *lēmma*. In this case, the *lēmma* spills over from one Homeric verse to the next: νευρὴν δ' ἐξέρρηξε νεόστροφον, ἣν ἐνέδησα | πρώϊον 'he [= the god] snapped my newly-twisted bowstring, which I strung to my bow this morning'. The speaker begins the discussion by focusing on the last word of the *lēmma*, taking note of an attested variant—πρῴην 'just now' instead of πρώϊον 'this morning'—and then adds, working backwards, that there is another case of variation earlier on in the *lēmma*, since 'we find' an attested variant ἐΰστροφον 'well-twisted' instead of νεόστροφον 'newly-twisted', just as πρῴην 'just now' was found instead of πρώϊον 'this morning'.

In the case of finding the different readings πρῴην and πρώϊον in different manuscripts, the authority is explicitly Aristarchus. In the case of the

---

2004 says (referring to the page-numbers of the version I published as N 2003b): "Nagy uses up more than two pages of *Gnomon* (491–3, small type) in a vain attempt to transfer this Didymean idiom back to Aristarchus." He gives no evidence to back up his claim that my attempt is in vain.

different readings ἐΰστροφον and νεόστροφον, the authority for finding the variant ἐΰστροφον is the ambiguous 'we' of the statement εὕρομεν 'we found'. Despite its ambiguity, this statement about the variants ἐΰστροφον and νεόστροφον is semantically and even syntactically integrated with the earlier statement about the variants πρῴην and πρώϊον. The authority that supports the comparison of different readings in different manuscript traditions is presented as the same. That authority is Aristarchus.

Not only do we see here that Didymus explicitly attributes to Aristarchus the finding of the variant reading πρῴην instead of πρώϊον. We can see also, from both scholia A and scholia T at O 470a, that Aristonicus is another witness to this reading. Moreover, Aristonicus specifies that Aristarchus found this reading in the Homer text of Zenodotus: ὅτι Ζηνόδοτος γράφει "πρῴην." The word ὅτι 'because' is used here by Aristonicus in order to explain why Aristarchus put a sign in the margin to the left of the verse (Erbse thinks that the sign here at verse O 470 was originally a διπλῆ περιεστιγμένη 'double mark with dots around it', not the plain διπλῆ 'double mark' shown by the Venetus A). In this context, it is essential to keep in mind that Didymus did not have access to the Homer text of Zenodotus.[90] Further, Didymus says explicitly that his information about the variant reading πρῴην comes from Aristarchus.[91]

Now we come to the fifth of the five instances adduced by West to support his claim that Didymus is the subject of the verb εὕρομεν 'we found' in the scholia A at A 423–424. The wording is as follows:

Scholia A at Π 636c. **ῥινοῦ τε βοῶν τ' εὐποιητάων:** "ἄμεινον εἶχε," φησὶν ὁ Ἀρίσταρχος, "εἰ ἐγέγραπτο 'βοῶν εὐποιητάων', ἔξω τοῦ τέ συνδέσμου." Aim. ἐν δέ τισιν <u>εὕρομεν</u> **ῥινῶν τε βοῶν τ' εὐποιητάων** κατὰ τὸ πληθυντικόν.

Scholia A at Π 636c. **ῥινοῦ τε βοῶν τ' εὐποιητάων:** "It would have been better," says Aristarchus, "if it had been written 'βοῶν εὐποιητάων', without the conjunction τέ." Aim. And in some texts <u>we found</u> ῥινῶν τε βοῶν τ' εὐποιητάων in the plural.

In this case, we see a collocation of εὕρομεν 'we found' with a direct quotation from Aristarchus himself, Moreover, it could be argued that the subject of εὕρομεν is likewise Aristarchus, since the statement that starts with the

90. West 2001b.56 acknowledges this point.
91. Perhaps the actual *lēmma* νευρὴν δ' ἐξέρρηξε νεόστροφον, ἣν ἐνέδησα | πρώϊον stems from Aristarchus himself. In that case, the length of the quotation is conditioned by the presence, within the quotation, of two cases of variant readings—not just one—chosen for discussion by Aristarchus.

phrase ἐν δέ τισιν εὔρομεν ... 'but in some texts we found...' may be a direct quotation in its own right.

Having surveyed West's five examples of usages involving *heuriskein* 'find', let us return to the wording that begins with οὕτως δὲ εὔρομεν καὶ ἐν τῇ Μασσαλιωτικῇ καὶ Σινωπικῇ καὶ Κυπρίᾳ καὶ Ἀντιμαχείῳ καὶ Ἀριστοφανείῳ 'this is the way we found it in the *Massaliōtikē* and the *Sinōpikē* and the *Kupria* and the *Antimakheios* and the *Aristophaneios*' in scholia A at A 423–424. From what we have seen so far, there is no support for West's claim that οὕτως δὲ εὔρομεν 'this is the way we found it' is the precise point where the "verbatim quotation" from Aristarchus stops and the discourse of Didymus begins.[92]

West goes even further in his discussion of this passage. Not only the wording but also the content, he claims, points to Didymus and not Aristarchus. As I argue in what follows, there is no support for this additional claim.

The wording that immediately follows in scholia A at A 423–424 is unproblematic: Καλλίστρατος δὲ ἐν τῷ Πρὸς τὰς ἀθετήσεις ὁμοίως, καὶ ὁ Σιδώνιος καὶ ὁ Ἰξίων ἐν τῷ ἕκτῳ Πρὸς τὰς ἐξηγήσεις 'Callistratus in his work Πρὸς τὰς ἀθετήσεις has it in a similar way; also [Dionysius] Sidonius, and [Demetrius] Ixion in the sixth volume of Πρὸς τὰς ἐξηγήσεις'. West is not alone when he says that Didymus must have been the originator of this statement highlighting Callistratus, Dionysius of Sidon, and Demetrius Ixion.[93]

It is quite another thing, however, for West to say that the man who consulted the *Massaliōtikē*, the *Sinōpikē*, the *Kupria*, the *Antimakheios*, and the *Aristophaneios* was not Aristarchus but Didymus himself. In order to justify such a claim, West would need to prove that Didymus had direct access to each of these five sources mentioned in the statement introduced by οὕτως δὲ εὔρομεν 'this is the way we found it'. As I hope to show in an overview of the five sources, West produces no such proof.

Viewing the list of these five sources in reverse order, I start the overview with the fifth, the *Aristophaneios*. West asks: "Was it still accessible to Didymus?"[94] He responds immediately: "His [Didymus'!] wording at A 423–4, οὕτως δὲ εὔρομεν [...], would suggest autopsy, as I remarked in connection with Antimachus' copy."[95] The reasoning is circular in the case of the *Antimakheios* as well as the *Aristophaneios*. The wording at A

92. West 2001b.70–72.
93. See the references assembled by West 2001b.71n9.
94. West 2001b.59.
95. West 2001b.59, referring to an earlier remark at his p. 54.

423–424, οὕτως δὲ εὕρομεν 'this is the way we found it', is in fact the only passage that West adduces to support his theory that Didymus had direct access to the *Antimakheios*.[96] The reasoning is also circular in the case of the *Aristophaneios* because, once again, the same wording at A 423–424 is the only passage West adduces to support his theory of an autopsy by Didymus. In the case of the *Aristophaneios*, moreover, I note that West himself observes: "In the final analysis, then, it remains doubtful whether Didymus had direct acquaintance with Aristophanes' text. All his knowledge of it may have come from Aristophanes' pupils Aristarchus and Callistratus."[97]

Continuing the overview, I turn to the fourth source in the listing of A 423–424, the *Antimakheios*. In this case, West expresses less doubt than in the case of the *Aristophaneios*, although the lack of evidence for direct access is just as pronounced.[98] In the case of the *Antimakheios*, moreover, there are indications that Aristarchus himself did indeed have direct access to it (perhaps by way of Hermesianax of Colophon, who may have brought the text to Alexandria).[99] As West himself observes, "[Aristarchus] did use Antimachus' text, at least sporadically."[100] The most justifiable inference, then, is that the *Antimakheios* is mentioned in the passage of the scholia at A 423–424 starting with οὕτως δὲ εὕρομεν 'this is the way we found it' simply because Aristarchus did indeed consult the *Antimakheios*.[101] The same inference applies to the mention of the *Aristophaneios* in this same passage. In the case of the *Aristophaneios*, moreover, we are dealing with the most basic relevant fact of them all: that Aristarchus regularly consulted the *Aristophaneios* as a base text.

I conclude the overview by turning to the three other mentioned sources in the passage starting with οὕτως δὲ εὕρομεν 'this is the way we found it': the *Massaliōtikē*, the *Sinōpikē*, and the *Kupria*. All three are representatives

96. West 2001b.54.

97. West 2001b.60.

98. West 2001b.52–54.

99. West 2001b.53.

100. West 2001b.54. I am indebted to Michael Apthorp for helping me sharpen the point I am making here. I should add that I find unclear West's formulation about "Antimachus' interpretations of Homer as reflected in his own poetry." The discussion of Pfeiffer 1968.94–95n8 is clearer, and on that basis I propose this reformulation of what West is saying: Antimachus actually used words in his poetry that match uncommon variants in his text of Homer.

101. West p. 54 remarks: "In order to argue that he [Didymus] derived their readings [that is, the readings of the five sources] from Aristarchus, we must postulate some Aristarchean source distinct from Aristonicus." Such a postulation, however, depends on West's more basic postulation that the οὕτως δὲ εὕρομεν passage of the scholia at A 423–424 is not

of the so-called 'city editions', the *politikai* (πολιτικαί). West describes as "a serious misconception" the idea that it was Aristarchus who collated the *politikai* (he gives a list of those who share this idea, including Ludwich, Erbse, Pfeiffer, Janko, and myself).[102] He claims that the *politikai*—that is, Homeric texts from Massalia (= ἡ Μασσαλιωτική / *Massaliōtikē*), Chios (= ἡ Χία / *Khia*), Argos (= ἡ Ἀργολική / *Argolikē*), Sinope (= ἡ Σινωπική / *Sinōpikē*), Cyprus (= ἡ Κυπρία / *Kupria*), and Crete (= ἡ Κρητική / *Krētikē*)—were collated not by Aristarchus but by Didymus (in the case of the *Massaliōtikē*, *Khia*, *Argolikē*, and *Sinōpikē*) and by Seleucus (in the case of the *Kupria* and the *Krētikē*). His claim is not based on any attempt to establish a relatively later date for the Homeric variants contained by the *politikai*—a date that would somehow suit the era of Didymus better than the era of Aristarchus. It is evident from his discussion that he can find no proof for any such redating.[103] Rather, the claim is based on West's examination of the patterns of associations linking the *politikai* with other sources named in the Homer scholia.[104] I propose here to re-examine these patterns.

To begin this re-examination, I offer a formulation that anticipates my conclusion. West's claim about the *politikai* seems to me impossible to sustain in view of the fact that the Homer scholia, especially those of Venetus A, refer consistently to these *politikai* as sources directly comparable with other sources that Didymus himself could not possibly have consulted. Such other sources include not only the Homer texts of Antimachus of Colophon and Aristophanes of Byzantium, as we see them mentioned in the scholia A at *Iliad* A 423–424 and elsewhere, but also the Homer text of Zenodotus. The scholia are in fact so consistent in comparing the texts of the *politikai* with the texts of Antimachus, Zenodotus, and Aristophanes—all three—that it becomes impossible or at least near-impossible to escape the conclusion that this consistency reflects a sustained system of collating choice texts. To accept West's theories about Didymus is to deny the existence of any system, let alone any system devised by Didymus, since there is no evidence that Didymus had any direct access to the Homer texts of Antimachus, Zenodotus, and Aristophanes. By contrast, Aristarchus did indeed have such direct access. As the testimony of the Homer scholia shows, Aristarchus had the opportunity to compare systematically the texts of Antimachus,

a direct quotation from Aristarchus. If it is a direct quotation, then that "Aristarchean source" of Didymus is Aristarchus himself.

102. West 2001b.69; he gives the list at p. 69n78.
103. The relevant discussion is in West 2001b.72.
104. West 2001b.67–72.

Zenodotus, and Aristophanes, whereas Didymus did not. Moreover, the testimony of the Homer scholia shows an ongoing systematic comparison of these texts with the texts of the *politikai*. On these grounds, I infer that it was Aristarchus and not Didymus who collated the texts of the *politikai* just as he collated the texts of Antimachus, Zenodotus, and Aristophanes.

For a test case, I turn to the scholia A at Ψ 870–871. Here the received text of Didymus is evidently this:

σπερχόμενος δ' ἄρα Μηριόνης ἐξείρυσε χειρός
τόξον· ἀτὰρ δὴ ὀϊστὸν ἔχεν πάλαι, ὡς ἴθυνεν.

Eagerly Meriones grabbed from his hand [= from the hand of Teucer]
the bow. But the arrow he [= Meriones] was already holding, taking aim.

Ψ 870–871 (via Didymus)

The scholia A first quote the variant verses found in the *Massaliōtikē*:

σπερχόμενος δ' ἄρα Μηριόνης ἐπεθήκατ' ὀϊστόν
τόξῳ· ἐν γὰρ χερσὶν ἔχε‹ν› πάλαι, ὡς ἴθυνεν.

Eagerly Meriones placed the arrow
on the bow. For he [= Meriones] was already holding it [= the bow] in
his hands, taking aim.

Ψ 870–871 (via the *Massaliōtikē*:)

The scholia A then quote the variant verses found in the *Antimakheios* (the reading seems to have been damaged in scholia A, but scholia T have preserved the undamaged reading, which is given below). Then the scholia A continue with a paraphrase of what Aristarchus had said in his *hupomnēmata*:

ὁ μέντοι Ἀρίσταρχος διὰ τῶν ὑπομνημάτων ἐπειγόμενον βούλεται τὸν Μηριόνην ἐκσπάσαι τῆς τοῦ Τεύκρου χειρὸς τὸ τόξον· καὶ γὰρ κοινὸν τῶν ἀγωνιζομένων αὐτὸ εἶναι ὥσπερ τὸν δίσκον. τὸ δὲ **ἀτὰρ ‹δὴ› ὀϊστὸν ἔχεν πάλαι** (871) ἐπὶ τοῦ Μηριόνου ἀκουστέον.

But Aristarchus in his *hupomnēmata* wants Meriones, in his eagerness, to grab the bow from the hand of Teucer. For it [= the bow], like the discus, was shared by those who were competing. The phrase ἀτὰρ ‹δὴ› ὀϊστὸν ἔχεν πάλαι is to be understood ['heard'] as applying to Meriones.

This paraphrase suggests that Aristarchus prefers the reading of the received text (and of the *Antimakheios*), which amounts to what survives as the received text of Didymus. There is further reinforcement in scholia T, where

the comment οὕτως Ἀρίσταρχος 'Aristarchus has it this way...' is followed by
this further comment: ἡ δὲ Μασσαλιωτικὴ οὕτω· ... 'but the *Massaliōtikē*
has it this way...' At this point the scholia T quote the same variant verses
from the *Massaliōtikē* that we have already seen quoted by the scholia A.
Then the scholia T follow up with this further comment: Ἀντίμαχος δὲ ...
'but Antimachus...' At this point the scholia T quote the variant verses found
in the *Antimakheios* (the reading of which seems to have been damaged in
scholia A), which agree with the sense of the received text and which disagree with the sense of the *Massaliōtikē*:

> σπερχόμενος δ' ἄρα Μηριόνης ἐξείρυσε Τεύκρου
> τόξον· χερσὶ δ' ὀϊστὸν ἔχεν πάλαι, ὡς ἴθυνεν

> Eagerly Meriones grabbed from Teucer
> the bow. But the arrow he [= Meriones] was already holding in his
>   hands, taking aim.

Ψ 870–871 (via the *Antimakheios*)

Throughout this discussion of variant verses at Ψ 870–871, I have spoken
in terms of quotations and comments by "scholia A" and "scholia T," as if
the scholiasts were speakers on their own. Of course the immediate speaker
is notionally Didymus himself, even if we cannot reconstruct his exact
words on the basis of the dual testimony provided by scholia A and T. As
for the ultimate speaker, however, I maintain that it must be Aristarchus:
what Didymus is saying is simply a reaffirmation of what Aristarchus had
said before him concerning the master's preference of the wording provided
by his received text as opposed to the wording provided, in this case, by
the *Massaliōtikē*. The wording of scholia T indicates that Aristarchus in his
hupomnēmata had expressed his preference in the context of juxtaposing
the reading of his received text with the reading of the *Massaliōtikē* and,
secondarily, with the reading of the *Antimakheios*. To repeat, in this case
the sense of the reading of the *Antimakheios* agrees with the received
text, whereas the sense of the reading of the *Massaliōtikē* disagrees with
it. The reference in the T scholia to the editorial choice of Aristarchus,
οὕτως Ἀρίσταρχος 'Aristarchus has it this way...' is being juxtaposed with
the reference to the reading of the *Massaliōtikē*. The οὕτω 'this way' in the
expression ἡ δὲ Μασσαλιωτικὴ οὕτω 'but the *Massaliōtikē* has it this way...'
marks the variant reading, while the οὕτως 'this way' of οὕτως Ἀρίσταρχος
'Aristarchus has it this way...' marks the judgment of Aristarchus.

West discusses these passages from scholia A and T at Ψ 870–871 after
having finished his discussion of the passage introduced by οὕτως ... εὕρομεν

'this is the way we found it' in scholia A at A 423–424.[105] He dismisses without justification Erbse's inference that Didymus took the testimony of scholia A and T at Ψ 870–871 from the commentaries of Aristarchus.[106] West now says about the same οὕτως δὲ εὕρομεν passage that he had discussed earlier: "I allowed earlier that he [Didymus] may not have had access to Aristophanes, but his εὕρομεν should be valid with respect to the items that head the list. The Massaliotica in particular has a strong claim to be among his direct sources in view of the frequency with which he cites it."[107] Here West has reminded himself of one of his allowances, that Didymus probably had no access to Aristophanes, and I think it should be linked directly with another allowance that West had made elsewhere: that Didymus probably had no access to Antimachus, either.

If Didymus had no access to either Antimachus or Aristophanes, then the systematic comparisons of their manuscript evidence with that of *politikai* like the *Massaliōtikē* must be Aristarchus' own. I infer, then, that Aristarchus did indeed collate manuscripts, and his procedure of collating is made explicit in expressions like ὁ μέντοι Ἀρίσταρχος… 'but Aristarchus…' in scholia A at Ψ 870–871. That Didymus mediated such information can be granted, but the point remains that the judgments and sources reported by Didymus go back to Aristarchus. Moreover, Aristarchus is the authoritative source not only where a judgment—stylistic or otherwise—is explicitly linked with him, but even where we find only bare statements of ancient variant readings.[108]

Besides Antimachus and Aristophanes, the Homer text of Rhianus was another source that seems to have been inaccessible to Didymus. West leaves open the possibility that Didymus could have consulted Rhianus, but without positive evidence. He tries to build a case for negative evidence by saying: "Aristarchus, so far as we can see, ignored Rhianus altogether. Aristonicus never mentions him. All the references come from Didymus."[109] Here it becomes essential to point out that Aristophanes of Byzantium was in fact interested in Rhianus, and that the Homer edition of Aristophanes did in fact contain Homeric variants that could be traced back to Rhianus.[110] West is not justified in inferring that these Homeric variants would have been ignored by Aristarchus. After all, Aristarchus' own Homer edition was

---

105. West 2001b.71.
106. Erbse 1959.282.
107. West 2001b.71–72, with reference to his earlier discussion at pp. 59–61.
108. In this paragraph, I have benefited from the help of José González.
109. West 2001b.57.
110. West 2001b.57n33.

directly linked with that of Aristophanes.[111] Aristarchus' *hupomnēmata* or 'commentaries' were based initially on the Homer edition of Aristophanes, which was only later superseded by the Homer edition of Aristarchus himself.[112] In this connection, it is easy for modern scholars to forget a central fact about the reputation of Aristophanes in the ancient world: he was considered to be the ultimate editor in his own time, while his student Aristarchus was primarily a commentator and only secondarily an editor.[113]

Here it is relevant to mention another student of Aristophanes, Callistratus, who made explicit references to the variants derived from Rhianus. It is understandable that Callistratus, who produced his own *ekdosis* 'edition' of Homer, would have named his teacher Aristophanes, not his peer Aristarchus, as the editorial source. It is also understandable that Didymus, who referred to both Aristarchus and Callistratus, would likewise have named Aristophanes, not Aristarchus, as the editorial source for variants derived from Rhianus. But the point is, the systematic consultation of Rhianus as a source of Homeric variants did not start with Didymus, nor even with Aristarchus, but rather with Aristarchus' mentor, Aristophanes.

In this connection, I note with interest what West says about Aristophanes and Callistratus taken together.[114] West's conclusion about them is linked with his conclusion about the inaccessibility of Aristophanes' text to Didymus: "In the final analysis, then, it remains doubtful whether Didymus had direct acquaintance with Aristophanes' text. All his knowledge of it may have come from Aristophanes' pupils Aristarchus and Callistratus."[115] In this context, West revisits the wording of scholia A at A 423–424, οὕτως δὲ εὕρομεν καὶ ἐν τῇ Μασσαλιωτικῇ καὶ Σινωπικῇ καὶ Κυπρίᾳ καὶ Ἀντιμαχείῳ καὶ Ἀριστοφανείῳ 'this is the way we found it in the *Massaliōtikē* and the *Sinōpikē* and the *Kupria* and the *Antimakheios* and the *Aristophaneios*'.[116] We have already seen that West is uncertain about the *Antimakheios* as a direct source for Didymus, and now we see that he is also uncertain about the *Aristophaneios* as a direct source. And yet, West persists in taking the

111. Montanari 1998.11–20.
112. Montanari 1998.11–20.
113. Pfeiffer 1968.174–175, 225.
114. West 2001b.59–61.
115. West 2001b.60. He shows two relevant passages: (1) scholia at T 327a, καὶ Ἀριστοφάνης προηθέτει τὸν στίχον, ὥς φησι Καλλίστρατος 'and Aristophanes already athetized this verse before [= before Aristarchus athetized it], as Callistratus says'; (2) scholia at Φ 130–135a, Ἀρίσταρχος διὰ τῶν ὑπομνημάτων Ἀριστοφάνη φησὶ στίχους ἓξ ἠθετηκέναι 'Aristarchus in his *hupomnēmata* says that Aristophanes athetized the six verses'.
116. West 2001b.59.

subject of εὕρομεν 'we found' as Didymus, not Aristarchus. He says: "his [= Didymus'] wording ... would suggest autopsy, as I remarked in connection with Antimachus' copy."[117]

In the case of the Zenodotean edition of Homer, the *Zēnodoteios* (Ζηνοδότειος), it is not just a probability but a certainty that Didymus had no direct access to it. When Didymus is reported as saying in scholia A at Δ 3a that the variant reading ἐνῳνοχόει comes from the edition of Zenodotus, he says explicitly that he gets this information from the *hupomnēmata* of Aristarchus; he also says explicitly that he gets the reading ἐῳνοχόει from the *ekdoseis* of Aristarchus.[118] On this basis, West acknowledges that Didymus had no direct access to an *ekdosis* of Zenodotus and instead consulted the two *ekdoseis* of Aristarchus and his *hupomnēmata*. West concludes: "It must be accepted that Didymus' knowledge of Zenodotus' text—like Aristonicus'—was indirect. Most of it probably derived from Aristarchus, partly indirectly (e.g. through Aristonicus), partly directly."[119]

West states that Didymus regularly consulted the two *ekdoseis* of Aristarchus and his *hupomnēmata*.[120] This statement requires a further observation: these two *ekdoseis* or 'editions' that Didymus attributes to Aristarchus may be described as modified base texts dating from a post-Aristarchean era and featuring the master's preferred readings as extrapolated from his *hupomnēmata* or 'commentaries', which had originally been published in volumes separate from the volumes of the base text. Aristarchus himself in his *hupomnēmata* must have used as his point of reference a relatively unmodified base text—a more "standard" version, so to speak, than the versions represented by the two later *ekdoseis* 'editions' attributed to him by Didymus. The left margin of the earlier standard version was marked by critical signs that referred to variant readings as discussed by Aristarchus in his *hupomnēmata*, where he indicated his preferred readings and the reasons for his preferences. This earlier standard

117. West 2001b.59.

118. West 2001b.64 appreciates the value of such testimony as proof that Aristarchus really produced his own base text in editing Homer, *pace* Erbse. The fact, however, that both of the two *ekdoseis* of Aristarchus had ἐῳνοχόει according to Didymus in scholia A at Δ 3a should be no surprise to West, since the base text of Aristarchus ordinarily defaulted to a "standard" version. See the next paragraph. I should stress that even the two *ekdoseis* of Aristarchus, the base texts of which contained post-Aristarchean extrapolations from his *hupomnēmata*, often defaulted to a "standard" version, as in this case.

119. West 2001b.56. His wording, "e.g. through Aristonicus," implies that Didymus would be two steps removed from Zenodotus as direct source, if indeed Aristonicus himself is one step removed.

120. West 2001b.56.

version used by Aristarchus was similar to, though slightly different from, the still earlier standard version used by Aristophanes. Aristarchus' system of critical signs and his verse-count of "genuine" verses were likewise similar to, though slightly different from, the corresponding system and verse-count of Aristophanes. The reasoning of Aristarchus was an exercise in balancing the evidence: he weighed the external evidence of variations in manuscripts against the internal evidence of Homeric diction as a system. Aristonicus must have used this same "standard version" as his own point of reference, systematically discussing variants signaled by the Aristarchean critical signs in its margins; these variants would be found not in the base text of the "standard version" but in the discussion provided by Aristarchus in his *hupomnēmata*.

With this observation in place, I proceed to one other passage cited by West as evidence to support his theories centering on Didymus. West draws attention to scholia A at *Iliad* Γ 406a, where Didymus comments on the *lēmma* θεῶν δ' ἀπόειπε κελεύθους at Γ 406.[121] West speaks about this *lēmma* as the wording that Didymus had read in "his own text" of Homer. Here is the passage in its entirety:

Scholia A at Γ 406a. **θεῶν δ' ἀπόειπε κελεύθους**: Ἀρίσταρχος "ἀπόεικε" διὰ τοῦ **κ**, καὶ χωρὶς τοῦ **σ** "κελεύθου." θαυμάσειε δ' ἄν τις, ἡ ἑτέρα διὰ τοῦ π πόθεν παρέδυ· οὔτε γὰρ ἐν ταῖς Ἀρισταρχείοις οὔτε ἐν ἑτέρᾳ τῶν γοῦν μετρίων ἐμφερόμενον πέφυκεν, καὶ οὐ μόνον ἐν ταῖς ἐκδόσεσιν, ἀλλὰ καὶ ἐν τοῖς συγγράμμασιν ἀπαξάπαντες οὕτως ἐκτίθενται. προσθήσειν μοι δοκῶ καὶ τὴν Ἀριστάρχου λέξιν οὕτως ἔχουσαν· "†τί δὲ† εἰς τὰς θεοὺς ὁδοῦ εἶκε καὶ παραχώρει, μὴ βαδίζουσα εἰς αὐτούς."

Scholia A at Γ 406a. **θεῶν δ' ἀπόειπε κελεύθους**: Aristarchus has "ἀπόεικε" with **κ**, and without **σ** the "κελεύθου." One could wonder about where the other reading with the π came from, for it is found attested neither in the *Aristarkheioi* [= the Aristarchean *ekdoseis*] nor in any other of the moderate ones [*ekdoseis*] at any rate.[122] And not only in the *ekdoseis* but also in the monographs [*sungrammata*] all sources feature it this way [= ἀπόεικε in place of ἀπόειπε]. I [= Didymus] think the *lexis* of Aristarchus will also add [to the evidence], which has it this way [= which has ἀπόεικε].[123] [Here Didymus quotes Aristarchus' paraphrase of the Homeric wording.]

121. West 2001b.51.
122. This translation follows in part the rendition offered by West 2001b.51–52.
123. Thanks to Michael Apthorp for his advice on interpreting this wording.

I interpret as follows: Didymus read ἀπόειπε in his received text, but he read ἀπόεικε in the two *ekdoseis* that he attributes to Aristarchus. Aristarchus referred to ἀπόεικε in his monographs, though he indicated somewhere else in his writings that he had manuscript evidence in favor of the reading ἀπόειπε. I infer that this indication was expressed in Aristarchus' *hupomnēmata*, though even there he must have discussed the merits of choosing ἀπόεικε on the basis of the internal evidence of Homeric diction. Aristarchus paraphrases the given Homeric passage in terms of the variant ἀπόεικε. His paraphrase is quoted here directly by the scholia, which refer to the quotation as the *lexis* of Aristarchus.

As West reports, what Didymus "has"—ἀπόειπε—is also attested for us in "five papyri, a quotation by Aristonicus, a late papyrus commentary, and the whole medieval tradition."[124] What, then, is exceptional about this reading? It is not that the *lēmma* itself is something out of the ordinary for Didymus. The reading that the *lēmma* gives, ἀπόειπε, is the received reading. Rather, what is exceptional in this case is simply that Didymus is not sure about the manuscript source of this received reading ἀπόειπε as given in the *lēmma* (θαυμάσειε δ' ἄν τις, ἡ ἑτέρα διὰ τοῦ π πόθεν παρέδυ 'one could wonder about where the other reading with the π came from'). Didymus is surprised because he had expected to find ἀπόειπε in the base text of at least one or the other of the two *ekdoseis* attributed to Aristarchus, or in one of Aristarchus' surviving monographs. What is exceptional is that ἀπόειπε can be found 'neither in the *Aristarkheioi* [= the Aristarchean *ekdoseis*] nor in any other of the moderate ones [*ekdoseis*] at any rate' (οὔτε γὰρ ἐν ταῖς Ἀριστάρχείοις οὔτε ἐν ἑτέρᾳ τῶν γοῦν μετρίων ἐμφερόμενον πέφυκεν).[125] It seems that the surprise here for Didymus is simply that Aristarchus in this case, exceptionally, cannot be used as a source of information—either indirectly by way of the two *ekdoseis* or directly by way of his own writings—about the actual manuscript source of this received reading ἀπόειπε.

West draws attention to the wording καὶ οὐ μόνον ἐν ταῖς ἐκδόσεσιν, ἀλλὰ καὶ ἐν τοῖς συγγράμμασιν ἁπαξάπαντες οὕτως ἐκτίθενται 'and not only in the *ekdoseis* but also in the monographs [*sungrammata*] all sources feature it this way [= ἀπόεικε in place of ἀπόειπε]'.[126] His interpretation of Didymus' reasoning, as reflected in the Greek wording, runs like this: not only does everybody in their editions read it this way—ἀπόεικε—but also everybody in their monographs. For West, such wording is proof that Didymus was

124. West 2001b.51.
125. See West 2001b.51–52.
126. This passage has the only attestation of ἐκτίθενται in the *Iliad* A scholia.

regularly "consulting" his own collection of Homeric manuscripts, rather than reporting on Aristarchus' survey of manuscript sources.

No doubt, Didymus regularly consulted the two Aristarchean *ekdoseis* as well as the monographs or *sungrammata* of Aristarchus—and most likely the *ekdoseis* of other scholars such as Callistratus. But I see no evidence here for a "consultation," as theorized by West, of alternative Homeric manuscripts unknown to Aristarchus. Let us look at the wording again: καὶ οὐ μόνον ἐν ταῖς ἐκδόσεσιν, ἀλλὰ καὶ ἐν τοῖς συγγράμμασιν ἁπαξάπαντες οὕτως ἐκτίθενται 'and not only in the *ekdoseis* but also in the monographs [*sungrammata*], all sources feature it this way [= ἀπόεικε in place of ἀπόειπε]'. The *ekdoseis* to which Didymus is referring here are I think primarily the two *ekdoseis* attributed to Aristarchus and, secondarily, to such *ekdoseis* as that of Callistratus. We may note that the emphasis in the Greek is on the monographs or *sungrammata*, in any case, and not on the *ekdoseis*.

Now let us look more closely at the wording that follows: προσθήσειν μοι δοκῶ καὶ τὴν Ἀριστάρχου λέξιν οὕτως ἔχουσαν· "†τί δὲ† εἰς τὰς θεοὺς ὁδοῦ εἶκε καὶ παραχώρει, μὴ βαδίζουσα εἰς αὐτούς." I translate this way: 'I [= Didymus] think the *lexis* of Aristarchus will also add [to the evidence], which has it this way'. Then, Didymus quotes Aristarchus' paraphrase of the Homeric wording.[127] I infer that Aristarchus was showing the merits of the variant reading ἀπόεικε on the basis of contextual evidence—hence his paraphrase of the relevant Homeric passage—while allowing for ἀπόειπε on the basis of the manuscript evidence. What was out of the ordinary in this case, and what surprised Didymus here, is that the manuscript source of the reading ἀπόειπε, which I think was being implicitly supported by Aristarchus in his *hupomnēmata*, was left unspecified in the two Aristarchean *ekdoseis*. I further infer that Aristarchus—that is, Aristarchus as represented by the two post-Aristarchean *ekdoseis* used by Didymus—in this case exceptionally failed to provide something that Didymus ordinarily expected him to be providing.[128] In this exceptional case, Didymus could not rely on the authority of Aristarchus concerning the manuscript sources for the reading ἀπόειπε; all he could report was the master's opinion that ἀπόεικε was preferable to the reading ἀπόειπε, at least in terms of the internal evidence provided by Homeric diction.[129]

Ordinarily, Aristarchus in his *hupomnēmata* would have specified whether

127. Thanks to Michael Apthorp for his advice on interpreting this whole passage.

128. I have changed the wording here from the wording I used in N 2003b.

129. Aristarchus may have been less scrupulous in discussing manuscript evidence in the case of verses that he considered un-Homeric. Such is the case with Γ 406, since Aristarchus in any case athetized all the verses of Γ 396–418.

a reading like ἀπόεικε is attested in the manuscript sources known as the 'more elegant ones', *khariesterai* (χαριέστεραι), also known as the 'more cultivated ones', *asteioterai* (ἀστειότεραι). Further, he could have specified, by way of expressions like αἱ πλείους 'the majority' and αἱ πᾶσαι 'all of them', whether the majority or all of the *khariesterai* (χαριέστεραι) showed this reading. By contrast, he could have specified that ἀπόειπε is the attested reading in the manuscript sources known as ἡ κοινή (*koinē*) or αἱ κοιναί (*koinai*) 'the common one(s)' or κοινότεραι (*koinoterai*) 'more common ones' or δημώδεις (*dēmōdeis*) 'the popular ones' or εἰκαιότεραι (*eikaioterai*) 'the more simple ones' or φαυλότεραι (*phauloterai*) 'the more base ones'. What is exceptional in this case is that the two Aristarchean *ekdoseis* used by Didymus had failed to specify either of these readings.[130]

I take special interest in West's discussion of Didymus' references to αἱ πᾶσαι 'all of them'.[131] This discussion can actually be used to support the argument that Didymus was simply reporting on 'all' the privileged textual sources—that is, on 'all' the *khariesterai*, which were regularly cited by Aristarchus. I infer that even the scholiasts who quote and paraphrase Didymus understand this rationale of the expression αἱ πᾶσαι 'all of them'. The references to the *khariesterai* 'more elegant ones' that disagree with the edition of Zenodotus, interchangeable with references to αἱ πᾶσαι 'all of them' that disagree with the edition of Zenodotus (scholia A vs. T at B 196c), show that the scholiasts who transmitted the work of Didymus understood their role: they were reporting on the sources of Aristarchus, not on Didymus' own sources.[132]

As West acknowledges, the term *khariesterai* (χαριέστεραι) 'more elegant ones' is a criterion of "support" for Aristarchean editorial preferences.[133] In the scholia A at B 12a, for example, where Didymus speaks of Aristarchus' reading being "supported" (so West) by αἱ πλείους καὶ χαριέστεραι τῶν ἐκδόσεων 'the majority of the *ekdoseis* that are *khariesterai*', it is evident that the tag *khariesterai* is an ex-post-facto validation of Aristarchean criteria. To put it another way, *khariesterai*—as this criterion is attested by way of Didymus—is a re-validation of Aristarchus' earlier validations in terms of the same word.

130. For a possible reason, see the previous note. In a separate project, I will explore the question of the formatting of the two Aristarchean *ekdoseis* 'editions'. I hope to produce evidence to support the argument that these *ekdoseis* stemmed from a post-Aristarchean era and featured abbreviated scholia extrapolated from the originally separate *hupomnēmata* of Aristarchus.

131. West 2001.51.

132. On scholia A vs. T at B 196c, see West 2001b.51.

133. West 2001b.51.

There is a comparable contrast made by Didymus in the scholia A at B 53a, where the category αἱ πλείους καὶ χαριέστεραι 'the majority that are *khariesterai*', in combination with ἡ Ἀριστοφάνους 'the text of Aristophanes' is being contrasted with the category αἱ κοιναὶ καὶ ἡ Ζηνοδότειος 'the *koinai* and the text of Zenodotus'.

Here is yet another comparable contrast, where once again we see Didymus highlighting a parallelism involving the *khariesterai* and the *Aristophaneios* as a point of contrast with less privileged Homer manuscripts:

> Scholia A at B 192b. **οἷος νόος Ἀτρεΐδαο·** "οἷος νόος Ἀτρείωνος" <u>κἂν ταῖς</u> <u>διορθώσεσι καὶ ἐν τοῖς ὑπομνήμασιν οὕτως ἐγέγραπτο</u> "Ἀτρείωνος." καὶ αἱ πλείους δὲ τῶν χαριεστάτων οὕτως εἶχον, καὶ ἡ Ἀριστοφάνειος. καὶ ὁ Σιδώνιος δὲ καὶ ὁ Ἰξίων οὕτως γράφουσιν.

> Scholia A at B 192b. **οἷος νόος Ἀτρεΐδαο·** This reading, "οἷος νόος Ἀτρείωνος," <u>even in the *diorthōseis* and in the *hupomnēmata*, is written</u> <u>this way,</u> with "Ἀτρείωνος." And the majority of the most elegant texts [*khariestatai* / χαριέσταται] had it this way [= Ἀτρείωνος in place of Ἀτρεΐδαο], as also the text of Aristophanes [*Aristophaneios* / Ἀριστοφάνειος]. Also, [Dionysius] Sidonius and [Demetrius] Ixion write it this way.

We can see from the wording here that the actual combining of manuscript evidence from the *khariestatai* (χαριέσταται) 'most elegant texts' with manuscript evidence from the *Aristophaneios* (Ἀριστοφάνειος) 'text of Aristophanes' is not the work of Didymus himself. The wording that I have highlighted makes it explicit, I think, that the information provided by the *khariestatai* and by the *Aristophaneios* has been mediated for Didymus by the authority of Aristarchus himself. Didymus is saying primarily that the relevant manuscript information is to be found in the Aristarchean editions (*diorthōseis* must refer to the two editions that Didymus attributes to Aristarchus) and in the commentaries (*hupomnēmata*). In saying this, Didymus focuses on the actual reading that Aristarchus preferred: κἂν ταῖς διορθώσεσι καὶ ἐν τοῖς ὑπομνήμασιν 'both in the *diorthōseis* and in the *hupomnēmata*'. For Didymus, it is of first priority that Aristarchus himself preferred the variant readings found in the *khariestatai* and the *Aristophaneios*. For Didymus, Aristarchus' specific choice of a reading is of first priority, while its corresponding source is only secondary. Accordingly, Didymus gives as his first category of evidence the actual judgment of Aristarchus as reflected in his preferred reading. Only after that does Didymus give, as his second category of evidence, the testimony of the choice manuscripts: καὶ αἱ πλείους δὲ τῶν χαριεστάτων οὕτως εἶχον, καὶ ἡ Ἀριστοφάνειος 'the majority of the most elegant texts [*khariestatai*] had it this way, as also the *Aristophaneios*. And only after that does Didymus add, as his third category of evidence, the supplementary testimony from (in this case) Dionysius Sidonius and Demetrius Ixion: καὶ ὁ Σιδώνιος δὲ καὶ ὁ Ἰξίων οὕτως γράφουσιν 'also, [Dionysius] Sidonius and [Demetrius] Ixion write it this way'.

This third category is analogous to what we have already seen in scholia A at A 423–424: Καλλίστρατος δὲ ἐν τῷ Πρὸς τὰς ἀθετήσεις ὁμοίως, καὶ ὁ Σιδώνιος καὶ ὁ Ἰξίων ἐν τῷ ἕκτῳ Πρὸς τὰς ἐξηγήσεις 'Callistratus in his volume Πρὸς τὰς ἀθετήσεις has it in a similar way; also [Dionysius] Sidonius, and [Demetrius] Ixion in the sixth volume of Πρὸς τὰς ἐξηγήσεις'. Just as Didymus must have been the originator of the statement highlighting Callistratus, Dionysius Sidonius, and Demetrius Ixion, the same can be said about the statement in scholia A at B 192b highlighting, again, Dionysius of Sidon and Demetrius Ixion. Conversely, I argue that Aristarchus must have been the originator of the preceding statement in scholia A at B 192b: καὶ αἱ πλείους δὲ τῶν χαριεστάτων οὕτως εἶχον, καὶ ἡ Ἀριστοφάνειος 'and the majority of the most elegant texts [*khariestatai*] had it this way, as also the *Aristophaneios*. So also I ascribe to Aristarchus the correspondingly preceding statement in scholia A at A 423–424: οὕτως δὲ εὕρομεν καὶ ἐν τῇ Μασσαλιωτικῇ καὶ Σινωπικῇ καὶ Κυπρίᾳ καὶ Ἀντιμαχείῳ καὶ Ἀριστοφανείῳ 'this is the way we found it in the *Massaliōtikē* and the *Sinōpikē* and the *Kupria* and the *Antimakheios* and the *Aristophaneios*'.

Working my way backwards in the scholia A at A 423–424, I now focus on the even earlier statement preceding the one I have just quoted about the *Massaliōtikē*, the *Sinōpikē*, the *Kupria*, the *Antimakheios*, and the *Aristophaneios*. In this earlier statement, which even West identifies as a direct quotation from Aristarchus, we see that the master adduces Sophocles (after having adduced "Homer" himself):

> <u>οὕτως</u> γὰρ νῦν Ὅμηρος τέθεικεν. ἔνιοι δὲ ποιοῦσι "[quotations]." χρῶνται δὲ καὶ πλείονες ἄλλοι τῶν ποιητῶν τῇ "[quotation]." Σοφοκλῆς (F 812 N = 898 P = R): "[quotation from Sophocles]."

> For <u>this is the way</u> [= κατὰ δαῖτα] that Homer's usage has it in this passage. Some poets use "[quotations]." But several others of the poets use "[quotation]." Sophocles has "[quotation from Sophocles]."

The wording οὕτως 'this is the way' in this statement, which signals the adducing of Homer and Sophocles, is picked up by the wording οὕτως δὲ εὕρομεν 'this is the way we found it' in the next statement, which signals the adducing of the *Massaliōtikē*, the *Sinōpikē*, the *Kupria*, the *Antimakheios*, and the *Aristophaneios*. Elsewhere too in the Homeric scholia, the adducing of evidence signaled by οὕτως εὕρομεν 'this is the way we found it' and related expressions conveys primarily the findings of Aristarchus, and only secondarily the findings of the Aristarchean speaker. Here are two telling examples where the speaker is the Aristarchean scholar Herodian, who flourished about 200 years after Didymus:

> Scholia A at Z 239c. **ἔτας {τε}**: ὁ Ἀσκαλωνίτης (p. 47 B) ψιλοῖ, [...] Ἀλεξίων (F 30 B) δὲ δασύνει. <u>ὁ δὲ Ἀρίσταρχος</u> οὐδὲν ἄντικρυς περὶ τοῦ πνεύματος <u>ἀπεφήνατο</u>. [...] ἡμῖν δὲ δοκεῖ ἀφορμῇ ἐκείνῃ χρήσασθαι· εἰ ἄδηλόν ἐστι τὸ πνεῦμα, τὰ δὲ τοιαῦτα πολλάκις ἐκ συναλιφῶν κρίνεται, <u>εὑρέθη</u> δὲ διὰ ψιλοῦ ἡ συναλιφή, οὐδέποτε δὲ διὰ δασέος, δῆλον ὅτι διὰ τοῦτο συγκαταθετέον τῷ Ἀσκαλωνίτῃ ψιλοῦντι. παρὰ γοῦν <u>Αἰσχύλῳ</u> (F 377 N = 530.28 M = 281a 28 R) <u>οὕτως εὕρομεν</u>· "[quotation from Aeschylus]," καὶ παρ' Εὐριπίδῃ (F 1014 N) τὸ "[quotation from Euripides]."

> Scholia A at Z 239c. **ἔτας {τε}**: Ptolemy of Ascalon gives smooth breathing [...] but Alexion gives rough breathing. <u>Aristarchus shows nothing contradictory</u> about the breathing.[134] [...] In my opinion, he used this rationale: if the breathing [that is, whether there is smooth or rough breathing] is not obvious—such cases can often be settled by examining contracted forms—and if the contraction <u>is found</u> to have smooth breathing, never rough breathing, then it is clearly for this reason that the form is configured this way by [Ptolemy] of Ascalon when he gives smooth breathing. <u>This is the way we find it</u> in Aeschylus: "[quotation from Aeschylus]." And in Euripides: "[quotation from Euripides]."

> Scholia A at M 201d. **ὑψιπέτης**: <u>Ἀρίσταρχος</u> ἐβάρυνεν <u>εὑρὼν</u> τὸ "ὠκυπέτα, χρυσέῃσιν ἐθείρῃσιν" (Θ 42) <u>οὕτως</u> κεκλιμένον, ὡσεὶ καὶ ἀπὸ τοῦ παντοπώλης παντοπῶλα. πρόδηλον δὲ κἀκ τῶν διαλέκτων· "ὑψιπέτας" γὰρ <u>εὑρέθη</u> κατὰ τροπὴν τοῦ η εἰς τὸ **α**,... τινὲς μέντοι ἐτόλμησαν τὸ ὑψιπέτης περισπάσαι, ἐπεὶ ἐν ἑτέροις ἔφη "ὥστ' αἰετὸς ὑψιπετήεις" (Χ 308). ὡς οὖν τὸ "τιμῆεις ἔσομαι" (ν 129) ἐγένετο τιμῆς, "οὐκέθ' ὁμῶς τιμῆς ἔσεαι" (Ι 605), <u>οὕτως</u> ὑψιπετήεις ὑψιπετῆς. ἀλλ' ἐπὶ μὲν τοῦ τιμῆς <u>εὕρομεν</u> αἰτιατικήν, "καὶ χρυσὸν τιμῆντα" (Σ 475), ἥτις ἐδίδασκε τὸ τῆς εὐθείας πάθος· ἐπὶ δὲ τοῦ προκειμένου οὐδὲν <u>εὕρομεν</u> τοιοῦτο. <u>ἔνθεν ἐπείσθημεν τῷ Ἀριστάρχῳ</u>.

> Scholia A at M 201d. **ὑψιπέτης**: Aristarchus gave non-oxytone accent, <u>having found</u> "ὠκυπέτα, χρυσέῃσιν ἐθείρῃσιν" (Θ 42), which shows it accented <u>this way</u>, as also in παντοπῶλα on the basis of παντοπώλης.

134. Ptolemy of Ascalon was a student of Aristarchus, and Herodian relies heavily on Ptolemy's reportage concerning Aristarchus' work on accentuation and related linguistic matters (see West 2001b.82). Questions of assigning smooth or rough breathing are an example of such related matters. Here and elsewhere, Herodian expresses his preference for Ptolemy's reportage.

It is evident also from the dialects: "ὑψιπέτας" was found, showing a switch from η to α ... Some have been so bold as to make a circumflex accentuation for ὑψιπέτης, since he [= Homer] says elsewhere "ὥστ' αἰετὸς ὑψιπετήεις" (X 308). Just as "τιμήεις ἔσομαι" (ν 129) becomes τιμῆς, as in "οὐκέθ' ὁμῶς τιμῆς ἔσεαι" (I 605), so also ὑψιπετήεις becomes ὑψιπετῆς. But in the case of τιμῆς we found [attested] the accusative, "καὶ χρυσὸν τιμῆντα" (Σ 475), which was instructive concerning the [accentual] behavior of the nominative. But in the previous case [= in the case of ὑψιπέτης], we found no such thing. On the basis of all this, we were persuaded by Aristarchus.[135]

Having examined the evidence of the Homeric scholia concerning the criteria of Aristarchus and Didymus, let us return one last time to the wording of scholia A at A 423–424, οὕτως δὲ εὕρομεν καὶ ἐν τῇ Μασσαλιωτικῇ καὶ Σινωπικῇ καὶ Κυπρίᾳ καὶ Ἀντιμαχείῳ καὶ Ἀριστοφανείῳ 'this is the way we found it in the *Massaliōtikē* and the *Sinōpikē* and the *Kupria* and the *Antimakheios* and the *Aristophaneios*'. On the basis of what we have seen, the *communis opinio* is confirmed: the subject of οὕτως δὲ εὕρομεν 'this is the way we found it' is Aristarchus. It is not Didymus, as the theory of West would have it.[136]

I conclude that it was Aristarchus, not Didymus, who developed a system for the collating of Homeric texts. And it was Aristarchus who led the way in searching for significant variations in the history of the Homeric textual tradition.[137]

135. The first-person subject of ἔνθεν ἐπείσθημεν τῷ Ἀριστάρχῳ 'on the basis of all this, we were persuaded by Aristarchus' is different from the first-person subject in the preceding οὐδὲν εὕρομεν τοιοῦτο 'we found no such thing', which is the final part of a series of 'findings' by Aristarchus, starting with the beginning of this extract, Ἀρίσταρχος ἐβάρυνεν εὑρών ... 'Aristarchus gave non-oxytone accent, having found ...'

136. West 2001b.54.

137. For further corroboration of my conclusion, see Rengakos 2002. He adduces a most telling example in the scholia at *Iliad* Z 4: here Aristonicus is specified as the authority for saying that Aristarchus found different readings of this verse in different *antigrapha* 'copies' at different stages in his investigations, and the word that Didymus (Z 4b) uses in this same context is *heuriskein* 'find'—with specific reference to the 'findings' of Aristarchus. As Rengakos concludes, "This clearly refutes the theory that Aristarchus did not consult different manuscripts." Rengakos goes on to discuss further pertinent evidence, especially the testimony of the scholia at *Iliad* I 401 and at T 386 (a particularly telling example, not considered by West 2001b). West 2004 replies to Rengkaos about the scholia at *Iliad* Z 4: "Aristonicus (copied by Didymus) reports that, after assuming one reading in his Hypomnemata, Aristarchus came across a different one and approved it [...]. This sounds like a casual discovery; at any rate it is not evidence of any systematic study of manuscripts." Such a scenario of casual discoveries seems to me unpersuasive. Also, I question West's claim that Aristonicus was "copied by Didymus."

CHAPTER 5

Aristarchean Questions:
Emerging Certainties
about the Finality
of Homer's Text

The New Companion to Homer, edited by Ian Morris and Barry Powell (1997), is bad company, for the most part.[1] Such is the opinion of Richard Janko in his review of this book, which had been meant to replace *A Companion to Homer*, edited by Alan J. B. Wace and Frank H. Stubbings (1962).[2] Preferring in many ways the "old" *Companion*, I too have my own negative opinions about various aspects of the *New Companion*, as is evident from my remarks in my earlier work.[3] But these aspects are not the same as those with which Janko is occupied. Aside from these differences, I disagree with much of what Janko has to say about my chapter in *New Companion*, "Homeric Scholia."[4] My concern here, however, is not to air all my disagreements with Janko's views. Rather, I propose simply to challenge certain assertions that he makes about Aristarchus as an editor of Homer, specifically with reference to my chapter "Homeric Scholia" (hereafter = HS),

* The original version of this essay is N 1998b.
1. Morris and Powell 1997.
2. Janko 1998a; Wace and Stubbing 1962. Since this review by Janko (1998a) was published in an electronic journal, I cannot assign page numbers wherever I quote him.
3. N 1997b = *HR* 4–7.
4. N 1997d = pp. 101–122 in Morris and Powell 1997 = Ch.1 in this volume.

which is linked to my book *Poetry as Performance* (1996; = *PP*). Essentially, Janko expresses doubts about the usefulness of Aristarchus as a source for genuine Homeric variants. To counter Janko's doubts, I return here to my ongoing project of defending the reliability of Aristarchus as a definitive source for establishing the history and prehistory of the Homeric textual tradition.

Janko criticizes me for claiming something that I know I did not claim in HS (or in *PP*): that Aristarchus and the two other major Alexandrian editors of Homer, Zenodotus and Aristophanes, never made emendations of the received text. What I do argue is that Aristarchus did not put his own emendations into the received text of Homer, confining them instead to his commentaries or *hupomnēmata*. Further, I have argued that the emendations of Aristarchus were generally based on variant manuscript traditions, not on his own conjectures.

In this context, it is important to distinguish between *emendation* and *conjecture*: you can emend a text (for example, by choosing one attested variant over another) without necessarily making conjectures (that is, proposing a form that is unattested in the manuscript evidence). Janko is saying "emendation" where I mean "conjecture." He writes: "To sustain the authenticity of all Alexandrian readings,... N. has to claim that they never emended the text (p. 114)." In my original version of HS in the *New Companion*, I never use the word "emend," nor do I make the claim attributed to me.[5] Instead, I criticize the stance of Homeric scholars who consistently dismiss variant readings attributed to Aristarchus on the grounds that they are "conjectures."[6]

Earlier in his review, Janko captures the essence of my argument when he says: "N. argues that the extent of rhapsodic variation in the text of Homer is so great that we cannot accept either an Aristarchean quest for *the* original reading, or Wolf's distrust that Aristarchus could recover authentic readings in general." But then he goes on to overstate my case, in order to create a foil for his own arguments, by paraphrasing me with these words: "all his [Aristarchus'] variants are authentic." To back up this overstatement, Janko quotes me as saying: "there is no reason to doubt that any Homeric variant attributed to Aristarchus can be considered *an* authentic reading."[7] The quotation is taken out of context. I repeat here my actual formulation:

5. HS 114.

6. Just to be double-sure, I ran a word-check on "emend" and "conjecture" in *PP*, and I found that there too as in HS I am consistently careful in maintaining a distinction between these two concepts.

7. HS 111.

To be sure, we may disagree fundamentally with the premise of Aristarchus, who searched for variants in Homeric textual transmission in order to find in each case *the* authentic variant. Instead, we may wish to argue for an evolutionary model, accounting for a plethora of different authentic variants at different stages (or even at any one stage) in the evolution of Homeric poetry *as an oral tradition*; variations in the textual tradition would reflect different stages in the transcribing of this oral tradition. Such a model is fundamentally at odds with the theories of Villoison, who puts his trust in Aristarchus, validating that Alexandrian scholar's case-by-case search for *the* authentic reading in the text of Homer.

Such a model is also at odds with the theories of Wolf, who distrusts Aristarchus' ability to recover authentic readings in general. Whereas Aristarchus—and Villoison—may have gone too far in positing *the* authentic reading in any given case throughout the Homeric text, there is no reason to doubt that any Homeric variant attributed to Aristarchus can be considered *an* authentic reading. For Wolf to cast general doubt on variant readings attributed to Aristarchus may well be going too far in the opposite direction.[8]

The emphatic *an* in the last part of my formulation was meant to contrast with the emphatic *the* in "*the* authentic reading."

My position on Aristarchus' editorial methods converges for the most part with that of Michael Haslam, whose chapter "Homeric Papyri and the Transmission of the Text," precedes my "Homeric Scholia" in *New Companion*.[9] The one major point of divergence between our positions is that Haslam subscribes to Janko's theory "that the Homeric texts were indeed written down from dictation during the eighth century."[10] By contrast, I argue for an evolutionary model.[11] To sum up my position, I can simply highlight from what I have said above: this evolutionary model accounts for a plethora of different authentic variants at different stages (or even at any one stage) in the evolution of Homeric poetry *as an oral tradition*; variations in the textual tradition would reflect different stages in the transcribing of this oral tradition.

Here is the crux of my disagreement with Janko's dictation model. In terms of my evolutionary model, the variant readings adduced for the Homeric text by the Alexandrians, most prominently by Aristarchus, can be viewed as reflexes of formulaic variation in an oral tradition. The

8. HS 110–111; see p. 13 in the present book.
9. Haslam 1997.
10. To quote from Janko 1998a; see Haslam 1997.80–81.
11. HS 111 = p. 13 in the present book. See also Ch.2 above.

variants themselves may *in theory* date from a wide range of chronological points extending from the second millennium BCE all the way to the era of Aristarchus. In reality, though, we may expect most of the surviving variants to stem from the latest recoverable phases of the oral transmission, especially from the timeframe spanning the last 500 or 600 years before Aristarchus. Even within this timeframe of half a millennium or so, we may expect the degrees of variation to drop off drastically during the last few centuries, as the Homeric oral tradition becomes ever less flexible while various political controls over performance conventions become ever more rigid.

In terms of Janko's dictation model, by contrast, the variant readings adduced by the likes of Aristarchus cannot really be products of an oral tradition, on the grounds that Homeric poetry had already become, by the eighth century BCE, a fixed text. At that point in time, we would still be well over 500 years away from Aristarchus. For over half a millennium before Aristarchus, according to Janko's explanation, Homeric poetry would have survived primarily as a text, not as a performance tradition. This is why Janko is forced to dismiss as "conjectures" some of the most significant surviving variants adduced by Aristarchus. This is why Janko must disagree with Haslam's analysis of such variants.

Janko highlights what Haslam says about the variant readings adduced by Aristarchus: "the prevailing opinion is that Aristarchus invented them, that is, conjectured them."[12] Calling Haslam's statement an "overstatement," Janko reacts by saying: "It is certainly not my opinion, only that he [Aristarchus] did venture *some* conjectures in his commentary (about thirty-three in the c. 3,000 lines of *Iliad* 13–16)." Janko's reference makes it clear that he is relying here on his own 1992 commentary on *Iliad* N-Π (hereafter = IC). Later on, when he is reacting to my position, Janko refers me as well to the same commentary, specifically to a specific page where he cites thirty-three "conjectures" supposedly made by Aristarchus.[13] In disputing me, however, he refers to the "thirty-three cases" as "emendations," whereas he had called these same cases "conjectures" in his earlier dispute with Haslam.

The basis for Janko's using this word "conjecture" is made clear when he says: "I agree with van der Valk and Kirk [vol. I p. 43] that most readings where the Alexandrians lack support in the papyri and early codices are conjectures."[14]

Prominent in Janko's sample list of Aristarchean "conjectures" is *Iliad* N

12. Haslam 1997.72.
13. IC 26.
14. IC 24–25. See van der Valk 1963/1964; Kirk 1985 I 43.

423.[15] In this Homeric line, as Janko argues, "Aristarchus altered στενάχοντα (read by Zenodotus and the vulgate) to -οντε, so that the bearers groan instead ([Aristonicus, Didymus]/A); a papyrus and some codices adopt this solution."[16] Hypsenor cannot be 'groaning', στενάχοντα, if he has already been killed at N 402–423. If we were to believe that the Iliadic text as we have it, with στενάχοντα at N 423, is the result of a performative blunder, then the short distance between N 423, where Hypsenor is badly wounded, and N 402–423, where he is already killed, makes the hypothetical blunder of the performer all the more pronounced.

But why reject the possibility that Aristarchus found textual evidence, inaccessible to us, that supported the reading στενάχοντε at N 423? That reading is in line with the context of N 402–423. Moreover, the form στενάχοντες in the hexameter at *Odyssey* ξ 354 is in fact attested in precisely the same metrical slot that στενάχοντε occupies in the hexameter at N 423. In other words, an argument can be made that the formulaic system of Homeric poetry, as attested in the surviving Homeric text, can generate στενάχοντε at precisely the point where Aristarchus adduces such a variant.[17]

To be sure, Aristarchus is not thinking in terms of an oral formulaic system. Instead, his editorial agenda are based on presuppositions of an original text that was supposedly *written* by Homer.[18] And yet, he adduces a form that could indeed have been generated by such an oral formulaic system. Here as elsewhere, the value of Aristarchus' testimony is not in his theories per se but in his editorial methods, which could occasionally yield information that would otherwise be lost. As I have argued in earlier work, Aristarchus "respected the reality of textual variants" because, from the standpoint of his own working theory, any one of these variants "could have been the very one that Homer wrote."[19]

From an evolutionary point of view, in terms of the model that I have already outlined, it would suffice to say that *Iliad* N 402–423 is incompatible with any version of *Iliad* N 423 that features στενάχοντα instead of στενάχοντες or στενάχοντε. Instead, Janko invokes his theory that the Homeric *Iliad* was dictated in the eighth century BCE, which would be the point of origin for the "blunder" of στενάχοντα.[20] For nearly half a

15. Janko lists this Iliadic passage first at IC 26n30 (N 28, N 191, and N 384 go into a secondary list), perhaps intending it as a premier case in point (cf. IC 37).

16. IC 99.

17. See also *HR* 67–68.

18. See Ch.1, p. 11.

19. *PP* 151.

20. IC 99–100 (also pp. 37–38).

millennium, according to Janko's explanation, N 402–423 happily coexisted with the version of N 423 that featured στενάχοντα—until Aristarchus in the second century BCE finally offered his "solution." According to Janko, "such blunders decisively support Lord's view that the *Iliad* is an oral dictated text."[21] I venture to ask, however, whether Lord's view is being used here and elsewhere to support Janko's view—rather than the other way around.[22]

I see a general problem with Janko's references to Albert Lord in this regard. Janko's own view of an oral dictated text of Homer is much narrower than Lord's. So too are various other views that I have criticized elsewhere.[23] Here I confine myself to pointing out some of the differences between Lord's and Janko's views. Lord's dictation theory stems from his article "Homeric Originality: Oral Dictated Texts,"[24] republished (along with a 1990 addendum) in his book *Epic Singers and Oral Tradition*.[25] In this article, Lord does not speculate on a specific time (or place) for his heuristic model, which is essentially comparative in nature. Further, Lord's model is not based on the theory of an eighth-century Homer. Nor is it tied to theories of a textual transmission that somehow persists for several centuries without the possibility of any further significant contact with oral transmission. Nor does it depend on theories about Aristarchean "conjectures." For all these reasons and more, I resist Janko's identification of his model with that of Lord.

In his review, Janko extends the theory of an orally dictated text of Homer, "which was absolutely fundamental to Albert Lord," to Milman Parry: "Indeed, Milman Parry never even considered any other explanation for the origin of the Homeric texts." In support of this assertion, Janko cites a single remark of Parry, recorded in fieldnotes published by his son Adam Parry in *The Making of Homeric Verse: The Collected Papers of Milman Parry* (1971).[26] We find Parry writing these informal notes to himself:

> I even figure to myself, just now, the moment when the author of the *Odyssey* sat and dictated his song, while another, with writing materials, wrote it down verse by verse, even in the way that our singers sit in the immobility of their thought, watching the motion of Nikola's hand across the empty page, when it will tell them it is the instant for them to speak the next verse.[27]

21. IC 99–100.
22. Again, see also *HR* 67–68.
23. N 1997b.
24. Lord 1953.
25. Lord 1991.38–48.
26. Hereafter cited as *MHV*.
27. *MHV* 451.

If Janko supposes that this thought of Parry amounts to the formulation of a theory—let alone a unique explanation for "the origin of the Homeric texts"—he should read on: Parry's linked thoughts, extending through the rest of the paragraph, need to be considered in their entirety. Parry's next sentence, for example, reads: "The reasons I have for such an opinion are many, some of them still very vague, some very exact."[28] I stand by what I said in *Bryn Mawr Classical Review* 1997: Milman Parry never formulated a "dictation theory."[29]

On the next page of this printed version of Parry's informal notes to himself, a different but related dimension of his thinking emerges: "The whole problem of the transmission of the poems once composed is also one which must be considered in detail."[30] Parry goes on to ponder "the alterations made to the Southslavic texts" by "unscholarly collectors and editors." At this point in his thinking, Parry is undecided about the relevance of these Southslavic typologies to the history of the Homeric textual tradition, though he seems to be leaning in the direction of discounting the variants: "A methodological study along such lines will probably show us much about the sources of the variants of the texts such as Ludwig [*sic*] and Allen give them in their editions, about the longer and shorter papyrus texts, and the action of the early editors."[31]

I note *en passant* that Adam Parry's edition of his father's work allows the name of Arthur Ludwich to be misspelled here. Moreover, Ludwich is missing altogether from the index of Parry's edition. Nor does this index record the reference by Milman Parry to T. W. Allen's work on the text of Homer.[32] It is not that I blame Adam Parry. My point is far more simple. I see here a minor symptom of a major trend: Homeric studies in the era after Milman Parry—an era that extends into the present—have tended to neglect the work of Ludwich, despite the signals that Parry had left behind. In this and in many other respects, I believe, things would have turned out differently if Albert Lord had been invited to edit Milman Parry's collected papers. My sense is that Lord's editing in such contexts would have been different: he would have followed up on all of Parry's inchoate signals, which lead in a variety of different directions—including the lines of thought represented by the likes of Ludwich.

The neglect of Ludwich's work is in turn symptomatic of another

28. *MHV* 451.
29. N 1997b.
30. *MHV* 452.
31. *MHV* 452.
32. *MHV* 452.

major trend: recent Homeric studies have tended to slight Aristarchus'
contributions to the textual history of Homer, treating the variants that he
adduces as mere conjectures. My book *Poetry as Performance* and Haslam's
chapter for the *New Companion* seek to reverse this trend.[33]

Here I return to a point I made earlier about Ludwich: he, along with
Karl Lehrs, was a premier defender of Aristarchus' editorial methodology
against the attacks of Friedrich August Wolf, as Rudolf Pfeiffer observes in
his *History of Classical Scholarship*.[34] With reference to Wolf's position, I
applied the term "Wolfian vulgate," as used by Michael Apthorp,[35] to what I
describe as "post-Wolf Homer editions that tend to discount the judgments
of Alexandrian critics."[36] Janko objects to my use of the term, particularly
with reference to the recent editions of the Homeric *Iliad* and *Odyssey* by
Helmut van Thiel,[37] claiming that Wolf did not produce his own editions of
Homer.[38] My point, in any case, is that the concept of a "Wolfian vulgate" is
antithetical to the concept of a unified edition. Moreover, it is antithetical
to the concept of an Aristarchean edition, as envisioned by Ludwich: for
Ludwich, the Alexandrian "edition" of Aristarchus represents a quantum
leap beyond the pre-Alexandrian "vulgate"; for van der Valk, by contrast,
the pre- and post-Alexandrian "vulgate" text is relatively superior to the
Alexandrian "edition" of Aristarchus, which may not even be deserving of
the term "edition."[39]

Milman Parry writes elsewhere about Ludwich's editions of Homer: "for
my purposes the traditional text is that of Ludwich."[40] He is careful to add:
"'traditional text' is of course a relative term."[41] Parry's understanding of this
"traditional text" of Homer is germane to the methodology of Aristarchus:

> We must go back to the principle of Aristarchus of getting "the solution
> from the text," but we must enlarge it until it covers not only the meaning

33. N 1996a = *PP*; Haslam 1997.

34. Pfeiffer 1968.215–218, with bibliography.

35. Apthorp 1980.xviii.

36. HS 115; see also above at p. 17; cf. *PP* 135n121.

37. See van Thiel 1996 and 1991 respectively.

38. But see now his retraction of that statement, published in *Bryn Mawr Classical
Review* 98.6.17, = Janko 1998d. In fact, Wolf did indeed publish his own editions of the
Iliad and *Odyssey*, in 1804 and 1807 respectively.

39. HS 114–115. See again Ch.1.

40. *MHV* 269n5. The editions of Ludwich are *Homeri Odyssea* I/II (Leipzig: Teubner
1889/1891) and *Homeri Ilias* I/II (Leipzig: Teubner 1902/1907). (As in the other instance
that I have already noted, this reference to Ludwich is likewise omitted in Adam Parry's
index of *MHV*.)

41. *MHV* 268n5.

of a verse or passage but the poems entire, and lets us know why the poet, or poets, of the *Iliad* and *Odyssey* made them as they are, or as they were at first. Whatever feature of poetic art we may study, *we must follow it throughout the traditional text*, and try to see it clearly and fully; *but our hope will not be to find places out of harmony with one another*, but instead, after finding all the elements of the poems which bear upon that feature, to draw from them when we can, but from them only, a new idea of poetic artistry [emphasis mine].[42]

This methodology is Parry's incipient answer to the Homeric questions that he says the "scholars of our time" are unable to answer. He describes these scholars as neo-unitarians who have succeeded in refuting the analysts—but who fail to give satisfactory answers to his questions, which he formulates as follows:

> ... what reasons have they had for passing over the fact pointed out by Wolf that a limited use of writing for literary purposes, which is the most one can suppose for Homer's age, must have made for a poetry very unlike ours? What source have they given for the tradition [Pausanias 7.26.13; Josephus, *Against Apion* 1.2.6] that Homer was recorded only at a later time? How have they explained the unique number of *good* variant readings in our text of Homer, and the need for the laborious editions of Aristarchus and of the other grammarians, and the extra lines, which grow in number as new papyri are found? Finally, have they shown why the poems should be of such a sort as to lend themselves to the many attempts to show the parts of which they were made, and have they told why these attempts were often made by men of the best taste and judgment?[43]

Parry's own answer, to repeat his wording, is that "we must look back to the principle of Aristarchus of getting 'the solution from the text.'" My book, *Poetry as Performance*, follows up on this principle by considering the "traditional text" in the relative sense of the term as Parry applies it, not in the absolute sense of Aristarchus.[44] Here I return to my earlier formulation, but now with three points of emphasis instead of two: "Whereas Aristarchus ... may have gone too far in positing *the* authentic reading in any given case throughout the Homeric text, there is no reason to doubt that any Homeric variant attributed to Aristarchus *can* be considered *an* authentic reading."[45]

To test this formulation, I return to Janko's sample list of thirty-three

42. *MHV* 268.
43. *MHV* 268.
44. *PP* Ch.5.
45. HS 111. See again above p. 13.

Aristarchean "conjectures," minus the lead-off example that I have already questioned, *Iliad* N 423.[46] In each of the thirty-two cases I am about to study, I will argue either (1) that the given form adduced by Aristarchus *can* be considered an authentic reading or (2) that the given form was only mentioned but not actually proposed by Aristarchus:

1. *Iliad* A 423–424 (IC p. 26n30): ἐπί vs. μετά at 423 and ἐπί vs. κατά at 424. Janko's observations here are most useful for arguing *against* the assumption of Aristarchean conjecture. It is clear from the verbatim quotations of Aristarchus at Didymus/A that he simply *glossed* μετά and κατά by way of ἐπί, while the paraphrase of Didymus/T misrepresents Aristarchus as if he had argued for ἐπί as a genuine variant. I agree with Janko's inference that the scholia often give "a false impression of his work" and, a fortiori, of the work of his predecessors. The same inference could have been invoked, I contend, in several other cases in Janko's present list. I invoke it also in general against some other claims that Janko adduces.[47] Aristarchus and his predecessors deserve the benefit of the doubt whenever they are paraphrased by indirect sources on the subject of variant readings.

2. *Iliad* I 222 (IC p. 26): ἂψ ἐπάσαντο or αἶψ' ἐπάσαντο vs. ἐξ ἔρον ἔντο. Here we see a case for arguing the second of the two alternatives, namely, that the given form was only mentioned but not actually proposed by Aristarchus. The scholia make it explicit that Aristarchus chose not to adopt in his base text such a different reading, ἂψ ἐπάσαντο (Didymus/A): ἄμεινον εἶχεν ἄν, φησιν ὁ Ἀρίσταρχος, [εἰ] ἐγέγραπτο "ἂψ ἐπάσαντο"· ἀλλ' ὅμως ὑπὸ περιττῆς εὐλαβείας οὐδὲν μετέθηκεν, ἐν πολλαῖς οὕτως εὑρὼν φερομένην τὴν γραφήν 'It would have been better, says Aristarchus, if it had been written "ἂψ ἐπάσαντο" or "αἶψ' ἐπάσαντο"; nevertheless, because of his extreme caution, he changed nothing, <u>having found in many of the texts this attested way of writing it</u> [= "ἐξ ἔρον ἔντο" instead of "ἂψ ἐπάσαντο"]'. The wording assumes that *some* of the texts did indeed feature ἂψ ἐπάσαντο instead of ἐξ ἔρον ἔντο.[48] (We may compare the parallel morphology of ἂψ ἐγένοντο at *Odyssey* κ 395; also the ἂψ vs. αἶψ' variation at *Odyssey* κ 405 and θ 92.) I infer that Aristarchus 'changed nothing' (οὐδὲν μετέθηκεν) *even though he could have made a change* on the basis of manuscript attestations of a variant reading. Moreover, he is quoted as considering the variant reading as a contrary-to-fact proposition. Accordingly, it seems unjustified to describe such readings as his own editorial conjectures.

46. See again Janko's list in IC 26.
47. I have in mind Janko 1998a.
48. See again my discussion in Ch.3 and Ch.4 of the scholia at *Iliad* I 222.

3. *Iliad* I 394 (IC pp. 26–7): γε μάσσεται vs. γαμέσσεται. I am not sure whether Janko was counting this case as one of his thirty-three examples, or whether he counted as two examples the case of A 423–4. In any event, it is not justifiable to assume that Aristarchus adduced μάσσεται mainly to avoid a violation of "Hermann's Bridge," as Janko claims. (Hermann's formulation dates back to 1805.) Also, the morphology of μάσσεται could have been generated by the formulaic system. Compare for example ἐπιμάσσεται at Δ 190.

4. *Iliad* Ξ 125 (IC p. 165): εἰ vs. ὡς, where ὡς is read "rightly" by the *dēmōdeis* (δημώδεις) 'popular' (Didymus/A), the papyri, and the codices. But how can Janko be sure that the reading ὡς is "right"? Granted, "ὡς is common after ἀκούω," but ἐτεόν, as here, is attested elsewhere with εἰ twenty-one times, by Janko's own count. Thus there are valid reasons to justify either reading, εἰ or ὡς, in terms of the formulaic system that generates Homeric diction. Janko's position is that he *has* to choose one or the other variant, and he *has* to discredit the variant(s) that he does not choose, because his dictation theory depends on one single text stemming from the eighth century. In *Poetry as Performance*, I questioned this position of Janko and summarized my counter-position as follows: "the empirical methods of comparative philology and the study of oral tradition can be used only to defend a variant reading as traditional, not to establish it as the superior reading—let alone the correct reading."[49]

5. *Iliad* O 197 (IC p. 248): βέλτερον vs. κέρδιον. Both are attested in manuscripts, but Janko claims that κέρδιον is "confirmed" on the grounds that he sees an "echo" at O 226 (another κέρδιον, but in a different verse-position) and that this word is "formular in this phrase, unlike the scholars' emendations." Although I find no instances of βέλτερον εἴη elsewhere in the Homeric corpus, there are attestations of βέλτερόν ἐστι at *Iliad* Σ 302, Φ 485, and *Odyssey* ρ 18 (all before the trochaic caesura, in a position that accommodates cognate phrases in verse-final position; all with infinitive constructions similar to the one at O 197).

6. *Iliad* Π 5 (IC p. 315): θάμβησε vs. ᾤκτιρε. Although θάμβησε in this verse is not attested in the manuscripts known to us, it is attested elsewhere, as at Ω 483, where Achilles is looking with wonder at Priam just after the old man has kissed his hands at 478—and just before Priam begins to speak at verse 486, appealing to Achilles to pity him. The exegetical reasoning of Aristarchus, as reported in Didymus/T, is called by Janko a "misjudgment," which "removes the central theme of pity from this central scene of the *Iliad*." I see no such removal and no such misjudgment as I read the contexts

49. *PP* 117–118, 132–152; the summary is at p. 133.

evoked by θάμβησε. The purported "misjudgment," according to Janko, "confirms that Aristarchus could emend on improper grounds." But we do not know his grounds, since we do not know of his manuscript evidence. Here and elsewhere, Janko has not been able to prove that Aristarchus would ever consider an emendation on the basis of content alone.

7. *Iliad* Π 50 (IC p. 322): εἴ vs. ἤν. "Aristarchus altered ἤν to εἴ (in no ms)." I agree with Janko that ἤν as in ἤν τινα οἶδα can be justified on the basis of parallels as at *Odyssey* α 415 and β 201; still, εἴ as in εἴ τινα οἶδα can also be justified on the basis of parallels as at *Odyssey* θ 145–6: πείρησαι ἀέθλων | εἴ τινά που δεδάηκας· ἔοικε δέ σ᾽ ἴδμεν ἀέθλους. Again, there are valid reasons to justify either reading at Π 50 in terms of the formulaic system that generates Homeric diction.

8. *Iliad* Π 638 (IC p. 392): Σαρπηδόνι δίῳ vs. Σαρπηδόνα δῖον. Janko assumes that Aristarchus emended from accusative to dative, without manuscript evidence. Again, an argument from silence. Also, compare συμφράδμονες plus dative at *Iliad* B 372; also συμφράζομαι plus dative at A 537, 540; I 374; *Odyssey* δ 462.

Janko's secondary list begins here:

9. *Iliad* N 28 (IC pp. 46, 122): ἠγνοίησαν vs. ἠγνοίησεν. There are other instances where a neuter plural subject takes a plural rather than singular verb, as at *Iliad* M 159, and I see no reason to assume that Aristarchus "normalized" from singular to plural on the basis of such examples. So I disagree with Janko's premise when he says: "it is wrong to normalize an oral dictated text."[50] I have already indicated my opposition to Janko's invoking "an oral dictated text" as a premise for his rejecting one given variant in favor of another.[51]

10. *Iliad* N 191 (IC p. 71): χρόος vs. χροός. I agree with Janko that Aristarchus interpreted χρόος as a diectasis of χρώς. It does not follow, however, that the form χρόος is an editorial conjecture in the sense of an alternative reading proposed by the editor to replace a supposedly false form as transmitted in the received text. For Aristarchus, accents were not part of the textual tradition of Homer.[52] At best, we may consider χρόος an exegetical reconstruction, however flawed, that Aristarchus must have considered in his commentary.

11. *Iliad* N 384 (IC p. 96): ἦλθ᾽ ἐπαμύντωρ (also O 540) vs. ἦλθεν

50. Janko IC 122.

51. On the principle of *lectio difficilior* in the analysis of variants stemming from an oral tradition, see *PP* 129n99. In the same note, I also adduce data collected by Ludwich to argue that Aristarchus' editorial priorities did not rank internal logic ahead of manuscript evidence.

52. *PP* 128–132.

ἀμύντωρ. Despite the parallel attestation in *Odyssey* π 263, Janko thinks that Aristarchus' reading "should be rejected," in view of ἦεν ἀμύντωρ at O 610. But compare the verse-final placement of the verb ἐπαμύνω as at *Iliad* Z 361 and M 369. I suggest that neither reading should be "rejected." Both forms could have been generated from the formulaic system of Homeric diction.

12. *Iliad* N 449 (IC p. 104): ἴδῃ vs. ἴδῃς. Aristarchus' adducing of the variant ἴδῃ alongside ἴδῃς here and elsewhere does not necessarily mean that he is "standardizing." Janko claims: "The Alexandrians wrongly standardize one way or the other." Rather, it may simply be a matter of consistently *reporting* such variants. Compare my remarks on "normalization" at *Iliad* N 28. Again, both forms could have been generated from the formulaic system of Homeric diction.

13. *Iliad* N 584 (IC p. 118): ὁμαρτήδην vs. ὁμαρτήτην. Janko claims that "this is a conjecture to avoid having two main verbs." But compare the interaction of adverbial -δην with other verbs, as in the case of such forms as κλήδην, ἐξονομακλήδην, ἐκ δ' ὀνομακλήδην at *Iliad* I 11, X 415 and *Odyssey* δ 278, μ 250.

14. *Iliad* N 599 (IC p. 120): ἐυστρεφεῖ vs. ἐυστρόφῳ. Given that the two forms are both morphologically predictable in Homeric diction, as Janko points out, I prefer to treat them as two interchangeable variants in the formulaic system. I disagree with Janko's description of the variant adduced by Aristarchus: "He is conjecturing to impose homogeneity." See also my remarks on N 28 and N 449.

15. *Iliad* N 810 (IC p. 145): αὕτως vs. οὕτως, attested in a papyrus and in "the good codices." I question such criteria involving "better" vs. "worse" manuscript readings.[53]

16. *Iliad* Ξ 72 (IC p. 158): ὅτε vs. ὅτι: "this needless conjecture has weak ms support." Janko argues that ὅτε "tidies up the syntax without altering the sense." Why assume, though, that it is the *editor* who tidies up? The formulaic system can generate either ὅτε or ὅτι in this context, and one of these alternatives happens to be more tidy than the other from Aristarchus' point of view. The adducing of the form by Aristarchus could simply be added to the manuscript evidence, however weak in this case, which points toward the existence of two variants in this context. Janko cannot prove that ὅτε is not an authentic variant. Giving Aristarchus the benefit of the doubt, I prefer to argue that he had access to two variants ὅτε vs. ὅτι, not that he conjectured ὅτε in order to oust a supposedly exclusive ὅτι that he found in the manuscripts. Aristarchus would then proceed to choose one variant

53. See above p. 61; also *PP* 148–149.

over the other, on the basis of the internal evidence. Janko's preference for the other variant, by contrast, is based on external considerations prompted by his theory of an eighth-century archetype that was dictated by Homer. In terms of such a posited archetype, ὅτι seems the plausible choice for Janko, since it seems to him the *lectio difficilior*; but you need to make a choice between the variants precisely because you are positing such an archetype. From an evolutionary point of view, by contrast, you do not need to choose one or the other variant as the true form. Rather, the choice is relative— depending on the given time and place in the history of the paradosis. In the case of Aristarchus, to repeat, his own need to make a choice in such cases is based on his theory of an archetype written by Homer.

17. *Iliad* Ξ 173 (IC p. 176): κατά vs. ποτί: "but Aristarchus' alteration is unjustified, since we are dealing with a misused formula." Rather, I argue that it is unjustified to claim an "alteration." Further, it is unjustified to claim that the expression ποτὶ χαλκοβατὲς δῶ is "misused" in this context, vs. the other contexts at *Iliad* A 426 and 438, Φ 505, *Odyssey* θ 321 and ν 4 (in the last case, the δῶ is that of Alkinoos, not of Zeus). The reading ποτὶ χαλκοβατὲς δῶ may be less "tidy" (to invoke Janko's criteria as applied to the previous case) than the reading adduced by Aristarchus, κατὰ χαλκοβατὲς δῶ, but it is still justifiable in terms of the formulaic system that generates Homeric diction. More important, expressions involving ποτὶ δῶμα (verse-final at *Odyssey* γ 488 and ο 186) and ποτὶ δώματ' (*Odyssey* ζ 297) are parallel to those involving κατὰ δῶμα (verse-final at *Iliad* X 442 and 478) and κατὰ δώματ' (*Iliad* Ω 512, *Odyssey* φ 372) in the formulaic system—both in terms of positioning within the hexameter and in terms of traditional themes at work in the given contexts. Finally, the thematic contexts of κατὰ δῶμα / δώματ(α) in verses like *Iliad* Ξ 257 and *Odyssey* δ 44 (cf. 72) are evidently cognate with the thematic context of *Iliad* Ξ 173 (about the wonders of the palace of Zeus).

18. *Iliad* Ξ 235 (IC p. 188): τοι χάριν εἰδέω vs. τοι ἰδέω χάριν (scanned – ◡ ◡ – ◡ ◡) in papyri and some codices; also vs. τοι εἰδέω χάριν in the *dēmōdeis* (δημώδεις) 'popular' texts (Didymus/A) and in our "vulgate." Janko says that Aristarchus' reading "removes the hiatus [between τοι and ἰδέω] and synizesis [the εω in ἰδέω]," citing *Odyssey* π 236. Actually, the prevalent manuscript reading there is ὄφρ' εἰδέω ὅσσοι τε …, which scans as – – – – – ◡. The synizesis there [the εω in εἰδέω] suggests to me that Aristarchus' reading could also feature synizesis: that is, τοι χάριν εἰδέω could scan as – ◡ ◡ – – as well as – ◡ ◡ – ◡ ◡ (with non-synizesis of εω but with correption of ω before the following vowel). The placement of χάριν εἰδέω before the bucolic diaeresis may be compared with the analogous placement

of χάριν ἴδε (scanned as ⏑ – ⏑ ⏑) at *Iliad* Λ 243. Note too the placement of εἰδώς before the bucolic diaeresis at *Odyssey* δ 818 and ε 250.

19. *Iliad* Ξ 485 (IC p. 220): Ἄρεω ἀλκτῆρα vs. ἄρεως ἀλκτῆρα. The latter "vulgate" reading, with synizesis of εω, is parallel to ἄρεως ἀλκτῆρες at *Iliad* Σ 213, again with synizesis; but ἄρης ἀλκτῆρα at Σ 100. Janko notes: "Aristarchus read Ἄρεω in all three places, but this too [like Zenodotus' reading ἄρης] is conjectural." How can Janko be sure? He explains thus about Ἄρεω: "this Ionic form, absent from the mss, first occurs in Archilochus [F 18]." But how can he be sure that such an Ionic form is excluded from Homeric diction? Janko continues: "The truth is surely as follows." He proceeds to argue that ἄρη (short α, as distinct from the long α of ἀρή 'curse') became "confused" with Ἄρης. "The poet let the barely intelligible formula [ἄρης ἀλκτῆρα] stand at [Σ] 100, but here [Ξ 485] and at [Σ] 213 he substituted Ἄρεος, a normal epic genitive of Ares, found in a few mss; because of the substitution, it has to be scanned (uniquely) with synizesis." Finally, "Ἄρεως will then be a superficial Atticism, also found as a variant at [*Iliad* T] 47." From an evolutionary point of view, by contrast, the formulation could be simplified: ἄρης ἀλκτῆρ- can coexist with an Ionicized variant Ἄρεω ἀλκτῆρ- as well as an Atticized variant Ἄρεως ἀλκτῆρ-.

Addendum: I agree with Janko (IC p. 37) that "the superficial Attic traits in the epic diction do prove that Athens played a major role in the transmission, and this must be related to the Pisistratids' patronage of Homeric poetry." But I disagree with Janko's linked idea (IC p. 37) that the Peisistratids "probably procured the first complete set of rolls to cross the Aegean." From an evolutionary point of view, the Attic phase of Homeric transmission was still a performative phase, not a textual phase (as required by Janko's theory of an eighth-century dictation). In such an Attic phase, it is important to note, we may expect the evolution of hyperionisms *in terms of the performative tradition.* That is, hyperionisms could be generated by performances in an Attic-speaking context. From Janko's point of view, by contrast, hyperionisms must be considered *only in terms of the textual tradition.* A case in point is the set of hyperionic forms adduced by Zenodotus for the Homeric text, as listed by Janko (IC p. 24). Janko dismisses all these forms as spurious editorial conjectures. In a forthcoming work, I will counterargue that such hyperionic forms are authentic performative variants stemming from an Attic phase of the performance tradition of Homer.[54]

54. With reference to an Attic phase, see also *PP* 134–136 on Zenodotean vs. Aristarchean editorial preferences concerning *Iliad* A 5.

20. *Iliad* O 82 (IC p. 237): μενοινήῃσι (in a few manuscripts) vs. μενοινήσειε (in most manuscripts, also in a papyrus). "An opt. is odd after an aor. subj., but so is a pres. subj., especially one formed like this ...; we are surely dealing with a conjecture." Janko cites Chantraine to justify his description of μενοινήῃσι as "odd."[55] But Chantraine in fact defends the authenticity of the form, in terms of the productivity of the ending -ῃσι in the *Dichtersprache*.[56] For a case in point, consider δώῃσιν at *Iliad* A 324, M 275. We may note such other "odd" forms as ἐπιπνείῃσιν at *Odyssey* δ 357, which scans like μενοινήῃσι, ⌣ – – – ⌣; both forms are located immediately after the trochaic caesura. Note too μενοινάᾳ at *Iliad* T 164: it scans ⌣ – – – and it too is located immediately after the trochaic caesura.

21. *Iliad* O 114 (IC p. 241): δ᾽ ἔπος ηὔδα vs. δὲ προσηύδα in most manuscripts. Similarly at *Iliad* O 398 and *Odyssey* ν 199. According to Janko, the Alexandrians "surely abandoned our vulgate δὲ προσηύδα (with its papyrus support) on the ground that it lacks an addressee in the acc., but this can be supplied from the context (cf. e.g. [E] 871)." I can understand how the Alexandrians could have used this kind of reasoning, but it does not follow that they should have conjectured δ᾽ ἔπος ηὔδα. I maintain that they would have "abandoned" δὲ προσηύδα only if they had δ᾽ ἔπος ηὔδα available as a textual variant. I am not persuaded by Janko's argument that verse-final ἔπος ηὔδα, as attested at *Iliad* M 163, could have been a source for conjecturing δ᾽ ἔπος ηὔδα as an alternative to δὲ προσηύδα. Rather, I view this attestation of ἔπος ηὔδα as a formulaic cognate of δ᾽ ἔπος ηὔδα. Janko adds that ἔπος ηὔδα "occurs 12x elsewhere, but its ϝ- is never 'neglected.'" But the "neglect" of ϝ- in δ᾽ ἔπος ηὔδα does not make this sequence any less formulaic than ἔπος ηὔδα. We may compare the notorious "neglect" of ϝ- whenever a female speaker speaks 'winged words': feminine φωνήσασ᾽ ἔπεα πτερόεντα προσηύδα vs. masculine φωνήσας ἔπεα πτερόεντα προσηύδα.[57]

22. *Iliad* O 252 (IC p. 253): ἵξεσθαι vs. ὄψεσθαι. Janko himself compares an interesting variation, attested in the manuscripts, between verse final ἵκηαι vs. ἴδηαι at *Odyssey* ρ 448. I contend that both pairs of variants, ἵξεσθαι vs. ὄψεσθαι and ἵκηαι vs. ἴδηαι, reflect a functional variation within the formulaic system of Homeric diction. Janko thinks that ὄψεσθαι "accords better with the stress on sight" in the present context. Well and good. But such an editorial preference for one variant over the other does not discredit

55. Chantraine *GH* I 77.

56. Here and elsewhere, I use "Dichtersprache" as a shorthand way of referring to poetic language as a meta-language that evolves from the grammar of everyday language but develops a distinct grammar of its own.

57. Parry *MHV* 397.

the other variant's authenticity. From an evolutionary point of view, I contend that both variants are authentic. See also my comments at *Iliad* N 810 on "better" vs. "worse" manuscript readings.

23. *Iliad* O 714 (IC p. 305): πέσον vs. πέσεν. Again, a case of neuter plural subject with a plural vs. singular verb. Janko refers back to his discussion of ἠγνοίησαν vs. ἠγνοίησεν at *Iliad* O 28, and I in turn refer back to my comments on that case.

24. *Iliad* Π 35 (IC p. 320): ὅτε vs. ὅτι: "a needless change lacking ms support." See my comments on *Iliad* Ξ 72.

25. *Iliad* Π 53 (IC p. 322): ὁππότε τις vs. ὁππότε δή. In support of his claim that "Aristarchus altered δή to τις," Janko says that there are twelve attestations of "ὅππoτέ (κεν) δή." I find, however, only three other cases of plain ὁππότε δή: *Odyssey* υ 386, ψ 345, ω 344. In each case, the verb is not in the subjunctive (two indicatives, one optative). In the present case, we see the subjunctive: ὁππότε τις [or δή] τὸν ὁμοῖον ἀνὴρ ἐθέλῃσιν ἀμέρσαι. I find two cases of verse-initial ὁππότε τις, and both feature the subjunctive: *Iliad* T 201 and Φ 112. The first of these two cases is strikingly parallel in syntax to the present case: ὁππότε τις μεταπαυσωλὴ πολέμοιο γένηται. The parallelism is in terms of "deep structure," not "surface structure," and it would be implausible, I think, to claim that Aristarchus was inspired by a verse like *Iliad* T 201 in preferring ὁππότε τις to ὁππότε δή at *Iliad* Π 53. I infer instead that Aristarchus had manuscript evidence for the reading ὁππότε τις alongside the "vulgate" reading ὁππότε δή. From an evolutionary point of view, however, there is no need to justify Aristarchus' preference, as opposed to Janko's preference. There is only the need to justify the authenticity of Aristarchus' reading, alongside the authenticity of the "vulgate" reading (as justified by Janko).

26. *Iliad* Π 106 (IC p. 330): καὶ φάλαρ' vs. καπ' φάλαρ' (all manuscripts and all papyri). Janko claims that the καί "is plainly a conjecture," because it turns the phrase βάλλετο δ' αἰεί at the end of the preceding line into a "parenthesis." We may restate Janko's claim this way: καί is an optional connector with the syntax of βάλλετο δ' αἰεί, while καπ' is an obligatory connector. But there are formulaic parallels to the "parenthetical" syntax of βάλλετο δ' αἰεί (if followed by καί): within the same "Adonic clausula" of the hexameter, scanned – ∪ ∪ – –, I find such constructions as τείρετο δ' αἰνῶς at *Iliad* E 352. Compare also ἵετο δ' αἰεί at *Iliad* N 424, which is not followed by "necessary enjambment" in this context, as opposed to the context of *Iliad* E 434, where we do find "necessary enjambment." Similarly with βάλλετο δ' αἰεί, we find absence vs. presence of "necessary enjambment" when followed by καί vs. καπ'. As for καί vs. καπ', compare the reverse situation in *Odyssey*

δ 72, where the manuscripts have καὶ δώματα ἠχήεντα vs. κατὰ δώματα ἠχήεντα in the scholia T at *Iliad* Ω 323. Compare verse-initial καὶ κεφαλῆς at *Odyssey* σ 355, where one of the manuscripts (Allen's "R12") reads κἆκε…, leading to the modern emendation κακ' κεφαλῆς.

27. *Iliad* Π 227 (IC p. 347): ὅτι μή vs. ὅτε μή. Janko says of ὅτι μή: "a common idiom in Herodotus and later, has no Homeric parallel." But ὅτι μή at this verse is attested in some manuscripts, so that it cannot simply be assumed to be non-Homeric. The four cases of ὅτε μή at *Iliad* N 319, Ξ 248, *Odyssey* π 197, ψ 185 do not disprove the potential presence of ὅτι μή in Π 227. Those four cases of ὅτε μή (aside from Π 227) introduce a verb in the optative, whereas we find no verb introduced by ὅτι μή / ὅτε μή at Π 227. For Janko to say that the expected verb "is easily supplied" does not explain why the verb is missing only at Π 227 but not elsewhere. The attested Ionic constructions introduced by ὅτι μή, which are regularly without a verb (compare Herodotus 1.18.3, 1.143.2, etc.), could supply an answer.

28. *Iliad* Π 252 (IC p. 351): σάον vs. σόον. "Aristarchus [Didymus/A] wavered [διχῶς] between σάον and σόον," while "the mss rightly read σόον." But compare σαόφρονα at *Iliad* Φ 462 and σαόφρων / σαοφροσύνης / σαοφροσύνῃσι at *Odyssey* δ 158 / ψ 13 / ψ 30. Janko explains that epic forms in σο- "arose by diectasis when the vernacular had contracted *σάϝος to σῶς, just as φόως replaced *φάϝος after it became φῶς." Still, as we see from Chantraine's Homeric grammar, φόως occurs when the second syllable is long by position (*Iliad* Θ 282, Λ 2, etc.) but φάος is the regular form when the next word begins with a vowel (unless a caesura intervenes, as at *Iliad* O 741).[58] Moreover, there are residual manuscript attestations of φάος before consonant, at *Odyssey* σ 317 and τ 34.

29. *Iliad* Π 504 (IC p. 381): ἔχοντο vs. ἕποντο. Janko rejects the form adduced by Aristarchus, saying: "it lacks ms support." But there are other kinds of support: for example, compare the syntax of the verse-final expression ποτὶ δὲ φρένες αὐτῷ ἔχοντο—if we admit ἔχοντο here as an authentic variant—with the syntax of the verse-final πρὸ δὲ δούρατ' ἔχοντο at *Iliad* P 355. I submit that the two constructions are cognate. Janko adds that "Aristarchus [Didymus/T] and nearly all mss read unmetrical ποτί in [Π] 504; προτί is a facile normalization of the rough-hewn text." But why should *brevis in longo* need to be "normalized" at a penthemimeral caesura? On this point, Parry's observations are telling.[59]

30. *Iliad* Π 522 (IC p. 383): οὗ παιδὸς ἀμύνει vs. ᾧ παιδὶ ἀμύνει. Janko contends that "this effort to emend away a hiatus is in no good ms." But why

58. Chantraine *GH* I 81.
59. Parry *MHV* 213–216.

assume that hiatus was Aristarchus' main concern? I suggest that he was interested in the *lectio difficilior* of the genitive vs. the dative with ἀμύνω. Janko himself cites *Iliad* M 402–3, Ζεὺς κῆρας ἄμυνε | παιδὸς ἑοῦ (vs. dative constructions at *Iliad* Π 265 and 512).

31. *Iliad* Π 668 (IC p. 396): Σαρπηδόνι vs. Σαρπηδόνα. "Aristarchus [Didymus/A] read Σαρπηδόνι, but verbs of cleansing can take a double acc. ([*Iliad* Λ] 572, [Σ] 345)." In this case, Aristarchus may be opting for the *lectio facilior*. Also, Janko compares Aristarchus' "change" at Π 638. But see my comments on that verse.[60]

32. *Iliad* Π 775 (IC p. 408): ὁ δ' ἐν στροφάλιγγι κονίης vs. ὁ δὲ στροφάλιγγι κονίης. Janko describes the form adduced by Aristarchus as "a facile. emendation." But note the prepositional construction at *Iliad* Φ 503: μετὰ στροφάλιγγι κονίης. The "deep structure" of the syntax in this case helps explain the ἐν in the other case. Further, the "surface structure" of μετὰ στροφάλιγγι κονίης seems to me too opaque to motivate ἐν στροφάλιγγι κονίης by some sort of analogy.

We have reached the end of Janko's list of his best-case arguments for doubting the testimony of Aristarchus. Having offered a counter-argument in each case, I conclude that Aristarchus deserves the benefit of the doubt.

There remains the theoretical possibility that a variant adduced by the Alexandrian scholars cannot be validated on the basis of what we know about the formulaic system inherited by Homeric poetry.[61] Even if we found such a case, it would not prove that the given variant had to be a conjecture. It could mean simply that we do not have enough data about the formulaic system. We know the workings of that system only to the extent of the surviving texts generated by the system. Even in the Homeric text as we have it we can find numerous unique occurrences, *hapax legomena*. A "hapax" occurrence in the Homeric text can be just as formulaic as multiple occurrences. The same principle holds for a "hapax" occurrence that exists not in the received text but as a variant adduced by an Alexandrian editor.

I close by signaling my intention to pursue further the rehabilitation of (1) the concept of an Aristarchean edition of Homer and (2) the importance of variant readings adduced by Aristarchus and other Alexandrian editors of the Homeric textual transmission.

60. At p. 121 above.
61. I am grateful to one of the two anonymous referees who alerted me to the necessity of addressing this theoretical possibility.

PART II

Language

CHAPTER 6

The Name of Achilles: Questions of Etymology and "Folk-Etymology"

In his book on the language of the Linear B tablets, Leonard R. Palmer explained the etymology of the name of Achilles, Ἀχιλ(λ)εύς, as a shortened variant of a compound formation *Akhí-lāu̯os, built from the roots of ἄχος 'grief' and of λαός 'host of fighting men, folk', morphologically parallel to such "Caland" compounds as Homeric κυδι-άνειρα and Οἰδι-πόδης.[1] The posited morphological shortening from *Akhílāu̯os to Ἀχιλ(λ)εύς, with optional doubling of the last consonant in the shortened variant, is paralleled by such forms as Χαρί-λαος and Χάριλλος (cf. also Φιλεύς vs. Φιλλεύς).[2] What follows is a reassessment of Palmer's explanation.

In my own work on the name of Achilles, I agreed with Palmer's reconstruction of *Akhílāu̯os, offering further evidence on the two distinct

---

* The original version of this essay is N 1994a.

1. Palmer 1963a.78–79. The original formulation for this kind of compound: Caland 1893; cf. Risch 1974.218–219. On the semantics of λαός 'host of fighting men, folk', see now Haubold 2000, especially pp. 2–3, 16, 43–45, 48–52, 76–78.

2. Palmer 1963a.79. On the morphology of -εύς, as in Ἀχιλ(λ)εύς, see Palmer 1963a.78; cf. Perpillou 1973.167–299. See also in general Schindler 1976, who demonstrates that this type of suffix is not a borrowing from a non-Indo-European language and that ευ-stems are in general secondary formations derived from o-stems. Further arguments in *BA* 70 par. 2n2 (cf. N 1976.209n9).

levels of linguistics and poetics.[3] The linguistic evidence was primarily
morphological, with a few additions to the examples already adduced
by Palmer.[4] The poetic evidence came mainly from the formulaic system
attested in the *Dichtersprache* of the Homeric *Iliad* and *Odyssey*.[5]

First of all, we may note that the noun ἄχος 'grief' is a functional synonym
of πένθος 'grief' in the Homeric *Dichtersprache*: for example, the personal
grief of Achilles over Briseis is ἄχος at *Iliad* A 188, Π 52, 55 and πένθος at *Iliad*
A 362; his grief over Patroklos is ἄχος at *Iliad* Σ 22, Ψ 47 and πένθος at Σ 73;
likewise, the collective grief of the Achaeans is ἄχος at *Iliad* Π 22 and πένθος
at I 3.[6] This thematic parallelism between ἄχος and πένθος is pertinent, I
argued, to the morphological parallelism between Palmer's reconstructed
"Caland" compounds *Akhí-lāu̯os* and *Penthí-lāu̯os*, matching respectively
the shortened "Caland" forms Ἀχιλ(λ)εύς and Πένθιλος.[7] Second, I argued
at length that the poetic evidence of the Homeric *Dichtersprache* reveals "a
pervasive nexus" between ἄχος and Ἀχιλ(λ)εύς, which is "integrated in the
inherited formulaic system and hence deeply rooted in the epic tradition."[8]

This statement is quoted, with approval, by Gary Holland, who then goes
on to summarize my overall interpretation of the *Iliad* along the lines of this
etymology:

> It also seems clear that Achilles' actions (or lack of action) lead to ἄχος for
> the host of fighting men. In Nagy's formula, Achilles' ἄχος leads to Achilles'
> μῆνις leads to ἄχος of the Achaeans. Furthermore, while the Trojans appear
> to be winning, that is, while they have the κράτος 'power', the Achaeans
> have ἄχος.... Thus, the thematic associations of ἄχος and λαός with the
> name of Achilles provide further corroboration for the etymology proposed
> by Palmer.[9]

Despite his agreement on the level of poetics, Holland has two objections
on the level of linguistics. First, he suggests that the thematic nexus between

3. *BA* 69–93; for the original formulation of the argument, see N 1976a. In his
commentary to Book I of the *Iliad*, Latacz 2000c.15 made a passing reference to this
formulation (which is the only reference by Latacz 2000a/b/c to any work of mine). On
the basis of this reference, it is not clear to me whether he understood my formulation.

4. *BA* 70 (cf. N 1976a.209–210).

5. This point, which I will reinforce in the present version of my essay, has not been
understood by all readers of previous versions. See above. For a working definition of
"Dichtersprache," see p. 125n56.

6. *BA* 94 (cf. N 1976a.221).

7. *BA* 72 (cf. N 1976a.210).

8. *BA* 79.

9. Holland 1993.22. For the original version of the formulation paraphrased here, see
N 1976a.216.

ἄχος and Ἀχιλ(λ)εύς may be a matter of "folk-etymology," not etymology: "the preponderance of ἄχος and its derivatives may simply be due to a folk-etymological association of the word with the name of Achilles on the part of the epic poet(s), and not to an actual etymological connection" (highlighting mine).[10] Second, he suggests that my translation of the "Caland" compound *Akhí-lāu̯os, 'whose λαός has ἄχος', "seems wrong for this compound type," because "dependent noun compounds are used very infrequently as the basis for bahuvrīhi or possessive adjective compounds."[11]

It is easier to begin with the second objection, if I am right in thinking that it is based on a misunderstanding. All along, I interpreted the reconstructed "Caland" compound *Akhí-lāu̯os as 'whose host of fighting men is sorrowful [= grieving]', where the syntactical function of the first component is indeed that of a possessive adjective.[12] Intending to convey a diathetical neutrality in the adjectival component,[13] which I am here rendering as 'sorrowful [= grieving]', I devised the translation 'whose lāu̯ós [λαός] has ákhos [ἄχος = sorrow, grief]'.[14] Similar translations can be applied to other "Caland" compounds, as with κυδι-άνειρα 'whose men are κυδροί', that is, 'whose men have κῦδος'; also, Οἰδι-πόδης 'whose feet are swollen', that is, 'whose feet have swelling = οἶδος' (in this case, the "Caland" simplex with suffix -ρός, alternate of the compound formant οἰδι-, is not attested).

Holland's second objection raises a more important question, which is central to this presentation: how to distinguish an etymology from a "folk-etymology." The latter term is misleading, I suggest, if it leads to the assumption that the only "genuine" etymology in comparative linguistics is one where a given reconstructed form can be traced all the way back to the parent language of the given languages being compared. According to such an assumption, a reconstruction like *Akhí-lāu̯os would be a "false" etymology if it cannot be traced back to "proto-Indo-European."

The term "folk-etymology" implies another, even more misleading, assumption: that any etymologically "wrong" derivation of one given form from another is purely a synchronic phenomenon. True, a functioning or living connection between a given set of forms that had once been unconnected must be assumed to have a starting point at some given synchrony. Still, any synchrony is destined to become, moving forward in time, simply a cross-section in the diachrony of language. As we reconstruct

10. Holland 1993.22–23.

11. Holland 1993.23, with reference to BA 69–70.

12. Cf. BA 78, 'he who has the host of fighting men grieving'.

13. By "diathetical neutrality," I mean that the opposition between active and passive usage is neutralized.

14. BA 69–70.

a given language forward in time, what may count as a "wrong" connection in an earlier cross-section can become a "right" connection in a later cross-section, from the standpoint of the evolving structure of that language. Here I refer to the classic work of Emile Benveniste on the necessity of combining synchronic with diachronic methods in the establishment of etymologies.[15]

In the case of a form like Ἀχιλ(λ)εύς, the question is not whether it had *always* been connected with the forms ἄχος and λαός. What matters instead is whether this connection is "deeply rooted," as I have described it, in the formulaic system of Homeric *Dichtersprache* and whether it can be traced far back enough in time to reach the remote stage when "Caland" formations were still a productive mechanism in the Greek language.

Moving diachronically forward, by the time we reach even the earliest attestations of the Greek language, we find that the "Caland" mechanism is already residual, clearly no longer productive: only such vestiges as κυδι-άνειρα vs. κυδρός are left.[16] What remains productive, however, as I argued, is the actual *Dichtersprache* that had preserved "Caland" formations like *Akhí-lāu̯os* vs. Ἀχιλ(λ)εύς and *Penthí-lāu̯os* vs. Πένθιλος.

Such a *Dichtersprache*, however, can be considered a system in its own right, capable of generating, analogically, such non-"Caland" formations as Χαρί-λαος vs. Χάριλλος, Σθενέ-λαος vs. Σθένελος, Νείλεως (Ionic, from *Nehélāu̯os*, apparently attested in the Linear B tablets as *ne-e-ra-wo*) vs. Νηλεύς (non-Ionic, from *Neheleús*), Ἰόλαος vs. Ἰόλη and Ἰόλεια (implying a corresponding *Ἰολεύς), Περίλαος vs. Πέριλλος.[17] Still other non-"Caland" types that could have been generated by the *Dichtersprache* along the lines of *Akhí-lāu̯os* and *Penthí-lāu̯os* include Πρωτεσί-λαος (*Iliad* B 698, etc.), Χαιρεσί-λαος, Πενθεσί-λεια.[18]

With reference to Πενθεσί-λεια, Holland remarks: "Although πένθος means 'pain' synchronically in Greek, further connections within Indo-European are semantically difficult."[19] I draw attention to his use here of "synchronically," since his purpose is to argue that seemingly related forms, such as πενθερός 'relative by marriage', are to be derived from the Common Greek root *penth- 'bind' (as in πεῖσμα 'rope'; the Indo-European root is *bhendh-, as in Sanskrit *bandh-), so that Πενθεσί-λεια should mean 'binding the λαός' rather than 'paining the λαός'.[20]

15. Benveniste 1966.289–307. Cf. Householder and Nagy 1972.48–58.

16. Cf. Risch 1974.218–219.

17. *BA* 71.

18. *BA* 71. On the capacity of Homeric *Dichtersprache* to generate new morphological categories, see e.g. Roth 1990.

19. Holland 1993.24.

20. Holland 1993.24.

The problem is, Holland's use here of "synchronically" implies that there is just one level of synchrony for the meaning of 'grief' or 'pain'—as if any previous level would default diachronically to the meaning of 'bind'. And yet, the possibility of reconstructing earlier levels of synchronicity for πένθος in the sense of 'pain' becomes open-ended if the root is derived from Common Greek *kʷenth- 'suffer' (cf. Lithuanian kenčiù, Irish cēssaim), as opposed to Common Greek *penth- 'bind'.[21]

It would be preferable in this case, I suggest, to keep in mind not the diachrony of the root πένθ- but also the synchronicity of a Dichtersprache that could generate, along with a morphological and thematic parallelism of ἄχος vs. πένθος, a morphological and thematic parallelism of *Akh(es)í-lāu̯os vs. *Penth(es)í-lāu̯ia. These parallelisms converge in the epic tradition of a mortal combat between the male warrior Ἀχιλ(λ)εύς and the female warrior Πενθεσί-λεια, as reflected in the Aithiopis (Proclus summary p. 105.22 Allen).

Up to now, I have offered linguistic arguments in support of Palmer's explanation of Ἀχιλ(λ)εύς. In terms of my argumentation, however, Palmer's explanation "will not carry conviction unless we can show that the meaning of *Akhí-lāu̯os is intrinsic to the function of Achilles in myth and epic."[22] In a later work, Palmer himself quoted and gave his approval to this formulation.[23] After he quotes my formulation about *Akhí-lāu̯os, Palmer goes on to say:

This poses the question of the function of ἄχος and λαός in the poetical tradition. His [= Nagy's] searching study brings out that the Leitmotiv 'pain, grief, distress' recurs at key points of the developing tragedy as the μῆνις of Akhilleus brought ἄλγεα on the Achaeans, as foreshadowed in the first lines of the poem. As C. H. Whitman [1958.182] has written, Homer handles his material in a 'profoundly organic' way, 'subordinating all characters to Achilles and all incidents of the Trojan War to the Wrath'. He adds that 'the Wrath of Achilles had probably been an epic subject for generations when Homer found it'.[24]

To restate my original formulation: "the ἄχος of Achilles leads to the μῆνις of Achilles leads to the ἄχος of the Achaeans."[25] As I also argued, the

21. The possibility of this derivation is raised by Chantraine DELG 862.

22. N 1976a.210. For a similar approach to the etymology of Ἀπόλλων / Ἀπέλλων, see the following chapter.

23. Palmer 1979.258. Also Palmer 1980.37 and 98. Neither work is mentioned by Holland 1993.

24. Palmer 1979.258. For a definitive work on the μῆνις of Akhilles, see now Muellner 1996.

25. N 1976a.216 (see n9 above). This article includes a thematic analysis of μῆνις in the

ἄχος experienced by warriors in the epic *Dichtersprache* is formulaically the converse of κράτος: that is, the λαός or 'host of fighting men' is conventionally described as having κράτος when they win, ἄχος when they lose.[26] It is crucial to note in this context Benveniste's demonstration that the semantics of κράτος are driven by a "zero-sum" mentality: the very fact that one of two sides gets κράτος necessitates that this side is thereby the winner and the other side, the loser.[27] Moreover, the thematic polarity of κράτος / ἄχος is mirrored by the morphological parallelism of Ἀχαιός / κραταιός, embedded in the formulaic system of the Homeric *Dichtersprache*, and the very name of the λαός, that is, the Ἀχαιοί, is synchronically derived from ἄχος—at least, within the framework of this *Dichtersprache*.[28]

How, then, could it happen that the naming of this host of fighting men was driven by a negative concept, as encoded in the word ἄχος? My answer centered on both the ritual and the mythological aspects of warfare, *as viewed within the epic tradition*.[29] Palmer asks a similar question about the naming of a hero like Achilles: it can only happen, he answers, if the very idea of **Akhí-lāu̯os*, 'whose λαός has ἄχος' had been generated by the themes of myth.[30]

And yet the name of Achilles is "attractively identified," as Palmer puts it, in the Linear B tablets: in the text of Pylos tablet Fn 70.2, a list of names in the dative includes *a-ki-re-we*, to be read as *Akhil(l)ēwei*.[31] As I commented on this attestation, "we must be ready to assume that the mythopoeic name of Ἀχιλ(λ)εύς inspired the naming of historical figures called Ἀχιλ(λ)εύς."[32] Palmer comments on my comment: "In fact, it is at the very least unlikely that any parent would have bestowed such a name on his son unless its

---

Homeric *Iliad*, where I argued that "the theme of Achilles' anger is singled out by the composition as the most central and hence most pervasive in the Iliadic tradition" (p. 211) and that the Homeric deployment of μῆνις indicates "a distinctive Iliadic association of this word with all the epic events that resulted from Achilles' anger against Agamemnon, the most central of which is the devastation [ἄλγεα] suffered by the Achaeans" (pp. 211–212). When I rewrote my arguments about Homeric μῆνις in *BA* 72–74, I adduced the important etymological and thematic observations of Watkins 1977 (that article does not mention the relevant thematic observations in N 1976a.211–212, 215–217).

26. N 1976a.216–232. Expanded version in *BA* 69–93.

27. Benveniste 1969 II 76–77; cf. *BA* 79–83.

28. *BA* 83–93.

29. *BA* 83–93. Cf. also *BA* 94–117 on the Homeric use of ἄχος and πένθος, both meaning 'grief', as programmatic indicators of ritual songs of lament (especially pp. 99–100 on *Odyssey* δ 220).

30. Palmer 1979.258.

31. Palmer 1979.258.

32. Palmer 1979.258.

inauspicious overtones had been masked by its occurrence as a heroic name in a famous story."[33] If Palmer's "chain of reasoning," as he calls it, is correct, "then the Pylian record may be construed as implying that a version of the 'Wrath of Akhilleus' was current at the time of the destruction of Pylos."[34]

All this is not to rule out an etymological connection, proposed by Holland, between the intermediate reconstructed Greek form *Ἀχιλος and "proto-Germanic" *Agilaz, from which the Old Norse name Egill can be derived.[35] Still, even though Holland allows for the possibility of an earlier reconstructed Greek form *Akhí-lāu̯os, the acceptance of a Germanic cognate *Agilaz leaves us with morphological as well as semantic problems that are unresolved.[36] In another connection, Palmer once called attention to "the first rule of etymology," attributed to Franz Skutsch: "Look for Latin etymologies first on the Tiber."[37] That "rule" is applicable to the name of Achilles.

33. Palmer 1979.258.

34. Palmer 1977.258–259. Moreover, there is an attestation of *a-ki-re-u*, to be read as *Akhilleus*, in Knossos-tablet Vc 106.

35. Holland 1993.25.

36. I am not persuaded by Holland's argument, p. 26, that ἄχος at *Iliad* XIII 86 and 417 is to be interpreted as 'fear', not 'grief'.

37. Palmer 1963b.90–91; cf. 1963a.187.

CHAPTER 7

The Name of Apollo:
Etymology and Essence

The etymology of Apollo's name, *Apóllōn*, has defied linguistic reconstruction for a long time.[1] A breakthrough came with a 1975 article by Walter Burkert, where he proposes that the Doric form of the name, *Apéllōn*, be connected with the noun *apéllai*, designating a seasonally recurring festival—an assembly or *thing*, in Germanic terms—of Dorian kinship groups.[2] The linguistic principles underlying Burkert's proposal have been definitively restated in a posthumously published work by Alfred Heubeck, who shows that the earliest recoverable form of the name is **apeli̯ōn*, built on a noun shaped **apeli̯a*: thus the meaning would be something like 'he of the assembly'.[3] The point of departure for my presentation is a Cypriote byform of Apollo's name, *Apeílōn* (to-i-a-pe-lo-ni = τῶι Ἀπείλωνι), showing the earlier e-vocalism as opposed to the innovative o-vocalism of *Apóllōn*.[4]

* The original version of this essay is N 1994b. From *Apollo: Etymology and Essence*, edited by Jon Solomon. © 1994 The Arizona Board of Regents. Reprinted by permission of the University of Arizona Press.

1. *DELG* 98.

2. Burkert 1975, especially p. 10.

3. Heubeck 1987. Particularly useful is his discussion, at p. 181, of the Pamphylian byforms of Apollo's name. Heubeck also surveys other attempts at explaining the etymology since the publication of Burkert's article.

4. For the attestation of the Cypriote form, see Masson 1983 no. 215b4; for a linguistic analysis, see Heubeck 1987.180–181.

Following up on a suggestion that I heard *viva voce* many years ago from Leonard Muellner, I propose to connect the name of Apollo, with recourse to this Cypriote by-form, to the Homeric noun *apeilḗ*, meaning 'promise, boastful promise, threat', and to the corresponding verb, *apeiléō* 'make a promise, boastful promise, threat'.[5] Offering arguments in support of this connection, I hope to show that the meaning of these forms *apeilḗ* and *apeiléō* is based on the concept of a speech-act, and that this concept dovetails with the meaning of *apéllai*, based on an actual context of speech-acts. Such dovetailing helps explain the essence of Apollo, 'he of the *apeliạ*', as the god of authoritative speech, the one who presides over all manner of speech-acts, including the realms of songmaking in general and poetry in particular.

Let us begin by reexamining the concept of a speech-act within the framework of archaic Greek society. In his 1989 book, *The Language of Heroes*, Richard Martin shows how Homeric narrative actually recovers, albeit in stylized form, the contexts of speech-acts such as formal boasts, threats, prophecies, prayers, laments, invectives.[6] The term "speech-act" derives from the theories of J. L. Austin and J. R. Searle concerning the performative aspects of language.[7] A speech-act, according to Austin and Searle, entails a situation where the antithesis of word and action is neutralized, in that the word *is* the action. When Diomedes utters a boast concerning his heroic identity in *Iliad* Ξ 126–127, to cite just one example, his self-praise is not just a set of words spoken by a Homeric character and quoted by Homeric narrative: it is a speech-act, brought to life by the narrative.[8] As Martin shows, a prime word used in Homeric diction to designate any such speech-act is *mûthos*, as in the example at hand concerning the boast of Diomedes (Ξ 126). Greek *mûthos* is the ancestor of our English word "myth." In Homeric diction, this Greek word *mûthos* reveals "myth" in its fullest meaning—not narrowly in the sense of made-up stories that are the opposite of empirical truth but broadly in the sense of traditional narratives that convey a given society's truth-values.[9]

The semantics of *mûthos* bring to life, in microcosm, the relationship between myth and ritual, word and action, in ancient Greek society.[10] In order to grasp the full meaning of *mûthos*, let us consider the distinction between marked and unmarked speech—to use the terminology of Prague

5. Muellner's original suggestion is recorded *en passant* in *BA* 43.
6. Martin 1989, especially pp. 12–42.
7. See Austin 1962 and Searle 1979.
8. Martin 1989.25.
9. *PH* 31–32.
10. *HQ* 128.

School linguistics.[11] We find that marked speech occurs as a rule in ritual contexts, as we can observe most clearly in the least complex or smallest-scale societies.[12] It is also in such societies that we can observe most clearly the symbiosis of ritual and myth, and how the language of ritual and myth is marked, while "everyday" language is unmarked.[13] So also with *mûthos* 'myth': this word, it has been argued, had at an earlier stage meant 'special speech' as opposed to "everyday" speech.[14]

From an anthropological point of view, "myth" is indeed "special speech" in that it is a given society's way of affirming its own reality. Edmund Leach offers a particularly useful synthesis:

> The various stories [i.e., the myths of a given society] form a *corpus*. They lock in together to form a single theological-cosmological-[juridical] whole. Stories from one part of the corpus presuppose a knowledge of stories from all other parts. There is implicit cross-reference from one part to another. It is an unavoidable feature of storytelling that events are made to happen one after another, but in cross-reference, such sequence is ignored. It is as if the whole corpus referred to a single instant of time, namely, the present moment.[15]

The Homeric sense of *mûthos*, in Martin's working definition, is "a speech-act indicating authority, performed at length, *usually in public* [italics mine], with a focus on full attention to every detail."[16] In fact, Homeric diction regularly associates *mûthos* with the verb *agoreúō* 'speak in public'.[17] There is a parallelism between this sense of *mûthos* and the sense of *apéllai* as 'public assembly' (Hesychius s.v. ἀπέλλαι· σηκοί, ἐκκλησίαι, ἀρχαιρεσίαι).[18] The **apelia* that gives Apollo his name is the context, as it were, of performing a *mûthos*. This implicit relationship between *mûthos* and the noun **apelia* as reflected in *apéllai* is made explicit in Homeric usage, if indeed the noun *apeilé* 'promise, boastful promise, threat' and the corresponding verb, *apeiléō* 'make a promise, boastful promise, threat' are formally related to *apéllai*. I cite the following Homeric collocation of *mûthos* and *apeiléō*:

11. *HQ* 128. Cf. Waugh 1982.
12. *PH* 31–32.
13. *PH* 31–32. Cf. Ben-Amos 1976.
14. N 1982; also *PH* 31–32.
15. Leach 1982.5. Cf. *HQ* 130–131.
16. Martin 1989.12.
17. Martin 1989.37.
18. See also Plutarch *Lycurgus* 6 and the other testimonia assembled at Tyrtaeus F 4 W. See also Burkert 1975.9, 16–17.

Ἀτρείωνα δ' ἔπειτα χόλος λάβεν, αἶψα δ' ἀναστὰς
ἠπείλησεν μῦθον, ὃ δὴ τετελεσμένος ἐστί

Iliad A 837–838

Then an anger took hold of the son of Atreus, and straightaway he stood
up
and boastfully promised [verb *apeiléō*] a *mū̃thos*,[19] which now has come
to fulfillment [= verb *teléō*, from noun *télos* 'fulfillment'].

In such contexts, the word *apeiléō* designates the actual performance of a
speech-act, a *mū̃thos*, while the word *teléō*, derivative of *télos* 'fulfillment'
guarantees that the speech-act is really a speech-act, in that the course of
events, which amounts to actions emanating from the speech-act, bears out
the speech-act. We may compare the Homeric instances where *apeiléō* can
be translated as 'vow' in the context of prayers addressed to gods (*Iliad* Ψ
863, 892).[20] In such cases the course of events in the future is predicated on
the value of the words spoken as a speech-act: if a god hears a prayer, then
the words spoken as prayer are a speech-act, and then the actions promised
by the one who prays can bear out the speech-act. Conversely, it is implicit
that if a god does not hear a prayer, then the words spoken as prayer are not
really a prayer: they turn out to have been not a speech-act after all, and the
actions promised by the one who intended a prayer need not be carried out.
I submit that the god who primarily presides over speech-acts, which are
then ratified by the actual course of events, is Apollo. It is for this reason that
he presides over oracles, including the great Oracle at Delphi.[21]

Ironically, the god who promises the fulfillment, the *télos*, of his own
speech-acts, is himself the incarnation of promise, not fulfillment. As we
see clearly from the Hesiodic *Theogony*, the lineage of purebred Olympian
gods comes to a halt, for all practical purposes, at the third generation,
with Zeus staying on as permanent executive of the universe. Once the
third generation is reached, the Olympian gods of this generation go on
propagating themselves by mating with mortals, not with each other. Mortal
genes, as it were, are dominant, while immortal ones are recessive, in that any
element of mortality in a lineage produces mortal offspring.[22] Thus all the

19. Cf. the comments of Martin p. 22.

20. On the subject of prayers as reported by Homeric narrative, see in general Muellner
1976.

21. On the role of Apollo's Oracle at Delphi as an implicit truth-value of Herodotean
narrative, see *PH* 215–249.

22. The topic of an enforced mortality for heroes is explored in *BA* 333–347.

progeny of third-generation Olympian gods is destined to be mortal. One of the few major exceptions to the short-circuiting of Olympian genetic self-perpetuation at the stage of the third generation is the god Apollo, fathered on the immortal Leto by the immortal Zeus. Burkert draws attention to the fact that Apollo is conventionally represented as beardless and unshorn, looking like an *éphēbos* 'ephebe', that is, a pre-adult male.[23] Unlike human pre-adult males, however, the god Apollo is a permanent ephebe. Unlike human males, he will never take over from his father.

The basic ephebism of Apollo can be connected with the semantics of *apéllai*. As Burkert points out, the feast of the *apéllai* at Delphi is technically a "Feast of Ephebes."[24] Moreover, we may consider the wording of the so-called Great Rhetra of Sparta, attributed to Lycurgus the lawgiver: ὥρας ἐξ ὡρᾶν ἀπελλάζειν 'to hold assemblies [*apéllai*], season [*hórā*] after season [*hórā*]' (Plutarch *Lycurgus* 6).[25] In this case the theme of seasonality, as conveyed by *hórā* 'season', can be connected with the celebration of young boys' coming of age, that is, of human seasonality, on the occasion of the *apéllai* of Delphi.[26] Moreover, the same theme can be connected with the very essence of the hero in archaic Greece, if indeed the *hórā* 'season' is etymologically connected not only with *Hérā*, the name of the goddess of seasonality, but also with *hérōs* 'hero'.[27] As we see most clearly in the case of Herakles = *Hēraklées* 'he who has the *kléos* of Hera', the Greek hero is unseasonal, off-balance, in terms of the myth that tells his or her story, and becomes seasonal, balanced, only with the completion of the myth, with the full telling of the story; the full narrative is realized in the hero's death, whether or not that aspect of the myth, the hero's death, is explicit in any individual narration.[28] Just as Apollo's ephebism embodies the god's promise, not fulfillment, so also the word *hérōs* conveys the promise of seasonality for the hero. It is no accident, I submit, that the premier hero of Greek epic, Achilles, shares in the ephebic features of Apollo: like the god, he wears his hair long—till the final moment of his realization, through the death of Patroklos, of his own self-fulfillment in death (*Iliad* Ψ140–153).[29] Observing such parallelisms between hero and god, Burkert has remarked that Achilles

23. Burkert 1975.18–19. For a basic work on the Greek concept of the ephebe, see Vidal-Naquet 1981, updated 1986.

24. Burkert 1975.11.

25. On which see Burkert 1975.9.

26. Detailed documentation and comparisons in Burkert 1975.10.

27. See the discussion by Pötscher 1961; further discussion by Householder and Nagy 1972.50–52. Further bibliography in *HQ* 47–48n79.

28. See Davidson 1980.197–202.

29. *BA* 142–144.

is a *Doppelgänger*, as it were, of Apollo.[30] In this light, it is also no accident that Achilles, like Apollo, is a singer of songs (*Iliad* I 186–191).

With these considerations in mind, I return to my argument that Apollo, 'he of the **apelia*', is the god of authoritative speech, the one who presides over all manner of speech-acts. For Austin and Searle, as we have seen, a speech-act is a situation where the antithesis of word and action is neutralized, in that the word *is* the action. Here I invoke Barbara Johnson's application of Austin's notion of speech-act to poetry—an application that Austin himself resisted.[31] This application is taken even further in Richard Martin's book, which applies the notion of speech-act to the oral performance of oral poetry.[32] The *mûthos* of Homeric poetry is not just any speech-act reported by poetry: it is also the speech-act of poetry itself, as also of song in general.[33] So also Apollo is not only the god of speech-acts: he is also the god of poetry and song. The god of eternal promise, of the eternity of potential performance, he is the word waiting to be translated into action. That is the essence of Apollo.

30. Burkert 1975.19. Cf. *BA* 143.
31. Johnson 1980.56.
32. Further discussion in *HQ* 132.
33. *HQ* 132.

CHAPTER 8

An Etymology for the Dactylic Hexameter

In his far-reaching survey of Indo-European poetics, Calvert Watkins remarks: "The origins of the Greek epic meter, the dactylic hexameter, are particularly challenging."[1] His own contribution to the ongoing debate concerning the hexameter's derivation is seminal. He writes: "I argued in passing in [Watkins] 1969 [p. 227] for a historical relation of the metrical contexts of the formula 'imperishable fame' in Greek and Vedic, and this topic was pursued in considerable detail in Nagy 1974, attacking the metrical problem via formulaics and formula boundary (typically corresponding to metrical boundary)."[2] The present inquiry pursues further the topic of metrical and formulaic boundaries, concentrating on the central question of finding a definitive etymology for the hexameter. The use of the word "etymology" will be explained at the end.

My 1974 book cited by Watkins followed methods pioneered by Milman Parry and Albert Lord.[3] My methodology combined the factors of *meter*, *formula*, and *theme* in oral traditions.[4] The alternative methods of those who

* The original version of this essay is N 1998d.
1. Watkins 1995.21.
2. Watkins 1995.21.
3. Parry 1971 = *MHV*; Lord 1960. For bibliography on Parry's and Lord's definitions of "formula" and "theme," see N 1996c.102–103.
4. N 1974; summarized in N 1979b.614–618; 1996c.100–103.

restrict their perspectives to quantitative metrics cannot succeed, I argued, in any attempt to arrive at a complete picture of the hexameter in its full diachrony.

As a metrical problem, the question of the hexameter's "origin" has led to a variety of proposed solutions. Watkins points to an outline of archaic Greek meters by West as a key to the answer.[5] But then he cautions: "The precise details of the origin of the hexameter still remain a matter of debate."[6] He mentions in passing the articles of Berg and Tichy as examples of alternative solutions.[7]

I propose to examine West's proposed solution for the derivation of the hexameter, which I will contrast with the solution that I proposed.[8] To begin, I draw attention to a basic contrast in linguistic perspectives. For West, as also for Berg and Tichy, the derivation of the dactylic hexameter is a question of *meter*.[9] For me, to repeat, it has to be a question of *meter* and *formula* and even *theme*.

The thesis of my 1974 book about the meters and formulas and themes of the hexameter can be summed up in this brief formulation: "the formula is a phrase that is diachronically generated by the theme which it expresses and synchronically regulated by the meter in which it is contained."[10] Similar arguments have been applied by Watkins to Indo-European poetics in general, summarized in the sections entitled "Formula and theme" and "Metrics" in his 1995 book.[11] His brief introductory section on "Metrics" concludes with this remark: "The quantitative metrics of Greek and Vedic, quite possibly reflecting a late dialectal protolanguage, will receive no further discussion in the present work."[12] Given the wealth of Indo-European evidence that Watkins successfully adduces throughout the rest of his book by way of combining the factors of meter and formula and theme, I take his

5. Watkins 1995.21, referring to West 1982.29–56.

6. Watkins 1995.21.

7. Berg 1978, Tichy 1981a and 1981b. See Magnelli 1996 for a brief survey of the explanatory models offered by Berg, Tichy, West, and myself. The list of other views that Magnelli surveys includes those of Campanile, Cantilena, Fernández Delgado, Gentili, Hoekstra, Hoenigswald, Horrocks, Itsumi, Ivanov, Jahn, Janko, Latacz, Peabody, Ritoók, Ruijgh, Sicking, Visser, and Vigorita.

8. My solution as published in N 1974 is supplemented in a later work, N 1979b, which offers a new dimension to the earlier solution.

9. See especially Magnelli 1996.123 on Berg's model.

10. N 1979b.617, reexamined in N 1996c.102.

11. Watkins 1995.16–19 and 19–21 respectively.

12. Watkins 1995.21.

remark as an implicit recognition of the relative impoverishment of metrical models that ignore the factors of formula and theme.[13]

Keeping in mind the interrelationship of meter with formula and theme, I propose to re-examine briefly the question of metrical and formulaic boundaries in the archaic Greek dactylic hexameter, especially in the hexameters of the Homeric *Iliad* and *Odyssey*. A convenient point of departure is the formulation of Daitz concerning the observance of pauses and non-pauses in the reading of Homeric hexameters. He advocates the reading of Homer (1) with pauses at verse-final position, regardless of enjambment and other factors, and (2) generally without pauses at verse-medial positions, regardless of caesura, diaeresis, and other factors.[14]

By "enjambment" I mean a syntactical runover from one verse to the next. By (1) "caesura" and (2) "diaeresis" I mean a word-break that is found respectively (1) within a foot and (2) between one foot and the next one. The "foot" in the dactylic hexameter is a quantitative sequence of one heavy syllable (–) followed by two light syllables ($\cup$ $\cup$), with the option of substituting – for $\cup$ $\cup$.

I propose that the formulation offered by Daitz, with modifications to be taken up below, needs to be extended. The question is not only how Homeric poetry was read but how it was performed and even how it was composed. The answer involves the patterning of metrical and formulaic boundaries in the hexameter.[15]

On the surface, the dactylic hexameter of Homeric poetry can be described in general terms as a self-contained syntactical unit. Allen quotes the observation of Kirk: "[the Homeric hexameter] tends to be more or less self-contained in meaning; its ending usually coincides with a major or minor *pause*, the end of a sentence or clause or at least the point at which a predicate is divided from its subject" (italics mine).[16] As Allen notes, similar observations can be made about other basic metrical units, such as the Latin Saturnian and the Indic *pāda*.[17]

Observations of this sort have led to the common assumption that there must have been a "pause" at the end of hexameter simply because there is a universal tendency for pauses to mark the end of basic syntactical units. Such an assumption is evident in the formulation of Lejeune as summarized by West: "[Lejeune] holds that a syllable followed by a *pause*, at verse-end

13. On theme and thematics, see already N 1974.229–261.
14. Daitz 1991. See now N 2000e.
15. Again, N 2000e.
16. Allen 1973.113 quoting Kirk 1962.60.
17. Allen 1973.113, with bibliography.

or in ordinary speech at sentence-end, has no definite quantity, because its duration is not 'limitée par l'attaque d'une syllabe suivante'" (italics mine).[18] West extends this formulation further by treating pause not only as a neutralizer of distinctness between long and short syllables but also as a generalizer that turns all verse-end shorts into longs: "I see no reason not to treat its [= the verse-end syllable's] duration as being what it would have been if another consonant+vowel had followed."[19] Still, his assumption appears to be essentially the same as that of Lejeune: that syntactical pause at verse-end causes metrical pause.

There is a basic question that arises from such an assumption: what, then, are we to make of a syntactical pause marked by a caesura or a diaeresis instead of a verse-end? Can a caesura or a diaeresis also cause a metrical pause? After all, a caesura or a diaeresis can coincide—much like a verse-end—with syntactical pause.[20]

A related question concerns the concept of the *colon* as demarcated by caesuras and diaereses. According to the colon-theory of Hermann Fränkel (1955), the hexameter is actually built by cola, with each hexameter comprised of four cola demarcated by an "A/B/C" pattern of word-breaking (four kinds of A, two kinds each of B and C):

$$- \, \| \, \cup \, \| \, \cup \, \| \, - \, \| \, \cup \, \cup \, - \, \| \, \cup \, \| \, \cup \, - \, \| \, \cup \, \cup \, \| \, - \, \cup \, \cup \, - \, \times$$

A1	A2	A3	A4		B1	B2		C1	C2

Something essential is missing in this picture. There is a "#" to be placed immediately after "×" (= the last syllable of the line, of indeterminate syllabic quantity). It is easy to forget that the metrical boundaries of these "cola" in the hexameter are not only (1) "‖" = caesura or diaeresis but also (2) "#" = the boundary for the end of the verse, which of course becomes *ipso facto* the boundary for the beginning of the next verse. The sequence of boundaries is ...A...B...C...#...A...B...C...#...A...B...C...# etc.

There is a vital distinction to be made here: whereas both "‖" (= A or B or C) and "#" can be markers of an optional pause in the syntax of the hexameter, only "#" may be described as the marker of an obligatory pause in the meter of the hexameter. In sum, the term "metrical pause" is appropriate only for verse-end, but it is inappropriate for a caesura (Fränkel's A1, A2, A4, B1, B2, C1) or for a diaeresis (A3, C2).

There are further qualifications to be made as we follow through on the

18. Lejeune 1955.259, 299, summarized by West 1982.9.

19. West 1982.9.

20. Cf. West 1982.36, with a map of "sense-pauses" marked by caesura, diaeresis, and verse-end in the hexameter.

assumption that syntactical pause causes metrical pause. Having addressed the basic question concerning syntactical pause as marked by a caesura or a diaeresis, we may proceed to some related questions concerning syntactical non-pause as marked by enjambment. Are we to consider the phenomenon of enjambment, especially the kind that is "necessary" from a syntactical point of view, to be a metrical irregularity? Since there is no syntactical pause in cases of "necessary" enjambment, are we to assume that there is no metrical pause in such cases? Further, are we to assume that syntactical non-pause at verse-end actually causes metrical non-pause?

Anticipating my conclusions, I propose that syntactical pause can be invoked as *causing* metrical pause at verse-end only if we take an exclusively diachronic point of view. From the synchronic point of view, metrical pause is independent of syntax.[21] A case in point is the phenomenon of necessary enjambment, where an obligatory metrical pause marked by verse-end (#) may intervene in the syntax without creating a syntactical pause in the transition from one verse to the next.[22] The work of Higbie (1990), Bakker (1990), and Clark (1994 and 1997) has proved that Homeric enjambment—including the "necessary" kind—is synchronically intrinsic, not extrinsic, to the formulaic system of Homeric diction.[23]

Conversely, again from the synchronic point of view, syntactical pause is independent of meter. A case in point is the phenomenon of the caesura or diaeresis, where an optional syntactical pause marked by verse-medial word-break (‖) may intervene in the meter without creating a metrical pause in the flow of the rhythm within the hexameter. To be more precise: a caesura or a diaeresis may optionally mark a syntactical pause, but it does not at the same time mark a metrical pause—in the sense of a pause in the flow of the rhythm.[24]

<u>Examples</u> ("#" = verse-initial / verse-final position; "‖" = caesura or diaeresis):

1 Metrical pause at verse-final position, regardless of syntactical non-pause (= enjambment): . . .ἠελίοιο # ἤσθιον . . . at *Odyssey* α 8–9. If there were no metrical pause at #, then the hiatus would not be allowed.[25] I suggest that there is a related phenomenon to be found in the observance of "movable

21. N 2000e.
22. See N 1974.120–35, with striking examples from lyric meters.
23. For a particularly useful sketch, see Bakker 1997a.149–155.
24. N 2000e.
25. Cf. Daitz 1991.152. Cf. also Higbie 1990.28 and 59n1 on non-elision between verses in Homeric diction.

v" at verse-final position in Ptolemaic papyri—regardless of what follows in verse-initial position.[26]

2 No metrical pause at verse-medial position, regardless of syntactical pause at caesura or diaeresis: χαλκοῦ τε χρυσοῦ τ᾽ ἀπολύσομεθ᾽. ‖ ἔστι γὰρ ἔνδον at *Iliad* X 50 (the A[t] scholia give ἀπολύσομεν). Compare βάλλ᾽· ‖ αἰεὶ δὲ … at *Iliad* A 52. This example has prompted the following remark: "A pause of one mora after βάλλ᾽ will have the effect of adding a syllable to the line, defeating the purpose of the elision."[27] We may compare also πλάγχθη· ‖ ἐπεὶ … at *Odyssey* α 2: a metrical pause would have canceled the correption (that is, the shortening of word-final vowel by way of juxtaposition with a succeeding word-initial vowel).[28]

Such examples of syntactical pauses at "‖" and of syntactical non-pauses at "#" point to a major problem with Fränkel's concept of the four-colon hexameter as the primary shaper of Homeric diction. Although his "A/B/C" system of caesurae and diaereses provides an elegant taxonomy for patterns of word-breaking within the metrical framework of the dactylic hexameter, it does not account for the actual mechanics of formulaic composition, which extend beyond that framework. Rather, it merely describes the surface conditions of word-placement within the hexameter.

It is essential to re-assess Fränkel's concept in light of Parry's demonstration that Homeric diction was built by a system of formulas. Within the larger context of this system of formulas, as Parry's work makes clear, there is a synchronic correlation of "#" and of "‖" with formulaic junctures in Homeric diction. Rossi (1965) and others have attempted to reconcile Parry's model of a formulaic system with Fränkel's model, which holds that Homeric diction was built by a system of four "cola" conditioned by the "A/B/C" patterning of "‖." Such attempts cannot succeed, in my opinion, if they are to be based

26. On the possibility that it was Aristarchus who initiated the new editorial policy of omitting verse-final movable ν, see S. West 1967.17, with further references. I think it is relevant that Aristarchus was relatively uninterested in the performance traditions of Homeric poetry, preferring instead to edit the Homeric paradosis as if it were a text originally written by Homer: see *PP* 130, 150–152.

27. Daitz 1991.155.

28. The stance of Aristarchus, as outlined in n26 above, helps explain the attitude of the later scholar Nicanor (fragments edited by Friedländer 1850), whose system for punctuating the Homeric text rules out the factor of performance. Cf. Daitz 1991.150, who shows that the various "morae" that Nicanor posits at syntactical pauses, especially at syntactical pauses marked by a caesura or a diaeresis, make it impossible for a performer / reader to maintain the rhythm of the hexameter. On Nicanor's system of morae, reflecting purely syntactical considerations rather than any sort of performative pause, see Blank 1983.

on the view that the meter of the hexameter actually generated the formulaic system of Homeric diction. Such a view shapes the theory of Rossi.[29]

My counter-theory about meter and formula in the hexameter can be summarized by way of three main points:[30]

1   From a diachronic point of view, meter is a result rather than a cause of traditional phraseology.

2   From a synchronic point of view, however, meter *contains* or *frames* the traditional phraseology that we call formulas. Further, "recent metrical developments may even obliterate aspects of the selfsame traditional phraseology that had engendered them, if these aspects no longer match the meter."[31]

3   As we switch from the diachronic perspective to the synchronic, the factor of *containing* is reversed: traditional phraseology contains rhythms that evolve into meters (diachronic perspective), and meters contain traditional phraseology that we call formulas (synchronic perspective).[32] Some of these formulas may preserve rhythmical patterns that had shaped the meters that now contain the formulas.[33]

Rossi rejects what he describes as "genetic" models of explaining the dynamics of Homeric hexameter.[34] As examples of "questa via genetica," he cites my model (N 1974, 1979b, 1992 = 1996c) and that of Gentili (1977 = 1996; with Giannini 1977). I object to Rossi's application of the term "genetic." Rather, my model combines the synchronic perspective with the diachronic.[35] As for Rossi's own model, it contains an implicitly "genetic" dimension of its own: by arguing that the dactylic hexameter, as analyzed by Fränkel, was and always had been the near-exclusive shaper of the Homeric system of formulas, he is in effect implying that the genesis of the Homeric

29. Rossi 1996.313. See Magnelli 1996.123–124 for a survey of other theories shaped by this view. An extreme example is Hoekstra 1981.33–53.

30. N 1996c.103.

31. N 1974.145. It goes without saying that meter, in any given historical situation, may even be extraneous to formula. For an extreme example, we may consider situations where the system of metrics is borrowed by one language from another: cf. Allen 1973.15.

32. For an illuminating discussion entitled "From Rhythm to Meter," see Bakker 1997a.146–155.

33. N 1974.140–149.

34. Rossi 1996.313–314.

35. I also object to the way in which my model is described by Gentili 1977 = 1996.35: his use of the word *priorità* (he says that one cannot establish "priority" between formula and meter) blurs the distinctions that I make between diachronic and synchronic perspectives.

formula as a phraseological system is to be traced back to the dactylic hexameter as a metrical system.

In the context of disputing "genetic" solutions in general, Rossi specifically rejects models that explain the hexameter in terms of a combination of two cola, as opposed to Fränkel's four-colon model.[36] It seems to me evident that Rossi is referring here to the formulation of Gentili,[37] who follows, with qualifications, the two-colon model of West.[38] Gentili speaks consistently of "cola" as the constituents of the hexameter.[39] In terms of his argument, these "cola" are derived from the "cola" attested in the meters of (1) archaic Greek verse-inscriptions and (2) archaic choral lyric poetry, especially the songs of Stesichorus.

Let us look more closely at the two-colon model as most recently outlined by West.[40] He starts with an eight-syllable lyric "colon" shaped $\times - \cup \cup - \cup$ $\cup \times$, and he posits two kinds of juxtaposition.

B1: $(\times) - \cup \cup - \cup \cup (\times) \# \times - \cup \cup - \cup \cup - \times$
B2: $(\times) - \cup \cup - \cup \cup - \times \# \times - \cup \cup - \cup \cup - \times$

I label the two kinds of juxtaposition "B1" and "B2" because West's intent is to make them correspond respectively to the main caesura patterns of hexameter, labeled B1 and B2 in Fränkel's scheme. There are problems, however, in making the numbers of syllables "add up" to the B1 and B2 patterns of hexameter. West is forced to cancel, without diachronic justification, the "$\times$" in three different places, as marked by the instances of parenthesized "$(\times)$" above. There are also problems in deriving hexameter sequence ... $- \parallel \cup \cup$ $- \ldots$ from West's posited sequence ... $- \parallel \times - \ldots$ (B1). Similarly, there are problems in deriving hexameter sequence ... $- \cup \parallel \cup \ldots$ from West's posited sequence ... $- \times \parallel \times \ldots$ (B2).

West's ingredient for the hexameter's "origin," the colon $\times - \cup \cup - \cup \cup - \times$, is a basic unit of dactylo-epitrite meters, still attested in the songs of the choral lyric poet Stesichorus (also in the songs of Pindar and Bacchylides, though their metrical systems are not nearly as archaic). A fundamental work on the dactylo-epitrite meters of Stesichorus is an article by Haslam (1978). As Watkins notes, Haslam is "assuming that it [= the metrical system of Stesichorus] was a development of the hexameter; but later West 1982:29–

---

36. Rossi 1996.314.
37. Gentili 1977 = 1996.31–32.
38. Gentili 1977 = 1996.31n56, citing West 1973.169n10.
39. Gentili 1977 = 1996.31–33; cf. Giannini 1977 = Gentili 1996.42.
40. West 1996.236.

56 showed that the hexameter could be derived from the Stesichorean line, and that this poet provided the critical link between choral lyric and epic."[41] More could have been said here. West's proposed solution is not the only one, and there may be preferable alternatives.

For my part, I prefer the arguments I presented in my 1979 article, where I proposed that some of the phraseology framed by the choral lyric meters of Stesichorus is cognate with some of the phraseology framed by the epic hexameter.[42] My 1979 arguments for a metrical *and* formulaic link between epic and choral lyric were later developed into the book *Pindar's Homer* (1990), containing an Appendix that offers a diachronic sketch of all metrical and formulaic components of epic and choral lyric.[43]

Although I disagree with Rossi's model, I agree with his main objection to the two-colon model proposed by West and followed in part by Gentili. West's scheme does not explain how a combination of two cola ever became a single unified metrical frame, the dactylic hexameter. My objection to the model of West applies even more to that of Gentili, who posits not only one combination of two "cola" but also many other combinations of other "cola": somehow, all of these different combinations of cola in different shapes and sizes are supposed to come together and become, here again, a single unified metrical frame, the dactylic hexameter. I infer that Gentili considers his own model "polygenetic," in view of his opposition to what he calls "soluzioni monogenetiche."[44] The scenario of polygenesis, a variation on West's model of bipartite genesis, makes it even harder to explain the synchronic metrical unity of the historically attested dactylic hexameter.

The alternative model that I offer, however, is not "monogenetic." It is

41. Watkins 1995.21. The two-colon model is evident from the discussion in West 1982.35–39.

42. N 1979b, especially p. 627.

43. *PH* 439–464 is the Appendix. The electronic publication of these printed pages is an improved version of this Appendix, because several typographical errors have been corrected: http://www.press.jhu.edu/books/nagy/PHTL/appendix.html. There is also a printed publication that incorporates these corrections and that recapitulates the results of all my work on formula and meter in epic and in choral lyric, N 1996c. For the record, I list here the corrigenda for the printed version of my Appendix to *Pindar's Homer*: p. 452 line 17, "D+D" not "B+D"; p. 459n108 line 2/ 1st metrical string, −∪∪−∪∪−x−∪∪−∪∪−− not −∪∪−∪∪x−∪∪−∪∪−− (x = "anceps"); p. 459n108 line 2 / 2nd metrical string, -uu-uu-n-uu-uu-- not -uu-uun-uu-uu-- (n = "anceps" *or* "biceps"/"macron"); p. 459n108 line 5, delete "IV 202,"; p. 459n108 line 6 / 2nd metrical string, −∪∪−∪∪−x−∪∪−∪∪−− not −∪∪−∪∪x−∪∪−∪∪−−; p. 459n108 line 9 / last metrical string, the initial o should be x; p. 463 line 13, delete the initial ∪∪−; p. 463n123 line 2, ἁλμυρὸν not ἄλμυρον; p. 463n123 line 3, ἁλμυρὸς not ἄλμυρος; p. 463n123 line 5, "ὕδωρ displaces πόντος" not "πόντος displaces ὕδωρ"; p. 464 line 1, "~*" not "*~."

44. Gentili 1977 = 1996.34.

not even "genetic," as I noted earlier, inasmuch as it combines a synchronic perspective with the diachronic. Applying as a metaphor the word *monophuḗs* 'single' in the botanical sense of describing a tree or herb with a single stem (Theophrastus *Historia Plantarum* 2.6.9, Dioscorides 4.114), I propose "monophysis" as a term for describing the synchronic reality of the hexameter as a singular and unitary metrical frame, in contrast to Gentili's "polygenesis." On the other hand, "polygenesis" is an apt term for explaining the diachronic reality represented by the vast variety of formulas, in all their different shapes and sizes, that are all ultimately accommodated by the unifying framework of the hexameter.

With these observations in mind, I arrive at the question: is there an etymology for the dactylic hexameter? My use of the word "etymology" in the wording of the question makes the answer difficult. This is appropriate, since the problem of the hexameter is complex and resists facile solutions. The search for etymologies entails the laborious process of linguistic reconstruction, demanding the rigorous application of all levels of linguistics—morphology and syntax as well as phonology. It also demands a combination of synchronic and diachronic perspectives. To explain the "origins" of hexameter by looking only at metrics and not at formulaics is the equivalent of arriving at an etymology by looking only at phonology and not at morphology and syntax. To ignore the synchronic point of view in the analysis of meter and formula is the equivalent of treating language merely as a mass of data, not as an integral system.

The "etymology" that I proposed for hexameter in the Appendix of my 1990 book involves both metrics and formulaics, both the synchronic and the diachronic perspectives. I offer here only a brief sketch of some of the essentials:[45]

1 The hexameter can be reconstructed as a single metrical frame, cognate with an Aeolic meter attested in the poetics of Alcaeus:

$$\times \times - \cup \cup - \cup \cup - \cup \cup - \cup \cup - \times$$

From a synchronic view of Aeolic metrics, this meter is not a distich. From a diachronic point of view, however, we may say that it evolved out of phraseology that could also produce, in other situations, metrical distichs. From a synchronic view of Homeric metrics, the hexameter is not a distich, either.[46] The common cultural perception of the hexameter in the historical context of the Classical period and later makes the unity of this meter

45. Besides the Appendix of *PH* = N 1990a, and the electronic version as cited at n43 above, I offer an overall exposition in N 1996c.

46. Still, the hexameter synchronically matches the length of a distich formally, esthetically, and even cognitively. See Bakker 1997a.148, who suggests that the hexameter,

unambiguously clear: the "hexameter" is exactly what the name says it is, a rhythmical frame that is measured in six parts—a *hexametros tonos* (Herodotus 1.47.2, 1.62.4, 5.60; cf. 5.61.1; iambic trimeter is a *trimetros tonos*: 1.174.5). The same perception could apply to the Aeolic meter from which I derive the hexameter.[47]

2 From a synchronic point of view, the formulas of Homeric diction are regulated by the metrical frame of the hexameter. From a diachronic point of view, the formulaic boundaries of Homeric diction coincide with the caesuras, diaereses, and verse-ends of the hexameter:

$$\dots \# \; - \; \| \; \cup \; \| \; \cup \; \| \; - \; \| \; \cup \; \cup \; - \; \| \; \cup \; \| \; \cup \; - \; \| \; \cup \; \cup \; \| \; - \; \cup \; \cup \; - \; \times \; \# \dots$$

A1   A2   A3   A4   B1   B2   C1   C2

3 From a diachronic point of view, the singular metrical frame of the hexameter accommodates a plurality of formulas.[48] Some of these formulas in hexameter are cognate with some of the formulas that evolved in the context of Aeolic meters. Examples include phraseology demarcated by C1___# and by B1___#.[49] Other formulas in hexameter are cognate with formulas that evolved in the context of "dactylo-epitrite" meters. Examples include phraseology demarcated by #___B1 and B2___#.[50]

4 Formulas are a synchronic reality in the traditional diction of lyric poetry, not just epic.[51] In comparing the meters of lyric and epic, the formulaic repertoires of both lyric and epic must be taken into account.[52]

My inquiry started with the argument that the principles of (1) pausing between hexameters and (2) non-pausing within hexameters need to be extended from the reading of Homer to the actual performing of Homer. For the sake of reconstructing backward in time, we must begin with the attested textual traditions of Homer, which reflect the historical context(s) of

in terms of cognitive psychology, "cannot be an original discourse unit: it is simply too long to be grasped in its entirety by the poet's and listener's consciousness."

47. On the evolution of the "Aeolic" base (= ××) into the first "foot" (= −− or −∪∪) of the hexameter, see the updated formulation in N 1996c.90.

48. On the "tricolon crescendo" effect of the pattern #___A4___C1___#, see Bakker 1997a.150–151.

49. On the application of the term "dactylic expansion" to the phenomenon exemplified by cognate phraseology shaped C1___# (shorter phrase) and B1___# (longer phrase), see N 1996c.83–85. The objections of Gentili 1977 = 1996.35–36 to my earlier analysis of "dactylic expansion" in N 1974.68–71 do not take into account the combination of synchronic and diachronic perspectives that I had applied to that phenomenon.

50. There is an extensive study of such patterns in N 1996c.

51. This is one of the basic arguments in N 1974, with detailed documentation; for a survey of examples, see N 1996c.93–94.

52. This point is missed by Hoekstra (1981.33–53) and others.

Homeric performances by rhapsodes. I have argued elsewhere that rhapsodic traditions of performance cannot be divorced from Homeric traditions of composition—if we take a diachronic point of view.[53] The diachrony of Homeric traditions involves performance, not just composition. The synchronic realities of composition-in-performance, observed by Albert Lord in living oral traditions,[54] need to be traced diachronically throughout the full historical range of Homeric performance traditions.[55] The principles of pause and non-pause in Homeric hexameter reflect these realities.

ADDENDUM

Testimonia concerning the observance of pause at verse-end (nos. 1, 3–5 after Daitz 1991):

1   Cicero *De oratore* 1.61.26l: ... et coniectis in os calculis, summa voce versus multos uno spiritu pronuntiare consuescebat '... and with pebbles inserted into his mouth, he [Demosthenes] grew accustomed to declaim, at the top of his lungs, many verses on a single breath' (tr. Daitz).

    Cf. Daitz p. 152, who argues that the regime of declaiming more than one verse in one breath implies that the normal practice was to declaim one verse with each breath.

2   In addition to the examples adduced by Daitz, we may note the following context of the Greek word *stikhos*, parallel to Latin *versus*, in Plutarch's *Life of Demosthenes* (11.1.1ff), where the same regime is described and where the source is said to be Demetrius of Phalerum *(FGH* 228 F 17), who reportedly heard Demosthenes himself tell about this regime:

> τοῖς δὲ σωματικοῖς ἐλαττώμασι τοιαύτην ἐπῆγεν ἄσκησιν, ὡς
> ὁ Φαληρεὺς Δημήτριος [*FGH* 228 F 17] ἱστορεῖ, λέγων αὐτοῦ
> Δημοσθένους ἀκοῦσαι πρεσβύτου γεγονότος· τὴν μὲν γὰρ
> ἀσάφειαν καὶ τραυλότητα τῆς γλώττης ἐκβιάζεσθαι καὶ διαρθροῦν
> εἰς τὸ στόμα ψήφους λαμβάνοντα καὶ ῥήσεις ἅμα λέγοντα, τὴν δὲ
> φωνὴν γυμνάζειν ἐν τοῖς δρόμοις καὶ ταῖς πρὸς τὰ σιμ' ἀναβάσεσι
> διαλεγόμενον καὶ λόγους τινὰς ἢ στίχους ἅμα τῷ πνεύματι
> πυκνουμένῳ προφερόμενον·

> For his physical disabilities he conducted the following regimen, as reported by Demetrius of Phalerum [*FGH* 228 F 17], who says that

53. *PP* 70–86; further arguments in *HQ*.
54. Lord 1960.
55. Cf. *HQ* Ch.2 and Ch.3.

he heard it from Demosthenes himself, who was by now an old man: that he [= Demosthenes] got under control and corrected, by way of physical training, the slur and lisp in his speech by putting pebbles into his mouth while delivering speeches, and that he exercised his voice by running and by going uphill while delivering verses within one concentrated breath.

3 Cicero *Orator* 9.4.108: ex hoc genere illud est Crassi: "missos faciant patronos; ipsi prodeant"—nisi intervallo dixisset "ipsi prodeant," sensisset profecto se fudisse senarium. 'An example of this type may be cited from Crassus: "missos ... prodeant." If he had not paused before (the words) "ipsi prodeant," he would have immediately recognized that he had produced a *senarius*' (trans. Cunningham).

   Cf. Daitz p. 154n9: "The clear implication of this passage is that the only element which identified Crassus' words as prose rather than poetry was the internal pause (*intervallum*) he had made at sense boundary. Hence we may conclude that in Cicero's time, poetry was normally not recited with internal pause at sense boundary."

4 Quintilian 9.4.93: ... in fine pro longa accipi brevem, quia videtur aliquid vacantis temporis ex eo quod insequitur accedere 'a concluding short syllable is usually regarded as equivalent to a long because the time-length which it lacks appears to be supplied from that which follows' (trans. Butler). Cf. Daitz 1991:152.

5 Quintilian 9.4.108: Sed hic est illud "inane" quod dixi: paulum enim morae damus inter ultimum atque proximum verbum (turpe duceret), et "turpe" illud intervallo quodam producimus 'This example also illustrates the "inane" I spoke of above, since we put a brief pause between the last two words (turpe duceret) and lengthen the last syllable of "turpe" by a kind of pause or delay in utterance' (trans. Cunningham). Cf. Daitz p. 154n8.

CHAPTER 9

Ellipsis in Homeric Poetry

This essay concentrates on four questions: (1) What is ellipsis? (2) How does ellipsis work in Homeric songmaking? (3) How does ellipsis typify Homeric songmaking? (4) How does Homeric songmaking use ellipsis to typify itself?

A WORKING DEFINITION

In the dictionary of Liddell and Scott, the verb *elleípō* (ἐλλείπω) is defined as (1) leave in, leave behind; (2) leave out, leave undone; (3) fall short, fail.[1] The abstract noun *élleipsis*, derived from this verb, designates a 'leaving out' of something, as we see from the use of the word in a grammatical sense: in Athenaeus 644b, for example, the term *élleipsis* (ἔλλειψις) is applied to explain the word *plakoûs* 'flatbread' as consisting of an adjective 'flat' plus substantive *ártos* 'bread' understood. That is, the substantive can be inferred *katà élleipsin* 'by ellipsis'. Where we would say "adjective with substantive understood," Athenaeus is saying "adjective with substantive by way of ellipsis."

* The original version of this essay is N 1997c.
1. LSJ 535–536.

Let us pursue the idea of "understood" elements in a given combination by highlighting the principle of the elliptic plural in ancient Greek. Ordinarily, the plural of a given entity, let us say A, will designate A + A + A + ... On the other hand, the *elliptic* plural of an entity A will designate A + B + C + ... Here are two examples:

1 τόξον [*tóxon*] 'bow' (as in *Iliad* Δ 124) vs. τόξα [*tóxa*] 'bow and arrows' (as in *Iliad* Φ 502) = 'bow + arrow + arrow + arrow + …'[2]
2 πατήρ [*patḗr*] 'father' vs. πατέρες [*patéres*] 'ancestors' = 'father + *his* father + *his* father + *his* father + …'[3]

Similarly, the elliptic dual will designate A + B, unlike the A + A of the "normal" dual. For example, Sanskrit singular *pitá* is 'father' but dual *pitárau* is not 'two fathers' but rather 'father and mother'.

What is "left out" by way of ellipsis need not be left out "for good," as it were. It may be a matter of shading over. What is shaded over in one place may be highlighted in another. In other words, the location of the ellipsis may vary: it can be at the ending, at the middle, or at the beginning of a sequence.

So far, we have seen examples of ellipsis at the beginning plus the middle or at the middle plus the ending. In the case of πατήρ [*patḗr*] 'father' vs. πατέρες [*patéres*] 'ancestors' = 'father + *his* father + *his* father + *his* father + …', for example, the father concludes a sequence of an unspecified number of ancestors, potentially starting with a first father.[4] Here I surmise that the beginning and middle are shaded over, while the ending—one's own father—is highlighted as an instance of all preceding fathers. In the case of τόξον [*tóxon*] 'bow' vs. τόξα [*tóxa*] 'bow and arrows' = 'bow + arrow + arrow + arrow + .. ', on the other hand, the bow initiates a sequence of an unspecified number of arrows, potentially ending with a last arrow. Here I surmise that the middle and ending are shaded over, while the beginning is highlighted.

Ellipsis can even highlight what is being said at the very end of a given sequence for the purpose of referring to the very beginning. For example, the ending of the first sentence of Herodotus' *History* signals the point of departure for the history: … τά τε ἄλλα καὶ δι' ἣν αἰτίην ἐπολέμησαν ἀλλήλοισι 'including all the other things [*álla*] but especially the cause for their entering into war with each other'. Each of the *álla* 'other things' is in

2. Cf. *PH* 177–178.
3. *PH* 177–178.
4. Cf. *PH* 155 and 192 (with n195) on *Peisistratídai* in the sense of 'Peisistratos + *his* son + *his* son + *his* son …'

effect an *állo* 'other thing': thus we have a sequence of *álla* = *állo* + *állo* + *állo* + ..., with the last element of the sequence referring back to the first element which had logically started the sequence of events—and which is yet to be stated by the *History*—that is, the original cause of the war about to be narrated.[5]

There is also ellipsis of the middle, the leaving out of the middle man or men, as it were. An example is the figure of the *merism*, in the sense of "a bipartite, commonly asyndetic noun phrase serving to designate globally an immediately higher taxon."[6] That is, the combination of two words can express a totality that is merely framed rather than filled by the two individual referents that match these two individual words. Thus for example the Hittite expression *ḫalkiš zíz-tar*, literally 'barley (and) wheat', designates *all* cereals, not just barley and wheat.[7] It is as if Hittite 'barley and wheat' were barley and wheat and every other kind of grain in between.

ELLIPTIC CONSTRUCTIONS IN HOMER

We turn to actual cases of ellipsis in Homeric composition. It is important to concede, from the start, that all discourse is to some extent elliptic. Still, keeping the focus on the formal mechanisms that make ellipsis possible, even explicit, I propose to offer a sample of some specific mechanisms, as attested in the *Iliad* and *Odyssey*.

It is instructive to begin with a striking example of a singular of a given noun where we might have expected the plural:

1a. ὣς ἄρα φωνήσασ᾽ ἀπέβη γλαυκῶπις Ἀθήνη	78
πόντον ἐπ᾽ ἀτρύγετον, λίπε δὲ Σχερίην ἐρατεινήν,	79
ἵκετο δ᾽ ἐς Μαραθῶνα καὶ εὐρυάγυιαν Ἀθήνην,	80
δῦνε δ᾽ Ἐρεχθῆος πυκινὸν δόμον. αὐτὰρ Ὀδυσσεὺς	81
Ἀλκινόου πρὸς δώματ᾽ ἴε κλυτά· ...	82

Speaking thus, [epithet] Athena [*Athénē*] went off	78
over the [epithet] sea, and she left behind lovely Skheria,	79
and she came to Marathon and to Athens [*Athénē*],	80
and she entered the well-built house of *Erekhtheus*.	
But Odysseus	81
went toward the renowned house of Alkinoos	82

Odyssey η 78–81

5. Cf. *PH* 218n23 and 220–221n34.
6. Watkins 1979.270 = 1994.645.
7. Watkins 1979.270.

We see here at verse 80 an exceptional attestation of the word for 'Athens' in the singular, *Athḗnē*. Elsewhere, 'Athens' is *Athḗnai*, in the plural. We see the plural form as we look ahead at text 1d below, verse 546, and we see it in general everywhere in ancient Greek literature.

As we look back at verse 80 of text 1a, we notice that this form *Athḗnē*, meaning 'Athens', is identical with the form that means 'the goddess Athene'—or Athena, in the Latinized spelling—as attested at verse 78 of text 1a and at verse 547 of text 1d. Why, then, is 'Athens' in the singular at verse 80 of text 1a? Second, can we even say that this is the same Athens that we know from later sources? Third, can we say that the plural *Athḗnai* in the sense of 'Athens' is a *functionally* elliptic construction?

Let us start with the first question, why is Athens in the singular here? On the level of surface metrical structure, we can justify the combination of singular substantive and singular epithet on the grounds that it *scans*, that is, on the grounds that it fits the metrical requirements of the dactylic hexameter, whereas the plural of this combination would clash with these requirements. If we look at text 1b, we can see what would happen if the plural of 'Athens' were slotted into the same metrical position within the dactylic hexameter and if it kept the same epithet assigned to the singular form as attested at verse 80 of text 1a:

1b.   *... εὐρυαγυίας Ἀθήνας [option canceled]

This combination is purely hypothetical (hence the prefixed asterisk) and in fact untenable for three mechanical reasons: (1) we expect the last syllable of the epithet εὐρυαγυίας to be long;[8] (2) the first syllable of the word for 'Athens' in this position has to be short; (3) the second syllable of the word for 'Athens' has to be long. These three specific reasons add up to one over-riding general reason: such a hypothetical combination of words would produce a rhythmical sequence of long + short + long (the criterion of measure is syllabic length), and this sequence is systematically shunned in Homeric diction.[9] I should add that the same idea, as expressed by this hypothetical epithet + noun combination, could indeed be expressed, *within the same metrical framework*, by another epithet + noun combination:

8. The α of accusative plural -ας in archaic (vs. innovative) situations is consistently long in Homeric diction: see Janko 1982.58–62, especially p. 61 ("the large number of older formulae with long endings that it [= the *Odyssey*] retained"); cf. *MP* 61–63.

9. *PH* 459n108. I need to correct three typographical errors in the 1990 printed version of that note (see also already p. 152n43, above): at line 2 (two times) and at line 6 (the second time), read –∪∪–∪∪–x ... not –∪∪–∪∪x ....

1c.   … εὐρυχόρους ἐς Ἀθήνας

'… to Athens, with its spacious area for song and dance'
Herodotean *Life of Homer*, par. 28

Moving to the second question, we may ask: can we even say that this 'Athens' in *Odyssey* η 80 is the same 'Athens' that we know from the historical period? The answer emerges from the next major relevant passage:

1d. οἳ δ' ἄρ' Ἀθήνας εἶχον, ἐυκτίμενον πτολίεθρον,   546
δῆμον Ἐρεχθῆος μεγαλήτορος, ὅν ποτ' Ἀθήνη   547
θρέψε Διὸς θυγάτηρ, τέκε δὲ ζείδωρος ἄρουρα   548
κὰδ δ' ἐν Ἀθήνῃς εἶσεν, ἑῷ ἐν πίονι νηῷ·   549
ἔνθα δέ μιν ταύροισι καὶ ἀρνειοῖς ἱλάονται   550
κοῦροι Ἀθηναίων περιτελλομένων ἐνιαυτῶν·   551
τῶν αὖθ' ἡγεμόνευ' υἱὸς Πετεῶο Μενεσθεύς.   552

And those who held Athens [*Athḗnai*], well-founded city   546
the *dḗmos* of stout-hearted Erekhtheus, whom once Athena
          [*Athḗnē*]   547
nourished,[10] daughter of Zeus, but the grain-giving earth
          gave birth to him.   548
And she established him in Athens [*Athḗnai*], in her own
          rich temple.   549
And there he is supplicated, with sacrifices of bulls and rams,   550
by the young men of Athens, each time the seasonal moment
          comes round.[11]   551
And their leader was Menestheus, son of Peteoos.   552

Iliad B 546–552

The 'Athens' of text 1d must surely be the same place as the 'Athens' of text 1a, as we see from the reference at verse 549 to the temple of Athena as the home of the goddess. At verse 547, we see that the temple is also home for the hero Erekhtheus, whom Athena establishes inside her temple, much as

10. We may note the wording in Plato *Menexenus* 237b on Mother Earth as being τῆς τεκούσης καὶ θρεψάσης καὶ ὑποδεξαμένης 'the one who gave birth, nourished, and accepted [them] into her care', with reference to the Athenians as her autochthonous children (cf. Loraux 1993.84n71; also pp. 58–59). I infer from this kind of phrasing that Athena in *Iliad* B was really pictured as nursing Erekhtheus. I see here a pattern of differentiation between older and newer concepts of the goddess.

11. Kirk 1985.206: the phrasing "suggests an annual festival; there may or may not be some idea of an early form of the Panathenaia, which was held in the month of Hekatombaion."

the goddess Aphrodite establishes the hero Phaethon inside her own temple in Hesiod *Theogony* 990–991.[12] Similarly in text 1a, the singular 'Athens' is the home of the hero Erekhtheus at verse 81, and it *seems* to be the home of the goddess Athena, who is described as going to the palace of Erekhtheus, situated in a place that has a name identical to the name of the goddess. While Odysseus proceeds to the *palace* of Alkinoos, Athena flies off to the *palace* of Erekhtheus. So Athena's city par excellence is presumably Athens.

It remains to determine, to be sure, how far back in time we may apply this formulation. Already in the era of the Linear B tablets, we find a distinct goddess named *Athā́nā* (spelled a-ta-na- in the syllabary), equivalent of Homeric *Athḗnē*:

1e. a-ta-na-po-ti-ni-ja = *Athā́nāi potníāi* (dative) 'to the Lady Athena'

Linear B tablet V 52 from Knossos

πότνι' Ἀθηναίη 'lady Athena'

Iliad Z 305

The Linear B tablets provide no direct information, however, about the name for the city of Athens. We need not assume that the goddess worshipped at Knossos in the second millennium BCE was known as the goddess of Athens. Still, the city of Athens was perhaps already then understood as belonging to the goddess.

Putting such questions aside, let us return to what seems more certain: that *Athḗnē* the goddess and *Athḗnē* the city in text 1a are the same as *Athḗnē* the goddess and *Athḗnai* the city in text 1d. True, *Athḗnē* and *Athḗnai* may be the appropriate designations of the same place at different times. The exceptional instance of singular *Athḗnē* in text 1a may reflect a relatively earlier context. According to Martin P. Nilsson, the relationship between goddess (Athene) and king (Erekhtheus) is here still in a "Mycenaean" stage in their relationship.[13] We see here the goddess as a patroness of the king in power and as a resident in his palace. She is his ultimate tenant, Mycenaean style, occupying as her abode a shrine-room within the palace. By contrast, the instances of plural *Athḗnai* as in text 1d reflect a later stage in the relationship of Athena and Erekhtheus, when the palace of the king has been transformed into the temple of the goddess. What we now see, from the perspective of a palace-turned-temple, is a hero who is worshipped within the sacred precinct of a goddess. From the viewpoint of the there-and-then identified with heroic times, Erekhtheus is a king empowered by Athena.

12. On the homology between Erekhtheus and Phaethon, see *BA* 191–192.
13. Nilsson 1921.

From the viewpoint of the narrator's here-and-now, by contrast, he is the protégé of the goddess, a cult-figure sharing in her overall cult.

In sum, the perspective of the distant past allows a residual situation, where Athens is in the singular, whereas the narrator's perspective of his own here-and-now requires Athens to be in the plural. We have yet to refine, to be sure, what it means to say "the narrator's perspective of his own here-and-now."

In fact, many questions remain about the semantics of any contrast between singular *Athénē* and plural *Athēnai*. Even when the singular is used to designate the whole city, is that usage not in itself an implicit ellipsis, as distinct from the explicit ellipsis of the plural? Does the identification of the name of the goddess with the name of the city imply that the concept of the goddess subsumes the concept of the city? Or, to put it another way, does the essence of the goddess lead into the essence of her population? Here is a list of some possible parallels:

1f Θήβη [*Thébē*] = Thebe the Nymph, vs. Θῆβαι [*Thēbai*] = Thebes[14]
1g Μυκήνη [*Mukénē*] = Mycene the Nymph, vs. Μυκῆναι [*Mukēnai*] = Mycenae[15]
1h Μεσσήνη [*Messénē*] = Messene the heroine;[16] cf. Linear B me-za-na[17]
1i Φίλιππος [*Phílippos*] = Philip, vs. Φίλιπποι [*Phílippoi*] = Philippi[18]
1j Modern Greek example, from the Island of Ikaria, where the town-name in the plural designates the town and its environs[19]

Of all available traces of residual ellipsis, the most striking example is this one:

2a. ἐκ μὲν Κρητάων γένος εὔχομαι εὐρειάων,
ἀνέρος ἀφνειοῖο πάις· ...

I proclaim that I am by birth from Crete [plural], the far-and-wide, the son of a rich man...

Odyssey ξ 199–200

14. Cf. Schwyzer 1939.638.
15. Schwyzer 1939.638.
16. Schwyzer 1939.638.
17. Pylos tablet Cn 3.1; see N 1970.148n187. On the basis of the forms *Mukénē* and *Messénē*, I suspect that even the suffix *-énē* is endowed with an elliptic function. Also, the element *mésso-* of *Messénē* implies the semantics of ellipsis, in that the idea of the middle is highlighted while that of the periphery is shaded over.
18. Schwyzer 1939.638.
19. Schwyzer/Debrunner 1950.43.

2b. ἐκ μὲν <u>Κρητάων</u> γένος εὔχεται <u>εὐρειάων</u>,
φησὶ δὲ πολλὰ βροτῶν ἐπὶ ἄστεα δινηθῆναι
πλαζόμενος·...

He proclaims that he is by birth from <u>Crete</u> [plural], the <u>far-and-wide</u>,
and he says that he has wandered around over many cities of mortals,
veering from his path.[20]

Odyssey π 62–64

There is of course only one island of Crete, and we may readily conclude that
the plural usage reflects the idea of "Crete and everything that belongs to it."
Such an idea corresponds to the historical construct of a "Minoan thalas-
socracy," as already intuited by Thucydides (1.4), who speaks of King Minos
of Crete as the founder of a prototypical naval empire extending throughout
the Cyclades Islands and beyond.[21]

So far, we have looked at elliptic constructions in Homer from a diachronic
viewpoint. But what are the implications of ellipsis from the synchronic
viewpoint of composition-in-performance? A case in point is the problem of
the dual of the heroic name *Aíās* 'Ajax', that is, *Aíante*. I will summarize the
key Homeric contexts of the dual Ajax, which I henceforth write simply as
Aiante, by quoting from a 1959 book on the *Iliad* by Denys Page, representing
what he himself calls an "analyst" as opposed to "unitarian" interpretation of
the epic.[22] Words emphasized by Page himself are left italicized, while those
highlighted by me are underlined. At key moments, I will interrupt Page's
words by noting salient opportunities for alternative explanations.[23]

Page's central argument is that the "original" meaning of Aiante is not
<u>Ajax Major (son of Telamon) and Ajax Minor (son of Oileus)</u> but <u>Ajax and
his half-brother Teucer</u>. He speaks of a place "where the <u>original</u> meaning of
Aiante, 'Ajax and his brother', is deeply embedded in the *Iliad*."[24] The passage
is *Iliad* N 177 and following, and here is what Page says about it:

> Ajax and his brother Teucer are fighting side by side. Teucer kills Imbrios:
> he therefore has the right to strip the body of its armour; and he sets out
> to do so. Hector intervenes, but is repelled by Ajax; *and the Aiante proceed
> to drag and despoil the body of Imbrios.* Here it is very obvious that Aiante
> means "Ajax and Teucer"; nobody else took part in the killing of Imbrios;

20. Cf. *Odyssey* α 1–2.
21. Muellner 1976.70.
22. Page 1959.
23. Footnotes within the quotations contain my own comments on Page's reasoning.
24. Page 1959.238.

nobody else has any interest in, or claim to, the spoils. It is indeed so obvious, that the later poets were inspired to correct what they thought to be a mistake. If the term Aiante was used, the smaller Ajax *must* have been engaged in the action; let us proceed at once to say "that the head of Imbrios was now cut off *by Ajax the son of Oileus.*" [N 203]. This we shall certainly not tolerate: what, we shall ask this bounding intruder, are you doing with a head which belongs to us? Imbrios was our victim, not yours: Teucer killed him, Ajax helped to secure the body; you had nothing whatever to do with him. The smaller Ajax pops into the scene suddenly, and out of it again immediately, having done his simple duty; which was, to bring the term Aiante into line with modern opinion.[25]

In the case of a similar problem, the use of the duals where we expect plurals in the "Embassy" passage of *Iliad* I, Page again resorts to the rhetorical device of an apostrophe addressed to a Homeric character: "Unhappy Phoenix, Achilles' oldest friend, not one single word of you; and if that were not enough, your leadership is instantly and silently taken from you."[26] In this case, Page thinks that Phoenix is the odd man out in the dual references to what seems to be a trio comprised of Phoenix, Ajax, and Odysseus.[27]

Let us return to the problem of the meaning of Aiante, as Page sees it:

> The trouble began in [M] 343 ff.: Menestheus sent a herald[28] to fetch Ajax, "*both*, if possible, otherwise Telamonian Ajax alone." In order that "both" might signify "both Ajaxes" instead of "Ajax and Teucer," a line was added, 350, "*and let Teucer come with him*" (repeated 363); the addition was properly athetized by Aristarchus as wanting in MS authority.[29] When he hears the message, Telamonian Ajax tells Oilean Ajax to stay where he is; he himself and Teucer go to help Menestheus. Thus in [M] 400 ff. Telamonian Ajax and Teucer fight side by side, having left Oilean Ajax in another quarter. And now Poseidon ([N] 46 ff.) speaks to the Aiante: who are they? Obviously Ajax and Teucer, for the poet has just gone out of his way to tell us that the two Ajaxes are *not* together. But once again the occurrence of the term Aiante leads to a jack-in-the-box intrusion by Oilean Ajax ([N] 66 ff.), just as it does in the later passage (197 ff.); in this

25. Page 1959.238.

26. Page 1959.300.

27. Cf. *HQ* 138–145.

28. The involvement of heralds in the narrative containing the Aiante problem, I suggest, is relevant to the involvement of heralds in the "Embassy" scene of *Iliad* I, containing the problem of the dual-for-plural usage.

29. The addition here of a third role—earlier in the narrative we saw only two roles—is comparable with the layering of two vs. three ambassadors in the "Embassy" scene of *Iliad* I.

case the confusion is great and obvious, since we were told a moment ago in so much detail that the one Ajax had separated himself from the other.[30]

I suggest, however, that there is no "confusion," and that it is inaccurate to speak of "intrusions." Instead, if we adopt an evolutionary model for the making of Homeric poetry, there are simply different levels of recomposition-in-performance, which are traces of an evolving fixity or textualization—and I use this term without implying the presence of written texts.[31]

ELLIPTIC MEANING IN HOMER

Here we reach the third question to be asked: how does ellipsis typify Homeric songmaking? A related question has just been raised as we contemplated the shift in the meaning of Aiante, from Ajax and Ajax to Ajax and Teucer: what are the implications of ellipsis from the synchronic viewpoint of composition-in-performance? Another related question is this: is it even possible to speak of a synchronic analysis of Homer? The evidence of ellipsis suggests that the answer has to be a complex one.

A case in point is the reference at *Iliad* M 335–336 to Αἴαντε δύω ... Τεῦκρόν τε 'the two Aiante ... and Teucer'. According to the commentaries, the explicit mention of Teucer here means that 'the two Aiante' must have been understood as Ajax Maior and Ajax Minor.[32] And yet, from a diachronic point of view, this kind of syntactic construction actually retains the elliptic function in the dual, thereafter highlighting what was initially shaded over by the ellipsis. That is, the implicit Teucer in the expression 'the two Aiante' is joined to an explicit naming of Teucer. We see parallels in other Indo-European languages, as for example in the Indic expression *Mitrā́ ... Váruṇo yáś ca* in *Rig-Veda* 8.25.2, meaning 'dual-Mitra [= Mitra and Varuṇa] and he who is Varuṇa' = 'Mitra and Varuṇa'; similarly in French, *nous deux Paul* means 'I and Paul' = 'the two of us, one of whom is Paul', not 'I and you (or he / she / it) and Paul'.[33] It is only if Paul gets stranded, as it were, from the two of us that the two of us—*nous deux*—could default to 'I and you (or he / she / it)'.

It is an elusive task, then, to establish the synchrony of the elliptic dual *Aíante* in the *Iliad*, or of the singular *Athḗnē* as opposed to the elliptic plural

30. Page 1959.272–273.
31. *HQ* 40.
32. E.g. Hainsworth 1993.355 (and, earlier, p. 346).
33. Puhvel 1977.399–400.

Athēnai in the *Odyssey*. And yet, surely there are synchronic mechanisms in Homeric diction—and surely there must have been at any given historical time and place a synchronic system for generating the language of epic in general. But the question remains: is there a synchronic reality to the world of the epic? My own answer is that there is no such thing. We may perhaps agree that the pattern or system of epic discourse has been for the most part set by, say, the middle of the eighth century BCE, an era of general cultural consolidation in the Greek-speaking world.[34] And yet, this epic discourse may continue to communicate different levels of perspective, even different levels of meaning. We outsiders looking in, as it were, on this system can reconstruct a diachronic dimension in order to highlight some of these different levels of perspective, but there seems to be no level playing field for producing a single perspective. I once said that Homeric diction defies synchronic analysis.[35] This is not to advocate any abandonment of the search for synchronic—or let us say "working"—mechanisms. Rather, it is to emphasize that there are different levels of meaning that cannot be reduced to any one single synchrony.

These considerations can be brought to bear on the specific problem of duals that seem to be used in the place of plurals in Homeric diction. While some experts have dismissed even the possibility that the dual can be used for the plural,[36] we now know for a fact that the Alexandrian scholars and poets not only admitted the possibility in their Homeric exegesis but also used the device of dual-for-plural in their own poetry when they wished to make specific "citations" of Homer.[37] It can be argued in general that *citation*, not *allusion*, is a more accurate term for references to Homeric poetry in Alexandrian poetry: for the Alexandrians, Homer was the absolute *source*, not only the unsurpassable *model*.[38]

In the Alexandrian poetics of figures like Apollonius of Rhodes and Callimachus, *citation* is a matter of reusing: a given archaic usage, no longer current in the spoken language, becomes re-used as a mark of the poetic language. In the oral poetics of the Homeric tradition, by contrast, there is no reusing, only *reactivation*. A case in point is Egbert Bakker's demonstration that Homeric diction can reactivate the use of verbs without

34. Janko 1982.228–231.
35. *MP* 29.
36. Page 1959.299.
37. Rengakos 1993.76–77; cf. *PP* 138. See also Matthaios 1999.378ff and the comments of Rengakos 2002.
38. Rengakos 1993.9; cf. *PP* Ch.5.

augment as a newly active mechanism in expressing "epic tense."[39] Another case, I suggest, is the "Embassy Scene" of *Iliad* I, where the use of the dual becomes reactivated to serve the special purpose of expressing an archaic situation where there *should* be only two ambassadors even though there are now three.[40] Thus the language of Achilles, in addressing two instead of three ambassadors, can develop the side-effect of effectively snubbing one of the three ambassadors in the context of a newer situation that is recreated out of an older one.[41] In both these cases, then, reactivation of older forms results in newer meanings.

If indeed there exist different levels of meaning that cannot be smoothed over as one single synchrony, then the elusiveness of a synchronic perspective in Homeric discourse may well be a mark of its essential fluidity. Here I return to the perceptive formulation of Albert Lord:

> Our real difficulty arises from the fact that, unlike the oral poet, we are not accustomed to thinking in terms of *fluidity*. We find it difficult to grasp something that is *multiform*. It seems to us necessary to construct an ideal text or to seek an *original*, and we remain dissatisfied with an ever-changing phenomenon. I believe that once we know the facts of oral composition we must cease trying to find an *original* of any traditional song. From one point of view each performance is an *original*.[42]

I might add that we must cease trying to find an absolutely *final* version of any traditional song.

Arguing that we cannot speak of a single "world of Homer" or a single "age of Homer," I return to my evolutionary model for the making of Homeric poetry.[43] Such an evolutionary model differs radically from some other explanations. Here I focus on two examples, formulated by Geoffrey Kirk (1985) and Richard Janko (1992), two of the contributors to *The Iliad: A Commentary* (produced under the general editorship of Kirk).

Kirk posits a "big bang" genesis of Homeric poetry. He argues for a one-time "oral" composition achieved by a so-called "monumental composer" sometime in the eighth century BCE, which then continues to be reperformed "orally" by rhapsodes for around two hundred years.[44] A second kind of "big

---

39. Bakker 1997b.

40. *HQ* 138–145.

41. Again, *HQ* 138–145. Cf. *PH* 5–6: when an older and a newer form compete for the same meaning, one of the things that can happen is that the older form, ousted from its old meaning, develops a newer meaning that becomes a specialized version of the older meaning now held by the newer form.

42. Lord 1960.100. The italics are mine. Already quoted in Ch.2.

43. See Ch.2.

44. Kirk 1985.1–16.

bang" theory is offered by Janko, who as we have seen thinks that the *Iliad* and *Odyssey* were dictated by Homer himself around the second half of the eighth century BCE[45]

So far, I have been testing my evolutionary model on the specific problem of dual-Ajax usages in the *Iliad*. Now let us test the "big bang" models of Kirk and Janko.[46] To start with Kirk, he says that the Aiante were understood as Ajax Major and Ajax Minor "by the monumental composer himself."[47] But then he adds: "Despite that association, the Locrian Aias [= Ajax] was not greatly admired in the heroic tradition, a reflection perhaps of his light-armed, unheroic and provincial ... side."[48] He recounts the reprehensible or "stupid" things done by this Ajax;[49] later on, commenting on *Iliad* Δ 272-3, he says that "there can be little doubt that here [the Aiante] are the greater Aias [= Ajax] *and Teukros* [=Teucer], since the Locrian Aias' light-armed contingent ... would hardly be described as 'bristling with shields and spears' as at 282 here."[50]

As for Janko, he says that the form of Aiante "was reinterpreted to mean two men called Aias [= Ajax], but Teukros [= Teucer] is always nearby; at [N] 202ff. the same hypothesis explains Oilean Aias' unexpected intrusion in a killing by Teukros and his brother [177–178]."[51] He goes on to say: "This verse [N 46] originally denoted Teukros and Aias, who clearly derives from Mycenaean epic ..., but the dual led Homer to insert Oilean Aias and then add Teukros (66f., 92)."[52] Commenting on *Iliad* N 177-178, Janko says that "the poet has momentarily confused Teukros with Aias 'son of Telamon', because he was unsure who was meant by 'the two [Aiante]' (46)."[53] In considering the mutually contradictory references to the positioning of the Aiante at the ships of the Achaeans, Janko says: "The contradiction over the [Aiante's] position surely derives from Homer's pervasive and creative misunderstanding of Aiante, originally 'Aias and Teukros' (46n)."[54] Commenting on *Iliad* Ξ 460, Janko says: "The unusual sense of Aiante in earlier stages of the tradition caused confusion over the [Aiante] and Teukros (13.46n); all three are present in this battle."[55]

45. Janko 1992.20–38, with reference to Janko 1982.228–231.
46. Underlines will indicate my highlightings.
47. Kirk 1985.201.
48. Kirk 1985.201.
49. Kirk 1985.201.
50. Kirk 1985.359.
51. Janko 1992.48.
52. Janko 1992.48.
53. Janko 1992.69.
54. Janko 1992.132.
55. Janko 1992.218–219.

We may have expected both these representatives of "big bang" models of composition in the eighth century to devise a corresponding set of "big bang" explanations for the complexities of the dual-Ajax constructions. Instead, they seem to be resorting to explanations based on assumptions of mostly random misinterpretations on the part of the poet.

From an evolutionary perspective, on the other hand, it is a question of systematic reinterpretations instead of unsystematic misinterpretations, and I find that the views of an old-fashioned "analyst" like Page are more useful for analyzing the complexities of reinterpretation.[56] I should stress at the outset, however, that I distance myself from Page's assumptions about older and newer poets, about original poets and later redactors, and, especially, about earlier texts and later texts. Still, his wording is replete with suggestive possibilities, as when he says:

> Certainly the poet, if asked, would say that Aiante means "the two Ajaxes"; and would admit that he has made a mistake. But he has not made a mistake, except in his interpretation of Aiante; he has preserved an almost obliterated truth, the usage of Aiante in the sense "Ajax and his brother." Tradition supplied him with a formula for addressing Ajax, *Aíante Argeíōn hēgétore*, in which Ajax's brother was included; in the early Epic this formula had been employed correctly; and the force of immemorial tradition has preserved it in a few contexts up to the end. It is very natural that the later poet should fail to notice the occasional confusion which is caused by the difference between the old and the new meanings of a word or formula; but no poet would of his own free will, as a positive and creative act, describe the two Ajaxes as joint commanders of an army comprising the regular Salaminians and the highly irregular Locrians.[57]

The notion of systematic reinterpretation may be described as a process of *mouvance*. For Paul Zumthor, who pioneered the term, *mouvance* is a widespread phenomenon in medieval manuscript transmission. He defines it as a "quasi-abstraction" that becomes a reality in the interplay of variant readings in different manuscripts of a given work; he pictures *mouvance* as a kind of "incessant vibration," a fundamental process of instability.[58] In another work, I have written extensively about this term, pointing out that

56. Again, underlines will indicate my highlightings.

57. Page 1959.237.

58. Zumthor 1972.507 ("le caractère de l'oeuvre qui, comme telle, avant l'âge du livre, ressort d'une quasi-abstraction, les textes concrets qui la réalisent présentent, par le jeu des variantes et remaniements, comme une incessante vibration et une instabilité fondamentale"). Cf. Zumthor pp. 43–47, 65–75.

there has been a great deal of *mouvance* even in the concept of *mouvance*.[59] Moreover, I suggest that the association of *mouvance* with "instability" may be misleading if it implies unsystematic change. To the extent that *mouvance* is the oral poetic process of recomposition-in-performance, it is a stabilizing rather than destabilizing force.

It is pertinent here to consider the semantics of the word *mímēsis* (henceforth spelled "mimesis") in the older sense of 'reenactment'.[60] A driving idea behind this word is the ideal of stability in the reenactment of the "same" thing by a succession of different performers.[61] It is as if the composition remained always the same, even though the performers kept changing.[62] It is as if there were no change in the process of recomposition-in-performance.[63]

There are numerous examples where the process of change through recomposition-in-performance is *not* recognized by a living oral tradition *as change*. A case in point is the following passage from Theognis:

> Κύρνε <u>σοφιζομένῳ</u> μὲν ἐμοὶ <u>σφρηγὶς</u> ἐπικείσθω
> τοῖσδ' ἔπεσιν, λήσει δ' οὔποτε κλεπτόμενα
> οὐδέ τις ἀλλάξει κάκιον τοὐσθλοῦ παρεόντος.
> ὧδε δέ πᾶς τις ἐρεῖ· Θεύγνιδός ἐστιν ἔπη
> τοῦ Μεγαρέως· πάντας δὲ κατ' ἀνθρώπους ὀνομαστός.
> <u>ἀστοῖσιν</u> δ' οὔπω πᾶσιν <u>ἀδεῖν</u> δύναμαι

> Kyrnos, let a <u>seal</u> [*sphrāgís*] be placed by me, <u>as I practice my skill</u>
>   [*sophía*],
>   upon these my words. This way, it will never be undetected if they are
>   stolen,
>   and no one can substitute something inferior for the genuine thing that
>   is there.
>   And this is what everyone will say: "These are the words of Theognis
>   of Megara, whose name is known among all mortals."
>   But <u>I am not yet able to please</u> [= verb *handánō*] all <u>the townspeople</u>
>   [*astoí*].

> Theognis 19–24

I have written about this passage:

59. *PP* chapter 1.
60. Detailed discussion in *PH* 42–44, 373–375.
61. *PH* 42–44, 373–375.
62. *PH* 42–44, 373–375.
63. *PH* 42–44, 373–375.

Like the code of [a] lawgiver, the poetry of Theognis presents itself as static, unchangeable. In fact, the *sphragís* 'seal' of Theognis is pictured as a guarantee that no one will ever tamper with the poet's words. Outside this ideology and in reality, however, the poetry of Theognis is dynamic, subject [like the law code of Lycurgus] to modifications and accretions that are occasioned by an evolving social order. And the poet is always there, observing it all—despite the fact that the events being observed span an era that goes well beyond a single lifetime.[64]

With his "seal," the figure of Theognis is authorizing himself, making himself the author. There is an explicit self-description of this author as one who succeeds in *sophía*, the 'skill' of decoding or encoding poetry.[65] On the basis of this success, the author lays claim to a timeless authority, *which resists the necessity of changing* just to please the audience of the here and now, who are described as the *astoí* 'townspeople'.[66] The author must risk alienation with the audience of the here and now in order to attain the supposedly universal acceptance of the ultimate audience, which is the cumulative response of Panhellenic fame:[67]

> οὐ <u>δύναμαι</u> γνῶναι νόον <u>ἀστῶν</u> ὅντιν᾽ ἔχουσιν·
> οὔτε γὰρ εὖ ἔρδων <u>ἀνδάνω</u> οὔτε κακῶς·
> μωμεῦνται δέ με πολλοί, ὁμῶς κακοὶ ἠδὲ καὶ ἐσθλοί·
> <u>μιμεῖσθαι</u> δ᾽ οὐδεὶς τῶν <u>ἀσόφων</u> δύναται.

> I am unable to decide what disposition it is that the <u>townspeople</u> [*astoí*] have towards me.
>   For I do not <u>please</u> [= verb *handánō*] them, either when I do for them things that are advantageous or when I do things that are disadvantageous.[68]

64. N 1985.33.

65. On *sophós* 'skilled' as a programmatic word used by poetry to designate the 'skill' of a poet in encoding the message of the poetry, see *PH* 148. See also *PH* 374n190: "A successful encoder, that is, poet, is by necessity a successful decoder, that is, someone who has understood the inherited message and can therefore pass it on. Not all decoders, however, are necessarily encoders: both poet and audience are decoders, but only the poet has the authority of the encoder."

66. In this and related contexts, *astoí* 'townspeople' seems to be the programmatic designation of local audiences, associated with the special interests of their own here and now. The anonymous referee draws my attention to Archilochus F 13 West, where the emotional state of the *astoí* seems to be contrasted with the stance of the poet: as I interpret this poem, the poet too is represented as feeling the same emotions of grief as felt by the rest of the community, but he urges all to transcend those emotions—as does the poem.

67. This theme of the alienated poet is examined at length in N 1985.30 and following.

68. The "doing," of course, may amount simply to the performative level of "saying" <u>by way of poetry.</u>

There are many who find blame with me, base and noble men alike.
But no one who is not <u>skilled</u> [*sophós*] can <u>reenact</u> [*mimeísthai*] me.

Theognis 367–370

Here the notion of mimesis becomes an implicit promise that no change shall ever occur to accommodate the interests of any local audience in the here and now, that is, of the *astoí* 'townspeople'. The authorized reperformance of a composition, if it is a true reenactment or mimesis, can guarantee the authenticity of the "original" composition. The author is saying about himself: "But no one who is not skilled [*sophós*] can reenact my identity."[69]

Here we see an ultimate ellipsis, formulated by poetry about poetry, where an entire succession of performers is being shaded over in order to highlight a single "original" composition-in-performance, executed by a prototypical poet who eclipses all his successors.

ELLIPTIC HOMER

We come now to the fourth and last question: how does Homeric songmaking use ellipsis to typify itself? A prime case in point is the Homeric "I," which highlights the prototypical singer of tales, elliptically shading over an open-ended succession of rhapsodes in the lengthy evolutionary process of countless recompositions-in-performance over time.

We have already seen an Iliadic passage that reveals a symbolic reference to such a diachrony of rhapsodes. While Achilles, becoming the ultimate paradigm for singers, is represented as actually performing the epic songs of heroes, *kléa andrôn* 'glories of men' at *Iliad* I 189, Patroklos is waiting for his own turn, in order to take up the song precisely where Achilles will have left off.[70]

I have argued that both the plural usage here of *kléa andrôn* 'glories of men' (as opposed to singular *kléos* 'glory') and the meaning of the name *Patrokléēs* are pertinent to the rhapsodic implications of this passage: "it is only through *Patrokléēs* 'he who has the *kléa* [glories] of the ancestors' that the plurality of performance, that is, the activation of tradition, can happen."[71] In this light, I repeat my earlier argument:

So long as Achilles alone sings the *kléa andrôn* 'glories of men', these heroic glories cannot be heard by anyone but Patroklos alone. Once Achilles leaves off and Patroklos starts singing, however, the continuum that is

---

69. For a fuller discussion, see *PP* 221–223.
70. *PP* 71–73.
71. *PH* 202. For a fuller discussion, see *PP* 71–73.

the *kléa andrōn*—the Homeric tradition itself—can at long last become activated. This is the moment awaited by *Patrokléēs* 'he who has the *kléa* [glories] of the ancestors'. In this Homeric image of Patroklos waiting for his turn to sing, then, we have in capsule form the esthetics of rhapsodic sequencing.[72]

By contrast, the "I" of Homer, as in the first verse of the *Odyssey*, implies that it will always be Homer who is told the tale by the Muse and who will in turn continue to tell it each time he invokes her:

ἄνδρα <u>μοι</u> ἔννεπε Μοῦσα ...

Narrate to me, Muse, ...

Odyssey α 1

Still, this "I" of Homer is interchangeable with a "we," as in the ἡμεῖς 'we' of *Iliad* B 486 or in the καὶ ἡμῖν 'us too' of *Odyssey* α 10, and I propose that such a "we" can refer elliptically to a whole vertical succession of performers.[73]

Still, no ellipsis can ultimately overshadow the lonely uniqueness of the performer when the vertical succession at long last reaches *him*, when *his* moment comes in the here-and-now of his own performance.[74] Though the present of performance, as Egbert Bakker notes, must be included into the "accumulated mass of the tradition,"[75] there must remain nevertheless "a certain distance" between the countless performances of the past and the unique performance of the present.[76] What must happen is a "reexperience."[77] The singer is just about to have such a reexperience when he says:

πληθὺν δ' οὐκ <u>ἂν</u> ἐγὼ <u>μυθήσομαι</u> οὐδ' <u>ὀνομήνω</u>,	488
οὐδ' εἴ μοι δέκα μὲν γλῶσσαι, δέκα δὲ στόματ' εἶεν	489
φωνὴ δ' ἄρρηκτος, χάλκεον δέ μοι ἦτορ ἐνείη,	490

---

72. *PP* 71–73. It can also be argued that Patroklos as the solo audience of Achilles becomes interchangeable with the general audience of the *Iliad*. See *PP* 72n37 for further discussion and bibliography on the Homeric device of creating an effect of interchangeability between characters of epic and members of an audience.

73. At *Odyssey* α 10, the expression τῶν ἁμόθεν γε 'from <u>one</u> point among these' seems to me pertinent to the idea of vertical succession in εἰπὲ καὶ ἡμῖν 'narrate to us too!' (addressed to the Muse).

74. Perhaps the expression κλέος <u>οἶον</u> at *Iliad* B 486 is pertinent: the singer hears the *kléos* or song "alone," as if he heard nothing else. Perhaps also pertinent is the singularity of the Muse invoked at *Iliad* A 1—and at *Odyssey* α 1.

75. Bakker 1997b.

76. Bakker 1997b.

77. Bakker 1997b.

εἰ μὴ Ὀλυμπιάδες Μοῦσαι, Διὸς αἰγιόχοιο   491
θυγατέρες, <u>μνησαίαθ</u>᾽ ὅσοι ὑπὸ Ἴλιον ἦλθον·   492
ἀρχοὺς αὖ νηῶν ἐρέω νῆάς τε προπάσας   493

But their number I <u>could</u> not <u>tell</u> nor <u>name</u>   488
(not even if I had ten tongues and ten mouths   489
and a voice that was unbreaking, and if a heart of bronze
    were within me)   490
<u>if</u> the Muses of Olympus, of Zeus the aegis-bearer   491
the daughters, <u>did</u> not <u>remind</u> me,[78] how many came to Troy.   492
But *now* I will say the leaders [*arkhoí*] of the ships, and all
    the ships.   493

Iliad B 488–493

All of a sudden, the singer steps out of the elliptic shade, and he starts to sing...

---

78. For subjunctive + potential particle ἄν in the apodosis and εἰ + optative in the protasis, Kirk 1985.167 compares *Iliad* Λ 386–387: "Your bow and arrows could not save you, if you did attack me face-to-face with your weapons." It seems to me that both constructions are contrary-to-fact: *if the Muses did not remind me (but they did)* and *if you did attack me face-to-face (but you did not).*

Allen, T. W. 1924. *Homer: The Origins and the Transmission.* Oxford.

——. 1931. ed. *Homeri Ilias.* I–III. Oxford.

Allen, W. S. 1973. *Accent and Rhythm. Prosodic Features of Latin and Greek: A Study in Theory and Reconstruction.* Cambridge.

——. 1987. *Vox Graeca: The Pronunciation of Classical Greek.* 3rd ed. Cambridge.

Apthorp, M. J. 1980. *The Manuscript Evidence for Interpolation in Homer.* Heidelberg.

——. 1990a. "Some Neglected Papyrus Evidence Against the Authenticity of *Iliad* 16.381." *Zeitschrift für Papyrologie und Epigraphik* 81:1–7.

——. 1990b. "Papyrus Evidence in Favour of Some Suspected Lines in Homer." *Zeitschrift für Papyrologie und Epigraphik* 82:13–24.

——. 1992. "*Nochmals* the Authenticity of *Odyssey* 10.475–9." *Classical Quarterly* 42:270–271.

——. 1993. Review of van Thiel 1991. *Classical Review* 43:228–230.

——. 1995a. Review of R. D. Dawe 1993. *The Odyssey: Translation and Analysis* (Lewes: The Book Guild). *Classical Review* 45:1–2.

——. 1995b. Review of J. R. Tebben 1994. *Concordantia Homerica*, Pars I: *Odyssea. A Complete Concordance to the Van Thiel Edition of Homer's Odyssey* 2 vols. (Zurich and New York). *Classical Review* 45:221–222.

——. 1995c. "Did Homer Give his Nereids Names? A Note on the Ancient Manuscript Evidence." *Acta Classica* 38:89–92.

——. 1995d. "*Iliad* 14.306c Discovered in the Syriac Palimpsest." *Zeitschrift für Papyrologie und Epigraphik* 109:174–176.

——. 1996a. "New Evidence from the Syriac Palimpsest on the Numerus Versuum of the *Iliad.*" *Zeitschrift für Papyrologie und Epigraphik* 110:103–114.

——. 1996b. "*Iliad* 18.200–201: Genuine or Interpolated?" *Zeitschrift für Papyrologie und Epigraphik* 111:141–148.

——. 1998. "Double News from Antinoopolis on Phoenix's Parricidal Thoughts (*Iliad* 9.458–61)." *Zeitschrift für Papyrologie und Epigraphik* 122:182–188.

——. 1999. "Homer's Winged Words and the Papyri: Some Questions of Authenticity." *Zeitschrift für Papyrologie und Epigraphik* 128:15–22.

——. 2000. "Did Athene Help Tydeus to Win the Cadmean Games (*Iliad* 5.808)?" *Zeitschrift für Papyrologie und Epigraphik* 131:1–9.

Austin, J. L. 1962. *How to Do Things with Words.* Oxford.

Bakker, E. J. 1997a. *Poetry in Speech. Orality and Homeric Discourse.* Ithaca.

——. 1997b. "Storytelling in the Future: Truth, Time, and Tense in Homeric Epic." In Bakker and Kahane 1997:11–36.

Bakker, E. J., and Kahane, A. 1997. eds. *Written Voices, Spoken Signs: Tradition, Performance, and the Epic Text.* Cambridge MA.

Ben-Amos, D. 1976. "Analytical Categories and Ethnic Genres." *Folklore Genres*, ed. D. Ben-Amos, 215–242. Austin TX.

Benveniste, E. 1966. *Problèmes de linguistique générale*. Paris.

———. 1969. *Le vocabulaire des institutions indo-européennes*. I. *Economie, parenté, société*. II. *Pouvoir, droit, religion*. Paris = *Indo-European Language and Society*. Translated by E. Palmer. London, 1973.

Berenson Maclean, J. K., and Aitken, E. B. 2001. eds. *Flavius Philostratus, Heroikos*. Atlanta.

Berg, N. 1978. "Parergon Metricum: Der Ursprung des griechischen Hexameters." *Münchener Beiträge zur Sprachwissenschaft* 37:11–36.

Bird, G. D. 1994. "The Textual Criticism of an Oral Homer." In *Nile, Ilissos and Tiber: Essays in honour of Walter Kirkpatrick Lacey* (ed. V. J. Gray), *Prudentia* 26:35–52.

Blackburn, S. H., Claus, P. J., Flueckiger, J. B., and Wadley, S. S. 1989. eds. *Oral Epics in India*. Berkeley and Los Angeles.

Bollack, J. 1994. "Une action de restauration culturelle. La place accordée aux tragiques par le décret de Lycurgue." *Mélanges Pierre Lévêque* (eds. M.-M. Mactoux and E. Geny) 13–24. Paris.

Bolling, G. M. 1925. *The External Evidence for Interpolation in Homer*. Oxford.

———. 1950. ed. *Ilias Atheniensium: The Athenian Iliad of the Sixth Century B.C.* Lancaster PA.

Bowie, A. M. 1981. *The Poetic Dialect of Sappho and Alcaeus*. New York.

Broggiato, M. 1998. "Cratete di Mallo negli scholl. A ad *Il.* 24.282 e ad *Il.* 9.169a." *Seminari Romani di Cultura Greca* 1:137–143.

Burgess, J. S. 1996: "The Non-Homeric Cypria." *Transactions of the American Philological Association* 126:77–99.

———. 2001. *The Tradition of the Trojan War in Homer and the Epic Cycle*. Baltimore.

Burkert, W. 1975. "Apollon und Apellai." *Rheinisches Museum* 118:1–21.

———. "Kynaithos, Polycrates, and the Homeric Hymn to Apollo." In *Arktouros: Hellenic Studies Presented to B. M. W. Knox*, edited by G. W. Bowersock, W. Burkert, and M. C. J. Putnam, 53–62. Berlin.

Caland, W. 1893. "Beiträge zur kenntnis des Avesta: Adjectiva auf -*ra* in der composition." *Zeitschrift für vergleichende Sprachforschung* 32:592.

Carnuth, O. 1869. ed. *ΠΕΡΙ ΣΗΜΕΙΩΝ ΟΔΥΣΣΕΙΑΣ*. Königsberg.

CEG. See Hansen.

Cerquiglini, B. 1989. *Eloge de la variante: Histoire critique de la philologie*. Paris.

Chantraine, P. 1968, 1970, 1975, 1977, 1980. *Dictionnaire étymologique de la langue grecque* I, II, III, IV-1, IV-2. Reissued 1999, with a Supplement (eds. A. Blanc, Ch. de Lamberterie, J.-L. Perpillou). Paris.

Citti, V. 1966. "Le edizioni omeriche 'delle città.'" *Vichiana* 3:227–267.

Clark, M. 1994. "Enjambment and Binding in Homeric Hexameter." *Phoenix* 48:95–114.

———. 1997. *Out of Line: Homeric Composition beyond the Hexameter*. Lanham MD.

Collins, D. 2001. "Improvisation in Rhapsodic Performances." *Helios* 28:11–27.

Cook, B. F. 1984. *The Elgin Marbles*. 2nd ed. 1997. British Museum Press. London.

Cramer, J. A. 1835–1837. ed. *Anecdota Graeca*. (Oxford mss) 4 vols. Oxford.

——. 1839–1841. ed. *Anecdota Graeca*. (Paris mss) 4 vols. Oxford.

D'Ippolito, Gennaro. 1977 *Lettura di Omero: Il Canto V dell' "Odissea."* Palermo.

Daitz, S. G. 1991. "On Reading Homer Aloud: To Pause or not to Pause?" *American Journal of Philology* 112:149–160.

Davidson, O. M. 1980. "Indo–European Dimensions of Herakles in *Iliad* 19.95–133." *Arethusa* 13:197–202.

Davies, A. M., and W. Meid, 1976. eds. *Studies in Greek, Italic, and Indo-European Linguistics Offered to Leonard R. Palmer.* Innsbruck.

DELG. See Chantraine 1968–1980.

Detienne, M. 1981. *L'invention de la mythologie*. Paris.

Dindorf, W. 1855. ed. *Scholia Graeca in Homeri Odysseam* I–II. Oxford.

——. 1875–1888. ed. *Scholia Graeca in Homeri Iliadem: ex codicibus aucta et emendata* I–VI. Oxford; V–VI contain the T scholia, edited by E. Maass 1887–1888.

Dougherty, C., and Kurke, L. 1993. eds. *Cultural Poetics in Archaic Greece: Cult, Performance, Politics.* Cambridge.

Drachmann, A. B. 1903–1927. ed. *Scholia Vetera in Pindari Carmina*. 3 vols. Leipzig.

Dué, C. 2001. "Achilles' Golden Amphora in Aeschines' *Against Timarchus* and the Afterlife of Oral Tradition." *Classical Philology* 96:33–47.

Dyck, A. 1993a. "The Fragments of Heliodorus Homericus." *Harvard Studies in Classical Philology* 95:1–64.

——. 1993b. "Aelius Herodian: Recent Studies and Prospects for Future Research." In W. Haase and H. Temporini, eds., *Aufstieg und Niedergang der römischen Welt* 2.34.1 pp. 772–794. Berlin.

Edwards, M. W. 1991. *The Iliad: A Commentary* V: Books 17–20 (general ed. G. S. Kirk). Cambridge.

Erbse, H. 1959. "Über Aristarchs Iliasausgaben." *Hermes* 87:275–303.

——. 1960. *Beiträge zur Überlieferung der Iliasscholien*. Zetemata 24. Munich.

——. 1969–1988. ed. *Scholia Graeca in Homeri Iliadem* I–VII. Berlin.

Esametro. See Fantuzzi and Pretagostini 1996.

Fantuzzi, M., and Pretagostini, R. 1996. eds. *Struttura e storia dell'esametro greco* I / II. Rome.

FGH. See Jacoby 1923–.

Finkelberg, M. 2000. "The *Cypria*, the *Iliad*, and the Problem of Multiformity in Oral and Written Tradition." *Classical Philology* 95:1–11.

Foley, J. M. 1999. *Homer's Traditional Art*. University Park PA.

Fränkel, H. 1955. "Der homerische und der kallimachische Hexameter." In *Wege und Formen frühgriechischen Denkens.* pp. 100–156. Munich. 2nd ed. 1960, 3rd ed. 1968.

Friedländer, L. 1850. ed. *Nicanoris ΠΕΡΙ ΙΛΙΑΚΗΣ ΣΤΙΓΜΗΣ reliquiae emendatiores*. Königsberg.

——. 1853. ed. *Aristonici ΠΕΡΙ ΣΗΜΕΙΩΝ ΙΛΙΑΔΟΣ reliquiae emendatiores*. Göttingen.

Gentili, B. 1977 [reprinted 1996]. "Preistoria e formazione dell'esametro." *Quaderni Urbinati di Cultura Classica* 26:7–37. Reprinted in *Esametro* II 11–41.

Giannini, P. 1977 [reprinted 1996]. "Preistoria e formazione dell'esametro." *Quaderni Urbinati di Cultura Classica* 26:38–51. Reprinted in *Esametro* II 42–55.

GMZ. *See* Grafton, Most, and Zetzel 1985.

Grafton, A., Most, G. W., and Zetzel, J. E. G. 1985. eds. *F. A. Wolf, Prolegomena to Homer*. Princeton.

Hainsworth, J. B. 1993. *The Iliad: A Commentary* III. Books 9–12 (general ed. G. S. Kirk). Cambridge.

Hansen, P. A. 1983. ed. *Carmina epigraphica Graeca saecularum viii–v a. Chr. n.* Berlin and New York.

Haslam, M. 1978. "Apollonius of Rhodes and the Papyri." *Illinois Classical Studies* 3:47–73.

———. 1990. "A New Papyrus of the Mythographus Homericus," *Bulletin of the American Society of Papyrologists* 27:31–36.

———. 1994. "The Homer Lexicon of Apollonius Sophista I: Composition and Constituents," *Classical Philology* 89:1–45.

———. 1996. "On *P.Oxy.* LXI 4096, Mythographus Homericus." *Zeitschrift für Papyrologie und Epigraphik* 110:115–117.

———. 1997. "Homeric Papyri and Transmission of the Text." In Morris and Powell 1997:55–100.

Haubold, J. 2000. *Homer's People: Epic Poetry and Social Formations*. Cambridge.

Henrichs, A. 1971 / 1974. "Scholia Minora zu Homer I, II, III / IV," *Zeitschrift für Papyrologie und Epigraphik* 7 (1971) 97–149; 229–260; 8 (1971) 1–12; 12 (1974) 17–43.

Heubeck, A. 1987. "Noch Einmal zum Namen des Apollon." *Glotta* 65:179–182.

Higbie, C. 1990. *Measure and Music: Enjambement and Sentence Structure in the Iliad*. Oxford.

Hoekstra, A. 1981. *Epic Verse before Homer*. Amsterdam / Oxford / New York.

Holland, G. B. 1993. "The Name of Achilles: A Revised Etymology." *Glotta* 71:17–27.

Householder, F. W., and Nagy, G. 1972. *Greek: A Survey of Recent Work*. The Hague.

Jacoby, F. 1923–. ed. *Die Fragmente der griechischen Historiker*. Leiden.

Janko, R. 1982. *Homer, Hesiod and the Hymns: Diachronic Development in Epic Diction*. Cambridge.

———. 1990. "The *Iliad* and its Editors: Dictation and Redaction." *Classical Antiquity* 9:326–334.

———. 1992. *The Iliad: A Commentary* IV. Books 13–16 (general ed. G. S. Kirk). Cambridge.

———. 1998a. Review of Morris and Powell 1997. *Bryn Mawr Classical Review* 98.5.20: http://ccat.sas.upenn.edu/bmcr/1998/98.5.20.html.

———. 1998b. "The Homeric Poems as Oral Dictated Texts." *Classical Quarterly* 48:1–13.

———. 1998c. Review of Nagy 1996a. *Journal of Hellenic Studies* 118:206–207.

———. 1998d. "Corrigendum." *Bryn Mawr Classical Review* 98.6.17: http://ccat.sas. upenn.edu/bmcr/1998/98.6.17.html.

———. 2000. "West's *Iliad*." *Classical Review* 50:1–4.

Jensen, M. Skafte. 1980. *The Homeric Question and the Oral-Formulaic Theory*. Copenhagen.

Johnson, B. 1980. *The Critical Difference: Essays in the Contemporary Rhetoric of Reading.* Baltimore.

Jong, I. de. 1985. "Eurykleia and Odysseus's Scar: *Odyssey* 19:393–466." *Classical Quarterly* 35:517–518.

———. 1989. *Narrators and Focalizers: The Presentation of the Story in the "Iliad."* 2nd ed. Amsterdam.

Katz, J. 1998. "AYTAP, ATAP, TAP: The Poetics of a Particle in Homer." *American Philological Association Abstracts* 128:81.

Kazazis, J. N., and A. Rengakos. 1999. eds. *Euphrosyne: Studies in Ancient Epic and Its Legacy in Honor of Dimitris N. Maronitis.* Stuttgart.

Keaney, J. J., and Lamberton, R. 1996. eds. *[Plutarch] Essay on the Life and Poetry of Homer.* APA American Classical Studies 40. Atlanta.

Kirk, G. S. 1962. *The Songs of Homer.* Cambridge.

———. 1985. *The Iliad: A Commentary* I. Books 1–4 (general ed. G. S. Kirk). Cambridge.

———. 1990. *The Iliad: A Commentary* II: Books 5–8 (general ed. G. S. Kirk). Cambridge.

Knight, R. Payne. 1820. ed. *Carmina Homerica, Ilias et Odyssea: a rhapsodorum interpolationibus repurgata, et in pristinam formam, quatenus recuperanda esset, tam e veterum monumentorum fide et auctoritate, quam ex antiqui sermonis indole ac ratione, redacta.* London.

Koller, H. 1972. "Epos," *Glotta* 50:15–24.

Kullmann, W. 2001. Review of Latacz 2000a/b/c and 2001. *Gnomon* 73:648–663.

Lamberton, R., and J. Keaney. 1992. eds. *Homer's Ancient Readers: The Hermeneutics of Greek Epic's Earliest Exegetes.* Princeton.

Langdon, S. 1997. ed. *New Light on a Dark Age: Exploring the Culture of Geometric Greece.* Columbia MO.

Lascaris, J. 1517. ed. *Scholia in Homeri Iliadem.* Rome.

Latacz, J. 2000a. ed. *Homers Iliad Gesamtkommentar. Prolegomena.* Munich and Leipzig.

———. 2000b. ed. *Homers Iliad Gesamtkommentar.* Band I. *1. Gesang.* Faszikel 1: *Text und Übersetzung.* Munich and Leipzig.

———. 2000c. ed. *Homers Iliad Gesamtkommentar.* Band I. *1. Gesang.* Faszikel 2: *Kommentar.* Munich and Leipzig.

———. 2001. *Troia und Homer. Der Weg zur Lösung eines alten Rätsels.* Munich and Berlin.

———. 2002. Response to Kullmann 2001. *Bryn Mawr Classical Review* 02.02.15: http://ccat.sas.upenn.edu/bmcr/2002/2002-02-15.html.

Leach, E. R. 1982. Critical Introduction to Steblin-Kamenskij, M. I., *Myth*, 1–20. Ann Arbor.

Leeuwen, J. van, and Mendes da Costa, M. B. 1906. eds. *Ilias.* 3rd ed. Leiden.

Lehrs, K. 1865. *See* Lehrs 1882.

———. 1882. *De Aristarchi Studiis Homericis.* 3rd ed. Leipzig; 1st / 2nd eds. 1833 / 1865.

Lejeune, M. 1955. *Traité de phonétique grecque.* 2nd ed. Paris. Superseded 1972 by *Phonétique historique du mycénien et du grec ancien.* Paris.

Liddell, H. G., Scott, R., and Stuart Jones, H. 1940. eds. *Greek-English Lexicon*. 9th ed. Oxford.

Loraux, N. 1993. *The Children of Athena: Athenian Ideas about Citizenship and the Division between the Sexes*. Translated by C. Levine from Loraux 1984, *Les Enfants d'Athéna: Idées athéniennes sur la citoyenneté et la division des sexes* (Paris). Princeton.

Lord, A. B. 1960 / 2000. *The Singer of Tales*. Harvard Studies in Comparative Literature 24. Cambridge MA. 2nd ed., with new Introduction (vii–xxix), by S. Mitchell and G. Nagy 2000.

———. 1991. *Epic Singers and Oral Tradition*. Ithaca.

———. 1995. *The Singer Resumes the Tale* (ed. M. L. Lord). Ithaca.

Lowenstam, S. 1997. "Talking Vases: The Relationship between the Homeric Poems and Archaic Representations of Epic Myth." *Transactions of the American Philological Association* 127:21–76.

LSJ. *See* Liddell, Scott, and Stuart Jones 1940.

Ludwich, A. 1884 / 1885. *Aristarchs Homerische Textkritik nach den Fragmenten des Didymos* I / II. Leipzig.

———. 1884. ed. *Didymi commentarii qui inscribebatur ΠΕΡΙ ΤΗΣ ΑΡΙΣΤΑΡΧΕΙΟΥ ΔΙΟΡΘΩΣΕΩΣ fragmenta*. = Ludwich 1884:175–631.

———. 1888–90. ed. *Scholia in Homeri Odysseam a 1–309 auctiora et emendatiora*. Königsberg.

———. 1898. *Die Homervulgata als voralexandrinisch erwiesen*. Leipzig.

———. 1902. ed. *Homeri Ilias*. I / II. Leipzig. Reissued 1995, Stuttgart.

Lührs, D. 1992. *Untersuchungen zu den Athetesen Aristarchs in der Ilias und zu ihrer Behandlung im Corpus der exegetischen Scholien*. Beiträge zur Altertumswissenschaft 11; Hildesheim.

Lünstedt, P. 1961. *Untersuchungen zu den mythologischen Abschnitten der D-Scholien*. Dissertation Hamburg.

Luzio, A. di. 1969. "I Papyri Omerici d' Epoca Tolemaica e la Costituzione del Testo dell' Epica Arcaica." *Rivista di Cultura Classica e Medioevale* 11:3–152.

Maass, E. *See* Dindorf.

McNamee, K. 1981. "Aristarchus and Everyman's Homer." *Greek, Roman and Byzantine Studies* 22:247–255.

———. 1992. *Sigla and Select Marginalia in Greek Literary Papyri*. Brussels.

Magnelli, E. 1996. "Studi recenti sull'origine dell'esametro: un profilo critico." *Esametro* II 111–137.

Marco, V. de. 1932. ed. "Sulla tradizione manoscritta degli 'Scholia minora' all'Iliade." *Atti della Reale Accademia Nazionale dei Lincei. ser. VI vol. IV*, 373–410. Rome.

———. 1941. ed. "Da un manoscritto degli Scholia minora all'Iliade." *Atti della Reale Accademia d'Italia, Rendiconti della classe di Scienze morali e storiche*, Serie VII, Suppl. al vol. II, 125–145. Rome.

Masson, O. 1983. *Inscriptions Chypriotes Syllabiques*. 2nd ed. Paris.

Matthaios, S. 1999. *Untersuchungen zur Grammatik Aristarchs: Texte und Interpretation zur Wortartenlehre*. Göttingen.

MHV. *See* Parry 1971.

Monro, D. B., and Allen, T. W. 1920. eds. *Homeri Opera*. 3rd ed. Oxford.

Montanari, F. 1979. *Studi di filologia omerica antica* I. Pisa.

——. 1994. ed. *La philologie grecque à l'époque hellénistique et romaine.* Vandoeuvres-Geneva: Entretiens sur l'antiquité classique XL, Fondation Hardt.

——. 1995. "Filologi alessandrini e poeti alessandrini. La filologia sui 'contemporanei." Aevum 8:47–63.

——. 1998. "Zenodotus, Aristarchus and the Ekdosis of Homer." In Most 1998:1–21.

——. 2002. "Alexandrian Homeric Philology: The Form of the Ekdosis and the Variae Lectiones." In Reichel and Rengakos 2002:119–140.

Morris, I., and Powell, B. 1997. eds. *A New Companion to Homer.* Leiden.

Most, G. W. 1998. ed. *Editing Texts / Texte edieren.* Aporemata II. Göttingen.

Muellner, L. 1976. *The Meaning of Homeric EYXOMAI through Its Formulas.* Innsbruck: Institut für Sprachwissenschaft der Universität Innsbruck.

——. 1996. *The Anger of Achilles: Mēnis in Greek Epic.* Ithaca.

N = Nagy.

Nagy, G. 1970. *Greek Dialects and the Transformation of an Indo-European Process.* Cambridge MA.

——. 1974. *Comparative Studies in Greek and Indic Meter.* Harvard Studies in Comparative Literature 33. Cambridge MA.

——. 1976. "The Name of Achilles: Etymology and Epic." In Davies and Meid 1976: 227–30.

——. 1979a. *Best of the Achaeans: Concepts of the Hero in Archaic Greek Poetry.* Baltimore: Johns Hopkins University Press. 2nd ed. 1999.

——. 1979b. "On the Origins of the Greek Hexameter." In *Festschrift Oswald Szemerényi,* ed. B. Brogyanyi, 611–631. Amsterdam.

——. 1982. Review of Detienne 1981. *Annales: Economies Sociétés Civilisations* 37:778–780.

——. 1983. Review of Bowie 1981. *Phoenix* 37:273–275.

——. 1990a. *Pindar's Homer: The Lyric Possession of an Epic Past.* Baltimore. Revised paperback version 1994.

——. 1990b. *Greek Mythology and Poetics.* Ithaca. Important corrigendum: on p. 203 between "same line)" and "specified," insert "of the marital bed; similarly, she 'recognizes' (ἀναγνούσῃ τ 250) as *sēmata* (same line) the clothes..." (in the present printed version, the reference to the marital bed as *sēmata* at ψ 206 is distorted by a mistaken omission of the wording that needs to be restored here: by haplography, the mention of the marital bed is omitted, and this omission distorts the point being made about the clothes and brooch of Odysseus as *sēmata* in their own right at τ 250).

——. 1992. "Metrical Convergences and Divergences in Early Greek Poetry and Song." *Historical Philology: Greek, Latin, and Romance,* ed. B. Brogyanyi and R. Lipp, II 610–631. Corrected version reprinted in Nagy 1996c.

——. 1994a. "The Name of Achilles: Questions of Etymology and 'Folk Etymology." *Illinois Classical Studies* 19, *Studies in Honor of Miroslav Marcovich* vol. 2:3–9. Recast as Ch.6 in this volume.

——. 1994b. "The Name of Apollo: Etymology and Essence." *Apollo: Origins and Influences,* ed. J. Solomon, 3–7. Tucson. Recast as Ch.7 in this volume.

———. 1996a. *Poetry as Performance: Homer and Beyond.* Cambridge.

———. 1996b. *Homeric Questions.* Austin TX.

———. 1996c. "Metrical Convergences and Divergences in Early Greek Poetry and Song." In *Esametro* II 63–110.

———. 1997a. "The Shield of Achilles: Ends of the *Iliad* and Beginnings of the Polis." In Langdon 1997:194–207.

———. 1997b. "An inventory of debatable assumptions about a Homeric question." *Bryn Mawr Classical Review* 97.4.18: http://ccat.sas.upenn.edu/bmcr/1997/97.04.18. html. Recast in N 2003a.4–7.

———. 1997c. "Ellipsis in Homer." In Bakker and Kahane 1997:167–189. Cambridge MA. Recast as Ch.9 in this volume.

———. 1997d. "Homeric Scholia." In Morris and Powell 1997:101–122. This piece is replete with printing errors. For a list of corrigenda, please write the author (gnagy@fas.harvard.edu). Recast as Ch.1 in this volume.

———. 1998a: "The Library of Pergamon as a Classical Model." *Pergamon: Citadel of the Gods*, ed. H. Koester, 185–232. Harvard Theological Studies 46.

———. 1998b. "Aristarchean Questions." *Bryn Mawr Classical Review* 98.7.14: http:// ccat.sas.upenn.edu/bmcr/1998/1998-07-14.html. Recast as Ch.5 in this volume.

———. 1998c. "Homer as 'Text' and the Poetics of Cross-Reference." *Verschriftung und Verschriftlichung: Aspekte des Medienwechsels in verschiedenen Kulturen und Epochen*, eds. C. Ehler and U. Schaefer, 78–87. ScriptOralia 94. Tübingen. Recast in N 2003a.7–19.

———. 1998d. "Is there an etymology for the dactylic hexameter?" *Mír Curad: Studies in Honor of Calvert Watkins* (eds. J. Jasanoff, H. C. Melchert, L. Oliver) 495–508. Innsbruck. Recast as Ch.8 in this volume.

———. 1999a. *The Best of the Achaeans: Concepts of the Hero in Archaic Greek Poetry.* 2nd ed., with new introduction, Baltimore.

———. 1999b. "Irreversible Mistakes and Homeric Poetry." In Kazazis and Rengakos: 259–274. Recast as Ch.3 of *HR*.

———. 1999c. "Homer and Plato at the Panathenaia: Synchronic and Diachronic Perspectives." *Contextualizing Classics*, ed. T. M. Falkner, D. Konstan, N. Felson Rubin, 123–150. Lanham MD.

———. 1999d. Foreword. In Dumézil 1999:vii–xi.

———. 1999e. "Epic as Genre." *Epic Traditions in the Contemporary World: The Poetics of Community*, ed. M. Beissinger, J. Tylus, and S. Wofford, 21–32. Berkeley and Los Angeles.

———. 1999f. "Comments" in "Symbolae Osloenses Debate: Dividing Homer: When and How were the *Iliad* and *Odyssey* Divided into Songs?" *Symbolae Osloenses* 74:64–68.

———. 1999g. "Les Éditions Alexandrines d'homère." *Homère en France après la Querelle* (1715–1900), ed. F. Létoublon and C. Volpilhac-Auger, 63–72. Paris.

———. 2000a. Review of West 1998b. *Bryn Mawr Classical Review* 2000.09.12: http:// ccat.sas.upenn.edu/bmcr/2000/2000-09-12.htm. Recast as Ch.3 in this volume.

———. 2000b. "Epic as Music: Rhapsodic Models of Homer in Plato's *Timaeus* and *Critias.*" *The Oral Epic: Performance and Music*, ed. K. Reichl, 41–67. Berlin.

———. 2000c. "Homeric *humnos* as a Rhapsodic Term." *Una nueva visión de la cultura griega antigua hacia el fin del milenio*, ed. A. M. González de Tobia, 385–401. La Plata.

———. 2000d. "Distortion diachronique dans l'art homérique: quelques précisions." *Constructions du temps dans le monde ancien*, ed. C. Darbo-Peschanski, 417–426. Paris.

———. 2000e. "Reading Greek Poetry Aloud: Evidence from the Bacchylides Papyri." *Quaderni Urbinati di Cultura Classica* 64:7–28.

———. 2001a. "Homeric Poetry and Problems of Multiformity: The 'Panathenaic Bottleneck.'" *Classical Philology* 96:109–119. Recast as Ch.2 in this volume.

———. 2001b. "The Textualizing of Homer." *Inclinate Aurem—Oral Perspectives on Early European Verbal Culture*, ed. J. Helldén, M. S. Jensen, and T. Pettitt, 57–84. Odense.

———. 2001c. "Reading Bakhtin Reading the Classics: An Epic Fate for Conveyors of the Heroic Past," In *Bakhtin and the Classics*, ed. R. B. Branham, 71–96. Evanston IL.

———. 2001d. "Éléments orphiques chez Homère." *Kernos* 14:1–9.

———. 2001e. "The Sign of the Hero: A Prologue." In Berenson Maclean and Aitken 2001:xv–xxxv.

———. 2001f. "Η ποιητική της προφορικότητας και η ομηρική έρευνα." *Νεκρά γράμματα· οι κλασσικές σπουδές στον 21ᵒ αιωνα* (ed. A. Rengakos) 135–146. Athens.

———. 2001g. Electronic publication of all nine Introductions and all nine Bibliographies for Nagy 2001h: http://chs.harvard.edu/chs_pubs/ninevol/index.htm.

———. 2001h. *Greek Literature*. 9 volumes, plus nine introductions written by editor. New York.

———. 2001h1. Volume 1. *The Oral Traditional Background of Ancient Greek Literature*. Introduction, pp. ix–xv.

———. 2001h2. Volume 2. *Homer and Hesiod as Prototypes of Greek Literature*. Introduction, pp. ix–xvi.

———. 2001h3. Volume 3. *Greek Literature in the Archaic Period: The Emergence of Authorship*. Introduction, pp. ix–xiii.

———. 2001h4. Volume 4. *Greek Literature in the Classical Period: The Poetics of Drama in Athens*. Introduction, pp. ix–xii.

———. 2001h5. Volume 5. *Greek Literature in the Classical Period: The Prose of Historiography and Oratory*. Introduction, pp. ix–xi.

———. 2001h6. Volume 6. *Greek Literature and Philosophy*. Introduction, pp. ix–x.

———. 2001h7. Volume 7. *Greek Literature in the Hellenistic Period*. Introduction, pp. ix–x.

———. 2001h8. Volume 8. *Greek Literature in the Roman Period and in Late Antiquity*. Introduction, pp. ix–xi.

———. 2001h9. Volume 9. *Greek Literature in the Byzantine Period*. Introduction, pp. ix–x.

———. 2002a. *Plato's Rhapsody and Homer's Music: The Poetics of the Panathenaic Festival in Classical Athens*. Cambridge MA and Athens.

———. 2002b. "The Language of Heroes as Mantic Poetry: Hypokrisis in Homer." In Reichel and Rengakos 2002:141–149.

———. 2002c. "Can myth be saved?" In *Myth: A New Symposium*, ed. G. Schrempp and W. Hansen, 240–248. Bloomington IN.

———. 2003a. *Homeric Responses*. Austin TX.

———. 2003b. Review of West 2001b. *Gnomon* 75:481–501. Recast as Ch.4 in this volume.

———. 2005. *Homer the Classic*. Berkeley and Los Angeles. Forthcoming.

Neitzel, S. 1977. ed. *Apions ΓΛΩΣΣΑΙ ΟΜΗΡΙΚΑΙ*. Sammlung griechischer und lateinischer Grammatiker III. Berlin and New York.

Neuschäfer, B. 1987. *Origenes als Philologe*. I/II. Schweizerische Beiträge zur Altertumswissenschaft 18.1/2. Basel.

Nickau, K. 1977. *Untersuchungen zur textkritischen Methode des Zenodotos von Ephesos*. Berlin and New York.

Nilsson, M. P. 1921. *Die Anfänge der Göttin Athene*. Copenhagen.

Page, D. 1959. *History and the Homeric Iliad*. Berkeley and Los Angeles.

Palmer, L. R. 1963a. *The Interpretation of Mycenaean Greek Texts*. Oxford.

———. 1963b. "The Language of Homer." *A Companion to Homer*, ed. A. J. B. Wace and F. H. Stubbings, 75–178. London.

———. 1979. "A Mycenaean 'Akhilleid'?" *Serta Philologica Aenipontana* III, ed. R. Muth and G. Pfohl, 255–261. Innsbruck.

———. 1980. *The Greek Language*. Atlantic Highlands NJ.

Parry, A. 1971. ed. *The Making of Homeric Verse: The Collected Papers of Milman Parry*. Oxford.

Parry, M. *See MHV* (= Parry 1971).

Pelliccia, H. N. 1997. "As Many Homers As You Please." *New York Review of Books* vol. 44 no. 18 [Nov. 20] 44–48.

Perpillou, J.-L. 1973. *Les substantifs grecs en -ΕΥΣ*. Paris.

Pfeiffer, R. 1968. *History of Classical Scholarship from the Beginnings to the End of the Hellenistic Age*. Oxford.

Pierron, P. A. 1869. ed. *L'Iliade d'Homère: texte grec, revu et corrigé d'après les documents authentiques de la recension d'Aristarque*. 2 vols. Paris.

Porter, J. I. 1992. "Hermeneutic Lines and Circles: Aristarchus and Crates on the Exegesis Of Homer." In Lamberton and Keaney 1992:67–114.

Puhvel, J. 1977. "Devatâ-Dvandva in Hittite, Greek, and Latin." *American Journal of Philology* 98:396–405.

Reichel, M., and Rengakos, A. 2002. eds. *Epea Pteroenta: Beiträge zur Homerforschung. Festschrfit für Wolfgang Kullmann*. Stuttgart.

Rengakos, A. 1993. *Der Homertext und die hellenistischen Dichter*. Hermes Einzelschriften 64. Stuttgart.

———. 2000. "Aristarchus and the Hellenistic Poets." *Seminari Romani de Cultura Greca* 3:325–335.

———. 2002. Review of West 2001b. *Bryn Mawr Classical Review* 2002.11.15: http://ccat.sas.upenn.edu/bmcr/2002/2002-11-15.html.

Richardson, N. J. 1974. ed. with commentary. *The Homeric Hymn to Demeter*. Oxford.

———. 1980. "Literary Criticism in the Exegetical Scholia to the *Iliad.*" *Classical Quarterly* 30:265–287.

———. 1993. ed. *The Iliad: A Commentary* VI: Books 21–24 (general ed. G. S. Kirk). Cambridge.

Risch, E. 1974. *Wortbildung der homerischen Sprache.* 2nd ed. Berlin.

Ritoók, Zs. 1970. "Die Homeriden." *Acta Antiqua* 18:1–29.

———. 1987. "Vermutungen zum Ursprung des griechischen Hexameters." *Philologus* 131:2–18.

Rossi, L. E. 1965. "Estensione e valore del colon nell'esametro omerico." *Studi Urbinati* 39:279–273. Reprinted in *Esametro* II 271–308, 315–320.

———. 1996. "Post-scriptum 1995." *Esametro* II 309–314.

Roth, C. P. 1990. *"Mixed Aorists" in Homeric Greek.* New York and London.

Schindler, J. 1976. "On the Greek type ἱππεύς." In Davies and Meid 1976:349–352.

Schloemann, J. 2001. "Der 'richtige' Homer und die Aufgabe der Textkritik." *Frankfurter Allgemeine Zeitung* 9 / 26 Nr. 224 p. 6.

Schmidt, M. 1854. ed. *Didymi Fragmenta.* Leipzig.

Schmidt, M. 1976. *Die Erklärungen zum Weltbild Homers und zur Kultur der Heroenzeit in den bT-Scholien zur Ilias.* Munich.

———. 1997. "Variae lectiones oder Parallelstellen: Was notierten Zenodot und Aristarch zu Homer?" *ZPE* 115:1–12.

Schmitt, R. 1967. *Dichtung und Dichtersprache in indogermanischer Zeit.* Wiesbaden.

Schrader, H. 1880–1882. ed. *Porphyrii Quaestionum Homericarum ad Iliadem pertinentium reliquiae.* Leipzig.

———. 1890. ed. *Porphyrii Quaestionum Homericarum ad Odysseam pertinentium reliquiae.* Leipzig.

Schwyzer, E. 1939. *Griechische Grammatik* I. Munich.

Schwyzer, E., and Debrunner, A. 1966. *Griechische Grammatik* II: *Syntax und syntaktische Stilistik.* Munich.

Searle, J. R. 1979. *Speech-Acts: An Essay in the Philosophy of Language.* Cambridge.

Severyns, A. 1928. *Le cycle épique dans l'école d'Aristarque.* Bibliothèque de la Faculté de Philosophie et Lettres de l'Université de Liège 40. Paris.

———. 1938. *Recherches sur la Chrestomathie de Proclos.* I / II. Paris.

Shapiro, H. A. 1993. "Hipparchos and the Rhapsodes." In Dougherty and Kurke 1993.92–107.

Sherratt, E. S. 1990. "'Reading the Texts': Archaeology and the Homeric Question." *Antiquity* 64:807–824.

Slater, W. 1986. ed. *Aristophanis Byzantii Fragmenta.* Berlin and New York.

Snodgrass, A. 1998. *Homer and the Artists: Text and Picture in Early Greek Art.* Cambridge.

Sodano, A. R. 1970. ed. *Porphyrii Quaestionum Homericarum liber I.* Naples.

Stallbaum, J. G. 1825. ed. *Eustathii Commentarii ad Homeri Odysseam* I–II. Leipzig.

Thiel, H. van. 1991. ed. *Homeri Odyssea.* Hildesheim.

———. 1996. ed. *Homeri Ilias.* Hildesheim.

———. 2000a. "Die D-Scholien der *Ilias* in den Handschriften." *Zeitschrift für Papyrologie und Epigraphik* 132:1–62.

————. 2000b. ed. *Proecdosis: Scholia D in Iliadem.* http://www.uni-koeln.de/phil-fak/ifa/vanthiel.

Tichy, E. 1981a. "Hom. ANΔPOTHTA und die Vorgeschichte des daktylischen Hexameters." *Glotta* 59:28–67.

————. 1981b. "Beobachtungen zur homerischen Synizese." *Münchener Studien zur Sprachwissenschaft* 40:187–222.

Valk, M. van der. 1963/1964. *Researches on the Text and Scholia of the Iliad* I/II. Leiden.

————. 1971–1988. ed. *Eustathii archiepiscopi Thessalonicensis Commentarii ad Homeri Iliadem* I–IV. Leiden.

Vidal-Naquet, P. 1981. *Le chasseur noir.* Paris.

————. 1986. "The Black Hunter Revisited." *Proceedings of the Cambridge Philological Society* 212:126–144.

Villoison, J. B. G. d'Ansse de. 1788. ed. *Homeri Ilias ad veteris codicis Veneti fidem recensita.* Venice.

Wace, A. J. B., and Frank H. Stubbings, F. H. 1962. eds. *A Companion to Homer.* London.

Waugh, L. R. 1982. "Marked and Unmarked: A Choice between Unequals in Semiotic Structure." *Semiotica* 38:299–318.

Watkins, C. 1969. *Indogermanische Grammatik* (ed. J. Kurylowicz) III.1: *Formenlehre, Geschichte der indogermanischen Verbalflexion.* Heidelberg.

————. 1977. "A propos de ΜΗΝΙΣ." *Bulletin de la Société de Linguistique de Paris* 72:187–209.

————. 1979. "NAM.RA GUD UDU in Hittite: Indo-European poetic language and the folk taxonomy of wealth." *Hethitisch und Indogermanisch. Vergleichende Studien zur historischen Grammatik und zur dialektgeographischen Stellung der indogermanischen Sprachgruppe Altkleinasiens,* ed. W. Meid and E. Neu, 269–287. Innsbrucker Beiträge zur Sprachwissenschaft 25. Innsbruck. Reprinted in Watkins 1994 II 644–662.

————. 1994. *Selected Writings* (ed. L. Oliver) I / II. Innsbruck.

————. 1995. *How to Kill a Dragon: Aspects of Indo-European Poetics.* New York.

West, M. L. 1973a. "Greek Poetry 2000–700 B.C." *Classical Quarterly* 23:179–192.

————. 1973b. "Indo-European Metre." *Glotta* 51:161–187.

————. 1982. *Greek Metre.* Oxford.

————. 1988. "The Rise of the Greek Epic." *Journal of Hellenic Studies* 108:151–172.

————. 1990. "Archaische Heldendichtung: Singen und Schreiben." *Der Übergang von der Mündlichkeit zur Literatur bei den Griechen,* ed. W. Kullmann and M. Reichel, 33–50. Tübingen.

————. 1995. "The Date of the *Iliad.*" *Museum Helveticum* 52:203–219.

————. 1998a. "The Textual Criticism and Editing of Homer." In Most 1998:94–109.

————. 1998b. ed. *Homeri Ilias* I. Stuttgart and Leipzig.

————. 1999a. "Frühe Interpolationen in der Ilias." *Nachrichten der Akademie der Wissenschaften in Göttingen* I. Philologische-Historische Klasse 3–11. Göttingen.

————. 1999b. "The Invention of Homer." *Classical Quarterly* 49:364–382.

————. 2000a. ed. *Homeri Ilias* II. Munich and Leipzig.

———. 2000b. "The Gardens of Alcinous and the Oral Dictated Text Theory." *Acta Antiqua Academiae Scientiarum Hungaricae* 40:479–488.

———. 2000c. *The East Face of Helicon: West Asiatic Elements in Greek Poetry and Myth*. Oxford.

———. 2001a. Response to 2000.09.12 and 2001.06.21. *Bryn Mawr Classical Review* 01.09.06: http://ccat.sas.upenn.edu/bmcr/2001/2001-09-06.html.

———. 2001b. *Studies in the Text and Transmission of the Iliad*. Munich and Leipzig.

———. 2003. "*Iliad* and *Aethiopis*." *Classical Quarterly* 53.1–14.

———. 2004. Reply to Rengakos 2002 and Nagy 2003b. *Bryn Mawr Classical Review* 2004.04.17: http://ccat.sas.upenn.edu/bmcr/2004/2004-04-17.html.

West, S. 1967. ed. *The Ptolemaic Papyri of Homer*. Papyrologica Coloniensia 3. Cologne and Opladen.

———. 1988. "The Transmission of the Text." In A. Heubeck, S. West, and J. B. Hainsworth, *A Commentary on Homer's Odyssey* I. Introduction and Books i–viii, 33–48. Oxford.

———. 1996. "Elements of Epic." *Times Literary Supplement*, 2 August 1996, 27. Review of N 1996a.

Wilson, N. G. 1967. "A Chapter in the History of Scholia." *Classical Quarterly* 59: 244–256.

———. 1990. "Thomas William Allen, 1862–1950." *Proceedings of the British Academy* 76:311–319.

Wolf, F. A. 1795. *Prolegomena ad Homerum, sive de operum Homericorum prisca et genuina forma variisque mutationibus et probabili ratione emendandi*. Halle.

———. 1804/1807. ed. *Homerou epe. Homeri et Homeridarum opera et reliquiae*. 4 volumes. Leipzig.

Wyrick, J. D. 1999. "The Genesis of Authorship: Legends of the Textualization of Homeric Epic and the Bible." Ph.D. dissertation, Harvard University.

Zumthor, P. 1972. *Essai de poétique médiévale*. Paris.

TRADITIONS

Baby and Child Heroes in Ancient Greece
  Corrine Ondine Pache

Homer's Text and Language
  Gregory Nagy

GREGORY NAGY is Francis Jones Professor of Classical Greek Literature and Professor of Comparative Literature at Harvard University, and Director of the Center for Hellenic Studies in Washington, D.C.

The University of Illinois Press
is a founding member of the
Association of American University Presses.

Composed in 10/12.5 Adobe Minion Pro
with ITC Stone Sans display
by Christopher Dadian
Designed by Copenhaver Cumpston
Manufactured by Thomson-Shore, Inc.

UNIVERSITY OF ILLINOIS PRESS

1325 South Oak Street Champaign, IL 61820-6903
www.press.uillinois.edu